CULTURE SHOCK!

Singapore

D1392399

JoAnn Meriwether Craig

·K·U·P·E·R·A·R·D·

In the same series

Australia	Ireland	South Africa	A Parent's Guide
Bolivia	Israel	Spain	A Traveller's Medical Guide
Britain	Italy	Sri Lanka	A Wife's Guide
California	Japan	Sweden	Living and Working Abroad
Canada	Korea	Switzerland	Living & Working in London
China	Laos	Syria	Living & Working in Rome
Czech Republic	Malaysia	Taiwan	Working Holidays Abroad
Denmark	Mauritius	Thailand	
France	Morocco	Turkey	
Germany	Myanmar	UAE	
Greece	Nepal	USA	
Hong Kong	Norway	USA – The South	
India	Pakistan	Vietnam	
Indonesia	Philippines		

Culture Shock! Singapore
First published in Great Britain 1993 by
Kuperard
No 7 Spectrum House
32-34 Gordon House Road
London NW5 1LP

Reprinted 1996, 1997

Kuperard is an imprint of Bravo Ltd.

Illustrations by TRIGG

Printed in Singapore

ISBN 1-85733-026-9

FOREWORD

More than a decade has passed since I wrote the foreword to my dear friend JoAnn Craig's first edition of this title.

Her book on Singapore/Malaysia was to spawn a world-ranging series of 'Culture Shock!' titles published from Singapore, all promoting the cause to which JoAnn herself is deeply devoted: the bringing together of different peoples and the breaching of cultural barriers through mutual understanding and respect.

Although Singapore has changed enormously since 1979, when JoAnn's book was first published – it is now a vastly more complex, sophisticated society and also a very affluent one – most of the cultural fundamentals described in the original book surprisingly have not. Singaporeans nowadays are also given to far more self-analysis and introspection than in the past, in their quest for identity. Many of them may therefore appreciate seeing themselves through others' eyes in this book every bit as much as the tourist visitor or expatriate resident will treasure JoAnn's invaluable guidance through the cultural quicksands of Singapore.

Singapore's skyscrapers are still great deceivers, as I said back in 1979. Let nobody be in any doubt – Singapore is Asia, and Asian. To peel away the cosmetic veneer of Westernization, outsiders will need this book.

For many non-Singaporeans, Singapore is something of a love-hate affair. But JoAnn is remarkable for never having suffered from any such dichotomous feelings. She speaks always from the standpoint of love.

Ilsa Sharp
(Writer, author of Culture Shock! Australia)
Singapore 1992.

CONTENTS

INTRODUCTION

THE CHAPTERS OF THIS BOOK

Chapter One provides some information about the physical aspects of living in Singapore. It is intended to help you settle in. Chapter Two – East Meets West explores some basic Singaporean values and the behaviour patterns which flow from them. Once you understand these patterns, your reaction to unfamiliar Singaporean ways should be a positive one – 'Ah ha! I see! So that is why they do that.' Chapter Three – Business Etiquette lists many 'Dos and Don'ts' to help you feel more competent and confident in your ability to work in a cross-cultural setting. The next three chapters on the Chinese, Malay and Indian communities give you a glimpse of the cultures of each of the three main ethnic groups in Singapore. They are intended to prevent or reduce culture shock on the level of the individual ethnic cultures of Singapore.

Chapter Seven takes a look at the phenomenon of culture shock, the problems caused by it, the experiences of it in Singapore, and what you can do to recover from it. Chapter Eight has two parts: part one discusses some of the problems and pleasures of the expatriate life in Singapore; part two gives tips on how to thrive in Singapore. A Cultural Quiz is included to help you gain confidence in your ability to deal with cross-cultural situations common in Singapore.

THE BACK-HOME SYNDROME

Back home – everyone makes sense! Here in the alien land, nothing makes sense!' Strangers can't help comparing the host country with the home country. The cultural differences are striking. Strangers are urged to treat Singaporeans as they themselves would like to be treated. Singaporeans are justly proud of their country and they resent

statements like: 'Back in the States we have bigger…better…more…';
and 'In France, our women are more…and our coffee is…'; and 'In
England, our pubs are…and our cheese is…'

A person is always free to criticize his/her own people, country,
values, behaviours, etc., but outsiders should never do it.

It is, of course, sometimes a truly disheartening experience to be
a stranger in a strange land, and Kipling's *Stranger* explains the real
distress felt by many strangers in a strange land.

THE STRANGER
The Stranger within my gate,
He may be true or kind,
But he does not talk my talk –
I cannot feel his mind.
I see the face and the eyes and the mouth
But not the soul behind.

The men of my own stock
They may do ill or well,
But they tell the lies I am wonted to
And they are used to the lies I tell;
And we do not need interpreters
(especially cultural ones*)
When we go to buy and sell.

The stranger within my gate,
He may be evil or good,
But I cannot tell what powers control –
What reasons sway his mood;
Nor when the Gods of his far-off land
May repossess his blood.

*I have taken the liberty of adding this line.

HOW THIS BOOK CAN HELP YOU

Many expatriates (expats) feel that to 'be yourself' is good advice. Why not be yourself – your own friendly and good-hearted self! This is dangerous advice! There are many reasons why an enlightened expat should learn the rules which regulate behaviours in Singapore. For instance: in a Western culture, it is good manners to walk into someone's home with your shoes on (it would be considered rude to remove them); it is considered friendly to shake hands with all people of both sexes whom we meet; it is permissible to give objects with either hand; it is often a normal social friendliness to hug or kiss the host or hostess when greeting them or when departing from their home; in Singapore all these customs are taboo in one or more of the different ethnic groups!

While in the throes of 'culture shock' (disorientation, stress and anxiety due to exposure to the thousand and one different habits of an alien culture) we may be trying to signal friendship when in reality we are communicating offence and disrespect by: touching when we should not be touching; wearing shorts when we should be covered up; inadvertently making 'obscene' gestures in front of our host's wife and children by using our own harmless gestures, etc.

The material in this book is not intended to make you worry and fret about what you are doing wrong. On the contrary, it is intended to help you have more accurate perceptions and assumptions. The most important way this book can help both foreigners and Singaporeans is to awaken warm feelings between guest and host people, and to enlighten the cultural mind through increased wisdom and compassion. The goals of this work are always to encourage better cross-cultural awareness and relationships; to relieve the pain and suffering of those who cross cultures; and to cure or mitigate the many problems of culture shock.

WE ARE ALL CROSS-CULTURAL PIONEERS

We also hope to assist those cultural nomads who travel from culture to culture with their briefcases and toolboxes in their hands. We are entering a new age! As adventurers and pioneers once crossed uncharted oceans in days gone by, they are now seeking to cross nothing less than the largely uncharted and dangerous cultural spaces of the cross-cultural mind. We are in the age of cultural expansion, and hopefully, it will not be an age of cultural imperialism and colonialism as well!

> *All people are the same – it is only their habits which are so different.*
>
> — Confucius

Welcome to Singapore. Photo: MITA (Ministry of Information and the Arts)

ACKNOWLEDGEMENTS

This book is a group-centered effort. Many people worked together to explain and interpret the information and to contribute materials. People from Singapore, and people from the Western world worked hand-in-hand and side-by-side to produce this book for you. It is for you, the people who cross cultures – and for you, the people who have your cultures crossed, that this book is intended. We hope that it will relieve the pain and suffering of your cross-cultural experiences and that it will ease your cultural paths.

Special thanks are due to old friends who helped to develop the original material in the 1979 edition: Cikgu Ehsan Haji Ali; Ilsa Sharp; C.M. Wong of the China Society; Lim Kim Guan, beloved tourist guide who did so much to help the foreigner love and appreciate Singapore; Chen Heng Wing; V.T. Arasu of the Ministry of Culture; Jalaja Menon; J. Verma; Yang Mohsin bin Abdul Rashid; Koh Ding Chiang; Sukianh binte Abu; Radiah binte Suri; Gan Siew Tin; Sharuddin bin Suri; Cikgu Abduhl Ghani of Bachok, Malaysia; Professor Michael A.H.B. Walter of Singapore University; Professor David Hammond-Tooke of The University of Witswatersrand, South Africa; Professor Chiew Seen Kong of the University of Singapore; Professor Robert C. Cooper of the University of Singapore; Captain A.P. Flip Johnson; Roy Ruderman; Zeke Feuerman; Bhopinder Singh; Raj Kumar; Yogi Yogarajah; Juanita Narona; A. Mani; Jayarani Pavadarayan; Nila Ibrahim; Joe and Patty Craig; Mead Scofield; Kevin Stein; Kevin Ching; Jim Langham, Mike Zenker, John Ahmed; Sunghee Kim; Danny Bronstein; and John Craig.

And now, we have new debts of gratitude to some new (and some old) friends who helped to update and revise the 1993 edition. A warm thank you to: Elizabeth Farol, my lovely and intelligent teaching assistant at San Francisco State University who helped so much with the research for this book; to Dr. Yaacob Ibrahim of the NUS (National University of Singapore) and Cikgu Ehsan Haji Ali who helped with the Malay customs and Esah Binti Susman who helped with the Hari Raya interpretation; Mah Singh of the Tourist Guide Association of Singapore who spent long hours reviewing the materials on the Chinese, Indians, and Malays; C. P. Cheng and W. T. Ong for help with the Chinese section; Professor Emeritus Maurice Tseng of the San Francisco State University and Lee Gek Ling of the NUS who helped with the linguistics; Bhopinder Singh and wife Shindi and father Joginder Singh who helped with the Sikh information; Raj Kumar and wife Yogi Yogarajah and R. Jaichandra who helped with the Indian interpretations; Ilsa Sharp and Paul Terrell who helped with logistics; Chris Treichler who helped with the religious systems; and to my dear friend June Khoo, who worked so hard to edit this work and to prepare the manuscript. We also wish to thank the many expatriates who helped to develop the section on the Expats in the 1979 book and in the 1992 book by filling out a very long and arduous survey. And, lastly, thank you to old friends Sawyer, Len, Ted, Ed, Yuri, Yanni, and Tiny.

Chapter One

SETTLING IN

When asked about their first impressions of Singapore, many newcomers express amazement at the pristine and spotless condition of this green and well-scrubbed city-state of a nation. Twenty years ago, it was a lovely city, but not quite the lovely and dynamic green garden city that it is today.

Much has happened to Singapore since the time it became independent from Malaysia in 1965. Below we take you on a small tour of some of the physical, social and cultural changes which have taken place since then.

MULTI-ETHNIC PEOPLE

The many ethnic groups which populate the tiny, jewel-like nation of Singapore consist of a polyglot mixture of Chinese, Malays, Indians, and others. In the early days of independence, they were often separated and divided by sometimes violent racial disagreements, but they are now harmoniously melded into a strong community who share a spirited national identity as Singaporeans.

According to the 1990 Singapore Population Census Report, the Chinese make up 77.7% of the population; Malays 14.1%; Indians 7.1% and Others 1.1%. Children of mixed marriages are usually classified under their father's ethnic group. Eurasians (descendants of mixed alliances between Europeans and locals) and small numbers of Armenians, Arabs, and Jews make up the numbers in the Others category.

Around the expat community, there has grown up a host of international schools. (An American school, a Japanese school, a French school, etc.) The social clubs (American Club, Japanese Club, British Club, etc.) to which Singaporeans can also belong provide an atmosphere of a home away from home for culture-shocked and homesick expats. There are international newspapers and restaurants which cater to international tastes; and shops featuring just about everything an expat could wish to find in his/her own home town. In the international arena, Singapore is now considered to be an 'easy duty' assignment.

CHANGES

Government policies have changed and shaped Singapore over the last twenty-seven years since independence from Malaysia. The most dramatic change is in the way Singapore, an Asian city, has at times the feel and pulse of a modern Western metropolis. This is seen in the gleaming skyscrapers, fast-food restaurants, endless shopping malls and the efficient system of road and rail network. Singapore is also linked to the rest of the world through its international telecommunications system. On the domestic front, the *kampung* have given way to modern housing estates with high-rise flats, landscaped parks and neighbourhood shopping centres. Concurrent with all this urban renewal is the conservation of historical buildings and nature reserves as well as the development of large scale leisure facilities such as marinas and theme parks.

These physical changes cannot be seen in isolation. They reflect the deeper changes which have occurred in the hearts and minds of the Singaporeans. The government perceives the nation as a 'Global City' connected to other global cities through the international networks of science and technology. English is the medium of instruction in all schools and colleges and is firmly established as the country's lingua franca replacing the bazaar Malay that was more commonly used twenty years ago. The English language has brought with it Western culture and the steady decline of traditional customs and ways of thinking.

PHYSICAL SHOCKS

If you come from a temperate climate, the first thing that hits you is the heat. Culture shock (anxiety, stress and disorientation due to exposure to the countless differences in an alien culture) comes in all forms. The first culture shock to assail the foreigner is usually the shock of being exposed to so many physical and tangible differences in the host culture.

Some practical information on coping with daily life in Singapore is provided in the rest of this chapter. By learning to quickly understand and cope with the physical differences, you can settle in much faster, and you can prevent, cure, or mitigate many of the *physical* aspects of culture shock.

PHYSICAL GEOGRAPHY

Singapore is very small. It has a total land area (including the offshore islets) of 626.4 square kilometres or 242 square miles. It is slightly less than 3.5 times the size of Washington, DC in the USA. It is approximately 136.8 kilometres (85 miles) from the equator and is therefore very hot. Temperature ranges from 24–31°C (75–88°F) with an average daily maximum relative humidity of 96.3%. The humidity wrecks havoc with sensitive electronic equipment and photographs get stuck to their transparent plastic pockets in albums.

Rain falls all year round but is most abundant from November to January. Rainfall occurs mostly as sudden showers. It is a good idea to carry an umbrella whenever you go out. Be careful about hanging your favourite dress or shirt out to dry in direct sunlight, the colour will fade. Wear light and cool clothing. Dressing is mostly casual and informal although Singaporeans dress more formally when they go to work. There is no countryside to speak of, nor are there any farms or orchards. In spite of its urban nature, there is greenery everywhere.

A teacher tells her nursery class about plants and the stages of plant growth. In an urban environment, nature has to be brought into the classroom. Photo: MITA (Ministry of Information and the Arts)

15

LANGUAGE

English, Chinese, Malay, and Tamil are the four official languages. English is considered to be the language of science and technology, and thus it is the medium of instruction in schools. All students in Singaporean schools must be proficient in English and their mother tongue. The mother tongue is the language of their ethnic group which transfers Asian culture and values to the person.

HOUSING

For the expat, housing tends to be very expensive, but many international corporations pay the costs of housing their employees. To be on the safe side, make sure there is ample provision for housing in your employment contract. Some choices of private housing for expats as well as locals are: condominiums, townhouses and apartments. Many of these offer luxurious facilities such as a 24-hour guard, a pool, squash courts, etc. There are also terraced and semi-detached houses. These houses are quite small compared to Western

There are landscaped parks and children's play areas within walking distance of the residents in every HDB estate. Photo: MITA

standards. Gracious, old-style colonial bungalows with their huge gardens and servant's quarters can still be found. They are often beautiful, pleasant, and quiet, but many are in need of repair. A glance at the properties page in the classified advertisements in the local newspaper will give you an idea of what sort of accommodation is available as well as the rental or purchase price.

Today, more than 85% of Singaporeans live in Housing Development Board (HDB) flats. They have the option of renting or buying their flats by using money from their Central Provident Funds (CPF).

FOOD

1. *Buying fresh food* Fresh food can be bought at supermarkets and wet markets. The gory aspects of wet markets take some getting used to. The smell of chicken droppings and fish are very strong. If you cannot get used to seeing piles of chicken gizzards and livers spread out on tables or pigs' heads hanging from hooks you can shop more comfortably at the supermarkets where everything is neatly cut and wrapped in cellophane.

2. *Water* It is perfectly safe to drink tap water in Singapore. To let your system get used to the change, boil your drinking water for the first week or two.

3. *Eating out* Singapore is a food lover's paradise. You can eat at inexpensive, clean, old-fashioned food stalls in hawker centres, fast food restaurants or expensive and exclusive air-conditioned restaurants. Eating out is a national pastime! One can literally eat out every night in Singapore at a different place and taste food of endless variety in every price range.

4. *Chillies* Singaporeans use chillies in much of their food, If you cannot take hot foods, be sure to inform the proprietor when you order, do not wait until after you have been served.

5. *Monosodium glutamate* Many Singaporean cooks use monosodium glutamate (MSG)as a flavour enhancer. However, this can cause adverse reactions in people who cannot take it (dry mouth,

swollen hands, palpitations, difficulty in breathing and a tightness at the back of the neck). If you are allergic to MSG, tell the proprietor to leave it out of your order.

6. *Utensils* When eating food from different hawker stalls, be sure that you do not mix the cutlery and plates of Muslim and non-Muslim food stalls. Muslims have very strict food taboos (eg. they must not eat pork). It will cause a lot of displeasure if a fork from a Muslim food stall was used to pick up a piece of pork from a Chinese food stall.

7. *Seating at hawker centres* Tables are fixed to the floors in most hawker centres. People are free to sit wherever they like and order food from any stall they fancy. There is no obligation to order food from the stall nearest your table although it is more convenient if you do. Stall holders are not allowed to drive you away from any of the fixed tables nearest their stalls just because you did not order your food from them.

The government makes regular checks at hawker centres to ensure that stall holders prepare food under hygienic conditions. Photo: MITA

18

8. *Dress in restaurants* Casual dress is appropriate although there are some which do not allow singlets, shorts or bermudas and slippers. Some first-rate restaurants and hotels require that men wear a jacket and tie or a long-sleeved batik shirt. You should check on this when making reservations.

9. *Summoning a waiter/waitress* Never hiss, whistle, snap the fingers or shout 'Boy.'

DOMESTIC SERVANTS

Foreign maids have generally replaced the Singaporean domestic servants of yesterday. The women who seek employment as household servants and childminders today come mostly from developing countries such as the Philippines, Thailand, Indonesia, and Sri Lanka.

The Black and White amah Not so long ago, even in the 1970s, the most prestigious housekeeper/childminder a person could have was a 'Black and White' amah. She was called a Black and White amah because she wore a spotlessly clean white blouse and a pair of black cotton or silk trousers. She also wore a long pigtail hanging down her back or coiled up at the back of her head (as a symbol of her eternal and voluntary spinsterhood). These women were highly valued domestic servants in wealthy families and it was considered a great coup to have one of these reliable and untiring Chinese women in a household.

Foreign maids today These women come to escape the depressing condition of economic hardship. They try to find a better life for themselves and for the families which they have left behind in poverty. Many of these women send much of their earnings home to help relieve the privation and suffering of their families.

These women often work long hours as live-in servants, making only about S$250-$500 a month. Many of these women work through agents who receive a percentage of their wages in the first three months of employment as payment for expenses incurred in getting the maids to Singapore. Before they come, they are bonded and given

19

Domestic maids from the Philippines on their Sunday 'day off' outside Wisma Atria. They exchange news from home, addresses and telephone numbers. It is a time of relaxation and fun. Photo: Nicky Moey.

pregnancy, hepatitis and Aids tests by the agency to ensure that they are fit and healthy. The Ministry of Labour has set up rules and regulations about employing foreign maids. This is to protect these maids from exploitative employers. Physical abuse of maids is viewed as a serious offence by the police. Employers who are found ill-treating their foreign maids are severely punished.

TRANSPORTATION

Getting around in Singapore is easy. Public transportation is cheap and convenient although taxi and bus drivers may not always understand your directions or questions because of your accent.

1. *Taxis* There are plenty of taxis except during rush hours and when it rains. They are affordable, clean and well regulated. The only

way you might get cheated in Singapore is if the driver suspects you don't know your way around town and then he might go by a circuitous route. If you are worried about it, check your route beforehand. Or you can query the route with the driver.

Fares are metered. There are surcharges for certain journeys at certain times:
- for a trip from the airport;
- between midnight and 6 a.m.;
- to dial for a taxi; or make a booking;
- to enter the restricted zone between 7.30 and 10.15 a.m. on weekdays and Saturdays and between 4.30 and 6.30 p.m. from Monday to Friday;
- for trips out of the restricted zones between 4 and 7 p.m. on weekdays and between 12 noon and 3 p.m. on Saturdays.

Taxis are allowed to carry a maximum of four adults. Children count roughly as two to an adult. Above the doors in all taxis is the taxi's registration number. If you have a problem, note it down.

If you have left something in a taxi, call the taxi company first. The driver hands it in to them and they pass it on to the registry of vehicles.

Taxis stop at taxi stands where orderly queues form. They also stop anywhere else that is safe and doesn't violate any laws. Stopping a taxi away from a taxi stand can be a frustrating business in busy places during rush hours. Someone else may walk twenty paces in front of you and hail the same taxi. This even happens at taxi stands. You are advised to step quickly if a taxi stops for you at a busy place during rush hours.

If the taxi you hail is empty but doesn't stop, it may be because the driver is on call or because he is changing shifts. If he wiggles his hand at you through the windscreen it means he's about to get his lunch or dinner.

2. *The Mass Rapid Transit (MRT)* The network links the four corners of the island with the centre. Tickets are bought from

machines at each station and costs are clearly mapped out. There is a time limit for use of the MRT and exceeding it involves a surcharge of $2. Eating, drinking and smoking are not allowed in the trains or on the platforms.

3. *Buses* Public buses cover the rest of the island and fares are very cheap. Some services are air-conditioned and slightly more expensive. A book of bus routes can be bought at most stationers. Not all bus drivers can understand or speak the English that you speak. To avoid bad feelings and frustration on both sides you should find out the bus route beforehand. Always have change ready because all buses are One-Man-Operated (the driver does everything and giving change is not his job). Passengers put in the correct amount of money and the driver punches out the ticket for them.

4. *Driving* Car ownership and use is extremely expensive in Singapore. Those who wish to own and drive their own cars are expected to pay for the privilege in a land-scarce country. You can drive in Singapore with a valid driver's licence from your own country for a year. After one year, you can apply for a Singapore driver's licence at the Traffic Police Headquarters in Maxwell Road. Bring your existing driver's licence along.

   Driving in Singapore can be quite harrowing. Singaporeans do not seem to mind being very close to one another, and they don't ordinarily leave large spaces between themselves and other cars as Westerners tend to do. Singaporean drivers often tailgate, or cut in on one another without giving the types of signals which

Westerners are used to, and they often change lanes indiscriminately, without realizing that they are offending anyone. Get used to drivers switching lanes as and when they see fit and often without indicating. It is quite customary for the driver on the inside lane to be travelling faster than those in the middle or outside lane and someone stuck behind a slow driver in the middle lane is just as likely to move into the inside lane as the outer lane to overtake.

Keep to speed limits. Maximum 80 km/h on expressways and 50km/h on busy and smaller roads.

Accidents must be reported within twenty-four hours to the police, even if there is no injury or major damage.

If a car breaks down, the local people put a branch in the bumper or rear mudguard, or they lift the hood. These are visible signs that the car is not working and that the traffic must go around it. If possible, the car should be pushed to the left side of the road so as to cause as little obstruction as possible to the flow of traffic.

Buses have total right of way in the bus lanes during peak hours. There are no bus lane restrictions on Sundays and public holidays. Automobiles should not be in the bus lanes during these hours unless turning left:

Weekdays: 7.30–9.30 a.m. and 4.30–7.00 p.m.

Saturday: 7.30–9.30 a.m. and 11.30 a.m.–2.00 p.m.

Singapore follows the British custom of driving on the left-hand side of the road. Be very careful if you are used to driving 'American' style where vehicles drive on the right-hand side of the road. As soon as you get into the car remember to 'Think Left.' Also, be very careful about stepping off the curb and looking in the wrong direction for the flow of traffic! Many an unsuspecting newcomer to Singapore has stepped right into the path of an oncoming vehicle because of this.

Before driving into the central area of town, called the Central Business District (CBD), it is necessary to buy a CBD sticker from one of the kiosks just outside the area selling them. They are sold at the moment on a daily basis and cost $3. They are only needed during the peak hours in the morning between 7.30 and 10.30 a.m. and early evening between 4.30 and 6.30 p.m.

If you break the law while driving in Singapore, you may be in for a surprise! The traffic police may not chase a violator in hot pursuit, but record the infraction and forward it to the perpetrator by mail weeks after the alleged offence. One pays the fine by a visit to the traffic police in Maxwell Road. It is possible to contest the fine, but you may notice that many junctions are fitted with automatic cameras.

5. *The Causeway* The only link by land between Singapore and Malaysia is the Singapore–Johor Causeway. Some points to be aware of are:

- At peak times very large traffic jams form behind the Malaysian immigration kiosks. Waiting time to get back to Singapore at the end of Chinese New Year or other long holidays runs into hours. If possible make the journey across by car in mid-morning or afternoon and avoid weekends.
- If you drive you must have your petrol tank at least three-quarter full when going from Singapore to Malaysia.
- If you have an employment pass or dependant's pass you do not need to fill out new entry permits for Singapore but you will need them for Malaysia.

SHOPPING AND BARGAINING

Singapore is a shopper's paradise! Newcomers to Singapore are often confused by the methods of shopping and bargaining in Singapore. The first thing to be aware of is that there are two price structures in Singapore (and many other countries in Asia for that matter): they are 'fixed' prices and 'bargaining' prices. There are no hard and fast rules but the following generalities apply:

1. *Fixed prices* In department stores, large emporiums, some large

There are grand department stores housed in air-conditioned shopping complexes selling expensive designer goods as well as inexpensive neighbourhood shops in the housing estates selling everything you would need to settle in comfortably. Photo: Munshi Ahmed

stores where prices are displayed and supermarkets, the prices are fixed and no bargaining is expected.

2. *No fixed price* The rules regarding bargaining in shopping centres are a little more complicated. You really have to know each shopping centre. In Chinatown Point, People's Park and the other shopping centres in Chinatown, except in the big emporiums, bargaining is mandatory. If the shop has fixed prices they will tell you. Similarly don't be fooled by the posh appearances of places in Wisma Atria, Lucky Plaza or Far East Plaza. Heavy bargaining is called for in many shops here. In the few *pasar malam* (night markets) in Singapore bargaining is also necessary.

3. *A quick guide to bargaining* It is important to know what the average prices are. Be sure to compare prices in different shops before attempting to seriously bargain for merchandise.

25

It is common to offer about 50% of the first asking price and then to begin the haggling back and forth until a mutually acceptable price is settled on. For instance, the merchant may reduce the price to 85% after your first offer, and then you can counter with about 60% of the original price, and the merchant then may counter your counter with about 75%. It is common to agree to about 75%–85% of the original price. Before the end of the session, you should ask: 'What is your best price?' The object of the game is to establish a relationship where both sides come out winners and no one comes out a loser. If a Westerner buys any merchandise without bargaining, he/she would be thought of as *bodoh* (Malay for 'stupid'). The local people normally bargain before they pay for any goods, and as a result, they may only pay about 60–80% of the first quoted price.

If you are not used to the process, don't know the rules and feel ill at ease you could try shopping with a local friend or just mention,'Can you offer any discounts?' This indicates that you are willing to buy but the quoted price is high; the sales attendant will normally give you a discount if he/she can and both parties are happy.

4. *Tactic* The best tactics to use are goodwill, friendliness, graciousness, warm-heartedness, and good fun. Try to be good-humoured about the whole thing. The worst tactics to use are hot-headedness, anger, shouting, suspicion, and paranoia.

5. *Beware of touts* If you have been around any other Asian city, you
   will by now have formed your own defensive measures against
   touts. The touts in Singapore sell anything from bad fake designer
   goods to sexual activity. Determinedly ignoring them is the best
   means of having a trouble-free stay in Singapore.

SCHOOLS

There are many expat schools in Singapore which follow the syllabuses
of the home country. Look up the telephone book or check with your
embassy for names, telephone numbers and addresses. Local schools
take in foreign students if there are vacancies.

MEDICAL FACILITIES AND HEALTH

Most expats and their families are enrolled in private health-care
schemes by their employers. Singaporeans pay a subsidized fee at
government health centres. There are also many private clinics, dental
surgeries and hospitals.

Singapore is the cleanest city in Southeast Asia. Sewage and
garbage disposal are not a problem. Daily trash collection is efficient.
Ants and cockroaches are more of a problem than they are in more
temperate climates.

There are few health hazards in Singapore. Dengue fever can be
a problem and may last for two or three months. Cholera occurs
occasionally, but an incidence is isolated immediately. Typhoid is
endemic, but cases are rare.

Children sometimes contract tropical fevers of unknown origin,
which may last from one to three days, but in general, Singapore
provides a good environment for young children. Occasional intestinal trouble may occur but serious dysentery is rare. Respiratory
ailments, however, are common. The country's humidity and heat
increase the incidence of skin problems. You are advised to seek
treatment at the first sign of trouble, as infections spread rapidly.

Facilities are good for most health problems, and there is adequate pediatric and obstetric care. Competent specialists in most fields practise in Singapore. Most doctors have been trained in Singapore, the United Kingdom, Australia, the United States or Canada. All hospitals are well equipped with the latest in diagnostic equipment.

POLICE AND SAFETY

Some of the major physical concerns people have when coming to work and live in a foreign country are always safety and security. If you come from a country where crime is not so well controlled, you may be pleasantly surprised to see that Singapore has a well-deserved reputation for being safe and relatively crime free.

1. *Neighbourhood Police Posts (NPP)* The police force, which had operated out of eight police stations or precincts in the past, was subdivided into locally-based Neighbourhood Police Posts (NPPs) in 1983. The police posts now number about eight per station, and they are built directly on the ground floors of high-rise blocks or

A policeman from a neighbourhood police post helps a schoolgirl and her mother with directions. Photo: MITA

in special kiosks in major residential areas, so that the 25 or more constables assigned to each post can be directly involved in the daily life of the residents. This follows the very successful Japanese *koban* system of crime control. The post constables make personal contact with every family in their post's jurisdiction, disseminate crime-prevention information and work with community organizations.

2. *Crime* Today, Singapore is relatively safe. The citizens are remarkably honest and taxi drivers have been known to chase after passengers who have left wallets, packages, and baggage behind. The society, in its media and newspapers, praises those citizens who have done astonishingly honest things, like returning a large amount of money found on the street to the owner.

Major crime is dealt with severely and swiftly. The death penalty is mandatory for possession or dealing in illegal drugs or firearms; for use of a firearm to cause bodily harm; and for murder and rape.

Vices are also considered crimes:
• public solicitation is forbidden;
• the only legalized gambling is horse-racing and the Singapore sweepstakes (both under government control);
• pornography in all forms is banned;
• public drunkenness is also banned.

3. *Advice to foreigners* At the street level, citizen exposure to law enforcement is more in reference to minor rules and regulations than major offences. All criminal laws are national laws and all laws apply equally to all citizens and to expats and their families as well. Expats who break the laws are subject to the same penalties as Singaporeans.

Much of the police service in Singapore is preventative rather than reactive. You may be surprised by the kindly community services offered by the friendly Singapore police. Not only are they polite, but if you let them know when you will be away, they will arrange a patrol to keep an eye on your home. Find out to which area you belong, and write down the number of your local police post for handy reference, because crimes must be reported in the area where they occur.

RELIGION

Singapore is a secular state where all religions are free to flourish. It strongly advocates religious tolerance, and encourages all minority religions to contribute to the harmony and welfare of the entire nation. The majority of Chinese are Taoists, Buddhists, or Freethinkers i.e., they hold to no particular religion, some are Christians; Malays are nearly all Muslim; most Indians are Hindus although there are many who are Muslims; and there are also Christians, Sikhs, Parsees, Confucianists, and mixtures of all of the above. The degree of religious tolerance in Singapore is amazing indeed.

TIPPING

In Singapore tipping is ordinarily taboo. It smacks of colonialism and imperialism. Singaporeans do not believe that they need extra money To Insure Prompt Service (TIPS)!

The local people generally do not tip taxi drivers, doormen, hairdressers, etc., but during Chinese New Year they ordinarily give a nice *hong bao* (red packet containing money) to those who do them a special service during the year, i.e. their servants, grocer, rubbish collectors, paper delivery person, etc.

1. Do not tip when there is a sign displayed which says 'No tipping'. Employees of private clubs and airport employees are not tipped. Government employees, meter readers, office clerks, etc., should never be tipped, not even on Chinese New Year, lest the tip be misconstrued as bribery or corruption!
2. Hotels usually add a service charge to the bill and this money is shared by all the employees in general so it is not necessary to tip unless someone does you a special service. If you wish to tip

an individual, then room and messenger service would warrant a tip of from 50 cents to $2.00.

3. Most restaurants add a 10% service charge to the bill, and this money is shared by the group (unlike in Western countries where each individual gets his/her own tips). If no service charge has been added, then a tip of 10–15% of the bill is fair, but not required.

TOILET FACILITIES

There are two types of toilets in Singapore: the 'sit down' type and the 'squat-on-the-floor' type.

1. *Toilet paper* It is wise to bring toilet paper with you when you go out. Toilet paper is not always available in many public toilets and in some homes, it is not the custom to use toilet paper.

2. *Public toilets* Many public toilets in shopping centres, restaurants, hawker centres are far from ideal. Very often the floors are wet, the flushing system has broken down and there is no toilet paper, a devastating combination when you are desperate. There is a fine of $150 for not flushing the toilet after use.

3. *Toilets in homes* In some homes, especially Malay and Indian homes, toilet paper is not provided. Malays and Indians splash-wash themselves with water after using the toilet. It would be polite to keep a bucket and bailing scoop in your own bathroom for use by local guests.

4. *Use of left hand* Among the Malays and Indians, the left hand is traditionally used for cleansing purposes. This is one of the reasons why the left hand is never used for any other reason except cleansing. For instance, it would be a gross insult to hand anyone anything with the cleansing left hand, to accept money with it, and so on.

Westerners might wish to follow this custom of using the right hand when dealing with Singaporeans (especially Malays and Indians) so as not to inadvertently cause offence.

DATES AND NUMBERS

The British system of writing dates is generally used, i.e., the day is placed first, then the month, and lastly, the year. Be careful if you are not used to this system because 6/9/92 is not June 9th, 1992, (like it is in the United States) but September 6, 1992. If you want to be cautious, always write out the month.

HOUSEHOLD PESTS AND WILDLIFE

Coming into contact with little creatures in and about the home that one has never seen before is one of the biggest shocks on the physical level which expats are exposed to.

- 'Is this insect poisonous?'
- 'Will that bug cause a painful rash?'

1. *Ants* These insects abound in Singapore. They can be black, brown, yellow or red; easily recognized by the constriction in the middle of the body. You can prevent ants from entering your home by keeping all areas (especially the kitchen) free of food particles and by sprinkling generous amounts of red chilli powder around the areas where they enter the house.

2. *Cicaks* (pronounced chee chaks) These are pale brown lizards that live in your home. Some Singaporeans believe they bring good luck. They are useful creatures because they eat other insects. They are harmless but their droppings can be a nuisance. The best thing to do is to seal up cracks and crevices in the home, this will deprive them of hiding places. To deprive them of food, keep the house free of other insects and human food particles.

3. *Cockroaches* These are insects with long feelers and a flat body. They can scramble away very fast. Control cockroaches by keeping your house clear of food particles and waste. Get rid of hiding places such as old newspapers, cartons and boxes.

4. *Flies* These are insects with compound eyes and hairy legs and bodies. They breed in decaying organic matter and hence transmit germs when they land on food meant for humans. Prevent flies

from infesting the home by keeping kitchens clean and rubbish bins covered.

I DON'T CALL EATING MOSQUITOES GOOD LUCK

5. *Lice* A louse is a small flat wingless insect with sucking mouth parts. Lice are parasitic on the skin on humans. There are different types of the lice, the most frequently seen ones in Singapore are the human body lice and the head lice.

If your children are scratching their heads all the time (and not just because of the hot weather) you should take a look at their scalps. See a doctor immediately if you find little white specks on the scalp. He will recommend treatment with a special shampoo.

6. *Mosquitoes* These insects can be dangerous because they carry the virulent diseases of malaria and dengue fever. The females feed on blood of humans and some animals. They have skin-piercing mouthparts by which they extract blood, thus transferring the illness when they sting.

Mosquitoes breed in stagnant water, so do not allow water to stagnate anywhere. There are strict fines for leaving standing water in plant trays, flower pots and clogged drains around the house. Officials from the Ministry of Environment make regional checks from time to time.

7. *Weevils and mealy bugs* These little creatures are a pestilence in the kitchen. They abound in the wet, humid, steamy atmosphere of Singapore. Their larvae feed on grains and other products such as flour. Keep all cereals and grains tightly closed in air-tight containers. Keep what you can in the refrigerator and buy in small quantities.

8. *Intestinal parasites* Hookworm and threadworm may be transmitted to children if they play about barefoot in the garden or sandpit. If you find your children complaining of itchy bottoms or

33

if you find little white squiggles in their stools, bring them to your doctor for deworming. A syrup that the doctor gives will do the trick.

9. *Snakes* Amazingly, Singapore still harbours a variety of snakes. While you may not see one in the strictly urban areas, there are still some areas which are rural enough to be attractive to them. Most hospitals carry anti-snakebite serum and no one has died of snakebite in Singapore for a very long time.

If you have a large, rambling garden (very rare) you might encounter a python or cobra during your stay. Most cobras are black with a beige patch which will only be seen when they rear up. They are spitting cobras and can cause blindness if they spit into your eyes. If you see one, leave the area quickly. If one enters your house, call the police. Unlike other species of cobras they will not attack unless they are threatened.

Pythons are not poisonous but their bite can inflict serious damage and anti-tetanus injections would be necessary. Other indeterminate coloured snakes are harmless. Blue coral snakes are probably no longer around but are very dangerous indeed.

10. *Spiders, scorpions and centipedes* There are poisonous spiders and scorpions but their bite is not fatal.

Children should not run around barefoot in the garden as there are centipedes which sting.

NATIONAL CAMPAIGNS AND LAWS

The Singapore government holds nation-wide campaigns whenever it wants to heighten public awareness of certain important issues such as safety for passengers in vehicles, dangers of smoking, healthy living etc. Fines are imposed to discourage anti-social behaviour. Following is a concise, but by no means complete, list of laws, rules and regulations of which the unwary should be aware.

1. *Breeding disease-bearing insects* It is an offence to create conditions that are favourable to the propagation or harbouring of

disease-bearing insects. For example, allowing water to stagnate in uncleared roof gutters or in drip dishes under potted plants. Disease-carrying mosquitoes breed in stagnant water. Persons found guilty of such an offence will have to pay a fine not exceeding $1,000 or face imprisonment not exceeding 3 months. The penalty is doubled for subsequent convictions.

2. *Chewing gum* Leaving chewed gum in a public place is an offence. There is a fine of $500. It is an offence to sell chewing gum, the penalty is a $2,000 fine.

3. *Copyright Law* The Copyright Act is very complex. In essence, acts *not* constituting an infringement of copyright works include copies made for private study, research, for criticism or review.

   It is an offence when copies are made for sale or hire or imported into Singapore, other than for private and domestic use. Anyone guilty of such an offence is liable on conviction to a fine not exceeding $10,000 or to imprisonment not exceeding 5 years or both.

   There is a fine of $1,000 for possession or sale of pirated videotapes. For subsequent offences – jail up to two years, or a fine of up to $2,000 or both.

4. *Cruelty to animals* There is a fine up to $500, or jail up to 6 months or both for this offence.

5. *Dogs and banned breeds* The number of dogs a household can have is restricted. People who live in an apartment are allowed only one dog (only small breeds). People with houses and a compound may keep three dogs. The Primary Production Department (PPD) deals with household pets. You will need to buy a dog licence from the PPD. The fine for an unlicenced dog is $500.

   The more ferocious breeds (American Pit Bull Terrier, Tosa, Akita, Neapolitan Mastiff and any cross breeds between them) are now banned following the recent attacks on humans in America and Europe.

   • These dogs must be muzzled and on a leash when outside the

owner's property or the owners will face a fine of up to $500.
- The dogs must have identification tattoos on their ears.
- The dogs must be sterilized.
- Owners must deposit a bond of $5,000 with the PPD.
- Owners must have third-party insurance of at least $100,000 per dog so that victims can claim compensation.

Other breeds such as Bull Mastiffs, Bull Terriers, Dobermans, German Shepherds and Rottweilers must be leashed and muzzled when they are outside the owner's property. The fine for violating the rule is $200.

There is a fine not exceeding $1,000 if your dog chases people, vehicles or bicycles.

6. *Drug trafficking* The government of Singapore takes a very serious view of drug offences. The maximum penalty for the misuse of drugs is death. Misuse of drugs includes possession and trafficking of controlled drugs.

7. *Fireworks* Banned fireworks include firecrackers, rocket fireworks, sand crackers (a pellet containing an explosive which will be activated when set on fire or rubbed on any abrasive surface) and others declared dangerous by the government. First offenders will be fined not more than $2,000. Second and subsequent offenders will be fined not more than $10,000 or jailed for not more than 2 years or both. Sparklers and party poppers are allowed and are on sale in shops selling party gear or stationery (especially in HDB estates).

8. *Jaywalking* There is a fine of $20 for all offences and that includes climbing over road dividers specially put up to encourage people to use overhead pedestrain bridges across busy roads. There is also a fine of $150 for motorists who do not give way to pedestrians at crossings.

9. *Littering and killer-litter* Do not throw your litter (candy wrappers, paper cups, bus tickets, etc.) on the streets or pavements. Use the litter bins near bus stops and along the streets. The maximum

fine for littering is $1,000. Throwing objects (killer litter) from high floors of flats and other tall buildings thereby causing serious injury to people below is a punishable offence. The penalty is a fine up to $250 or jail for up to 3 months or both.

10. *Road traffic offences*
- Speeding, reckless driving and driving under the influence of drink (alcoholic) or drugs are punishable offences. The penalty is a fine not exceeding $1,000 or jail not exceeding 6 months or both. The penalty is doubled for subsequent offenders who may also be disqualified from holding a driving licence.
- Motorcyclists and pillion riders must wear protective helmets approved by the government. There is a fine not exceeding $200 for contravening this regulation.
- Seat belts and child restraints. Children under eight years of age must be strapped in with seat belts or harnesses when in the front seat or back seat of cars, pick-ups and trucks. It is an offence for an adult to put a child on the lap with the seat belt over both adult and child. There is a fine of $120 for those not complying with the rule.

11. *Smoking* There is a ban on smoking in most public places. Smoking is prohibited in enclosed, air-conditioned buildings (for example, cinemas, theatres, lifts, restaurants). The maximum fine for smoking in a prohibited place is $1,000. There is a heavy duty on cigarettes in Singapore and you are restricted to bringing in two packets if you enter Singapore from Malaysia.

12. *Spitting* There is a fine not exceeding $1,000 for spitting on the street or any public place.

13. *Toilet flushing* There is a fine of $150 for not flushing a public toilet after use. Many public toilets now have automatic flushing systems, so do not be alarmed at the sudden gush of water sometimes even before you have finished.

14. *Touting* There is a fine of not more than $5,000 or 6 months

imprisonment or both for touting and selling of fake goods. The penalty is doubled for subsequent offenders.

15. *Weapons and arms* Unlawful possession of weapons and arms is a serious offence. Maximum punishment includes life imprisonment and caning (not less than 6 strokes).

SINGAPORE'S FASCINATING LINGUISTIC STYLE

Most Singaporeans are fluent in two or three languages, and some are also fluent in two or three dialects. The English spoken by Singaporeans (especially those who are more comfortable in their mother tongue) is influenced by many factors: the grammar rules, syntax and phonology of the mother tongue (Chinese, Malay Indian), slang from American television programmes and from the movies, national service where the influence of Hokkien is very strong, and other factors such as the working environment and age of the speaker. Singapore-English has its own style and form, its own charm. Some refer to this particular style of English as a hybrid which they call Singlish – a colourful mixture of Singaporean and English words and grammar rules!

Children learn English as well as their mother tongue in school. Sometimes the lines separating the two languages became blurred, intertwined, and merged. Out of this rich co-mingling and blending of cultures and languages, the English of Singapore continues to thrive and to go through ceaseless social change.

SOME SINGAPORE-ENGLISH LANGUAGE PATTERNS

I wish to thank my very dear friend, Professor Emeritus Maurice Tseng, of San Francisco State University, for assistance with this section. Professor Tseng explained and interpreted many of the patterns and the reasons for the linguistic patterns which follow.

1. *Accent and pronunciation* Heard in a flash, some of the English spoken by Singaporeans might sound like another language

An English lesson in a primary school. English is the language for international interaction in industry, commerce, science and technology. It is also the language for inter-ethnic communication in Singapore today. Photo: Nicky Moey

entirely to native English speakers. The influence of the mother tongue is evident in the way Singaporeans pronounce English words. For example, a 50 year-old bus driver who is more comfortable with Chinese might not be able to help you when you ask him, 'Does this bus go to Holland Road?' because he pronounces Holland Road as 'Ho-lahn Lood' and as far as he knows there is no Holland Road along his route.

2. ***Double words used for emphasis*** When any word is said twice in rapid succession, it accentuates the meaning. For instance 'thin-thin' means that the person is bone thin.

3. ***Words ending with 'L'*** Many Chinese in Singapore tend not to

pronounce the ending 'L' sound in words that end with 'L', for example:

- 'wall' sounds like 'war'
- 'example' sounds like 'examper'
- 'file' sounds like 'fa' or 'fy'

However, Chinese do not seem to have any problem at all with 'L' sounds at the *beginning* of words and many of their words begin with 'L.'

4. ***'Lah' used at the end of a phrase*** Singaporeans of all ethnic groups often use the expression 'lah' at the end of a statement. You may be surprised to learn that the 'lah' is not used at random, and that there is a definite logic associated with using it, and that the expression has a meaning and a purpose all its own. Generally, 'lah' is a suffix which emphasizes the point made in a sentence, for example:

- 'No lah!'
- 'Don't be like that lah.'
- 'She can do it lah. No problem.'

The expression 'lah' could have come from the Chinese 'le' (from the north of China), or from the 'la' (from the south of China). When used according to the Chinese pattern, it is used as a particle, and denotes:

- a completed action
  'They met already lah.'
- a situation different from the one perceived or expected
  'Too expensive lah!'

5. ***'One' used in place of the possessive pronoun*** Instead of using an English-style possessive pronoun such as 'mine', 'his', Singaporeans often use their version of distinguishing possession. It is a direct translation of the Chinese expression *de,* and the Malay expression *punya*, for example:

- My one (*Wo de* in Chinese, *saya punya* in Malay) – Mine.
- His one – His.

6. *Opposing choices – used for requests, statements, possibility and questions* Words which suggest possibility – or conditional words like could/should, may/might, shall/will are often absent in Asian conversation. Instead, the use of 'opposing forces' is substituted. In the Chinese language, whenever a question is asked; a request is made which requires an answer; or a statement is made which suggests a possibility; or when a person is given a choice; it is considered very polite to offer the person a choice of both possibilities (positive and negative).

For instance, when asking a friend if he/she wants to eat now, to Chinese ears, it would not be so polite to say: 'Do you want to eat now?' because there has been no range of alternatives presented. The more polite Chinese way would be: (literally translated) 'Eat now, want or not want?' (*yao bu yao*)? Other examples:

- 'I offer you a price of $15.00; good or not?' (*hao bu hao*)
- 'Go to the movies, can or cannot?' (*ke yi bu ke yi*)
- 'Do you like it or not?' (*xi huan bu xi huan*)

41

These very polite Singaporean forms which present the full range of choice, though very polite in Chinese, may sound strange and harsh to Western ears when they are directly translated into English. Some examples of cultural courtesy cues:

- English style – 'Do have a cup of tea!' This could sound pushy and bossy to Asian ears because it implies that there can be only one choice: 'yes'.
- American style – 'Would you like a cup of tea?' This could sound impolite to Asian ears because it does not present a positive and a negative choice.
- Singaporean style – 'You want to drink tea or not?' This could sound impolite to Western ears because it sounds harsh and pushy, as if one was being dared to make the choice!

With everyone trying to be very polite to each other, and with everyone sounding not so polite to each other because of cultural differences, what should one do to come out looking like a polite person? The best thing to do, of course, would be to show kindness. Kindness is always a mark of courtesy, no matter where you are. Be aware of the politeness of each culture, and adjust yourself to each one.

7. *Tag ending: 'Isn't it?'* Singaporeans of all ethnic groups use the tag ending 'Isn't it?' with great frequency.

The words always mean:
- Isn't it so?
- Don't you agree?
- Isn't that right?

If a Singaporean says to you: 'You are from America, isn't it?' It does not mean that the Singaporean does not know how to use correct English grammar! He/She is not making a grammatical error because he/she is not saying: 'You are from America, aren't you?' The Singaporean is saying, 'You are from America

– isn't that right?' There are many reasons why Singaporeans use this tag so much:

- It is a consensus-building device – The tag 'Isn't it' does not pose a question. It asks for consensus, group agreement, and verification of what is being said. It is an attempt to make for harmony in the group and it draws the listener into the circle of the group and invites him/her to participate.

- It shows deference – The polite 'Isn't it' leaves the final say up to the one being spoken to – it courteously gives him/her the final choice or thought. In this context, if a Singaporean of lower status is speaking to a person of higher status, he/she would probably use more tags to show more deference and politeness to the elder/teacher/parent/boss.

- It shows modesty – The superior person is unpretentious, modest, and humble. By saying 'Isn't it,' a person is showing a sign of uncertainty (even if he/she is positively right) which shows that he/she is not a know-it-all and definitely not a braggart. All this implies that the person speaking is polite, modest and of a superior character!

8. ***Tense determined by time words and phrases*** The word 'tense' comes from the Latin, and it means: 'time'. It refers to changes in the form of the verb to indicate the time of the action. English verbs have six tenses: present, past, future, present perfect, past perfect, future perfect. By using these tenses, everyone knows exactly when an action takes place, or will take place, or had taken place, or will have had taken place, etc.

The Chinese (and the Malays) on the other hand, do not use tenses in their language structure. They do not use auxiliary verbs either. Seen from the Western point of view, all of their verbs are in the present tense only.

If they do not use tenses, how then do they make sure that one knows whether something has happened in the past, the present, or the future? They simply use a literary device called a time phrase. A time phrase is a word or phrase such as: tomorrow afternoon, last night, 24 hours from now, next time, last time, formerly, etc.

The time phrase is simply tacked onto the present tense of the verb form:

- Tomorrow he go, today he not free. (Future and Present)
- I see that show already. (Past perfect)
- Today I eat with my friend. (Present)

These time words and phrases are then directly translated into English words and phrases, and we can see that Westerners wrongly judge Asians as using improper grammar form when they are in fact following very strict grammar rules of their *own* culture.

9. *Common Singlish words/expressions*
- aiyah (aiyoh) – indicates that the user has just had some sort of setback. (Malay, Chinese, Indian)
- ang moh – literally this means 'red hair' in Chinese-Hokkien. It refers to Caucasians/Westerners.
- blur – confused or confusing. 'I feel so blur' (derived from Chinese for 'not clear', used especially among national servicemen during training).
- buaya – a girl chaser. It is the Malay for crocodile.
- can – used in many instances when agreement is requested:
  Can? – Is that O.K?
  Can! – Yes! That's fine.
- cheem – difficult, complicated, profound. (Chinese-Hokkien for deep)
- frus – short for frustrated.
- gone case – said when someone or something is beyond hope, cannot be saved.
- kay poh – nosy.
- kiasu – afraid of being left out or of failing. (Chinese-Hokkien)
- catch no ball – don't understand.

- makan – a meal; to eat. (Malay)
- malu – embarrassed. (Malay)
- minah – girlfriend. (Malay)
- my rice bowl – my living.
- now then you know – you've found it out only now/so late.
- orang puteh – Malay for 'white man' refers to Caucasians/ Westerners.
- quai lo – 'devilish person' Chinese-Cantonese for foreign devils, refers to Caucasians.
- see first – to wait and see (to avoid committing oneself right now).
- shiok – fantastic, good, particularly food. (Malay)
- towkay – boss; head of an establishment. (Chinese-Hokkien)
- ulu, swaku – unsophisticated, countrified, wet behind the ears.
- zap – to photocopy something.

TRIGG.

— *Chapter Two* —

EAST MEETS WEST

The country of Singapore is a plural society, comprising a multi-lingual, multi-ethnic and multi-religious people. These people have created a new society in which different ethnic groups have blended together to become one people; yet each group has retained its own special charm, uniqueness, and individuality which adds to the exotic flavour of Singapore.

In many ways the local customs and courtesies of Singapore are very different from the traditional good manners of a Western culture. Westerners tend to think that basic good manners and etiquette are universally understood and practised in the same way; after all, we are all humans here, and we all feel the same way – we love, we grieve, we rejoice – but we may not realize that not all humans do things the same way. What constitutes good manners in one society may have exactly the opposite effect in another.

ETHNOCENTRISM

Ethnocentrism has always been one of the biggest dangers in the cross-cultural world. Anthropologists, business people, housewives, students, teachers, and all who cross cultures can fall victim to it. In Webster's dictionary, ethnocentrism is defined as: 'The emotional attitude that one's own ethnic group, nation, or culture is superior to all others.'

According to an anthropological definition, it means that one compares every other culture unfavourably with one's own culture; that one looks at other cultures through one's own cultural eye – and closed cultural mind; that one reacts in a bigoted, prejudiced, and intolerant way towards other cultures; that one sees ones own culture as virtuous or select and feels that one's own standard of values and behaviour is universally and intrinsically true, and that one views one's own customs as the original human ones, and views all other customs as somehow inferior.

It is often seen in the 'Back home, we do it this way' attitude. It creeps in when it is least expected. It can even occur when one is determined to appreciate everything about the foreign culture one is visiting or living in. An obvious example of this can be seen during the durian season in Singapore (June–July and December). This season is characterized by Singaporeans dragging home huge sacks of this peculiar-smelling fruit. The odour lingers for hours in lifts stairwells and cars. Your Singaporean companion raises her nose and breathes in the sweet aroma of durian and sighs in delight. To you it smells like a very bad gas leak laced with sulphur or worse. Elsewhere in town serious negotiations are going on between stall holders and durian connoisseurs as to the exact degree of ripeness, sweetness and texture of the prickly fruit. Physiologically speaking, human noses work in the same manner, but culturally speaking, what constitutes a good smell in one culture is not necessarily so in another. To understand and appreciate each other – one must have an open mind – and in this case, an open nose! In the matter of durians, foreigners who enjoy it are considered to be honorary Singaporeans.

DANGERS OF ETHNOCENTRISM

In spite of the hints, courses, and books which advise Westerners on how to understand the Asian psyche, many an unwary expat still feels that the safest policy is to 'be yourself: your open, friendly, frank, outspoken, and up-front self.' These qualities are supposed to be what Asians admire about Westerners. However, Asians are less likely to admire these 'qualities', than they are to view the Westerners as lacking in grace, manners, and cleverness when these same qualities cause hurt feelings, lost face, business breakdowns and unwitting hostility.

Remember that behaviours are culturally-bound! A smile and laughter in an Asian culture can signal many things (happiness, joy, sorrow, embarrassment, shame, lost face, shyness, coolness, etc.) while the same smile and laughter in the West usually signals only one thing: joy or amusement! When the Asian hides sorrow behind a smile, and the Westerner wrongly takes that smile for a heartless and cruel reaction to something, then, sadly, ethnocentrism can result and the wrong information can be processed: 'These people are barbarians, their culture is perverse, they have no heart, and so on.'

CULTURAL PROFILES

A Singaporean ideology was published by the Singapore Institute of

Policy Studies in October 1988. The ideology promotes racial and religious understanding; tolerance and harmony; honest government; the harmonizing of individual and communal interests; respect for the family as a basic institution of society; compassion for the less fortunate; and the use of consensual means to resolve major issues. This ideology strives to successfully combine the best parts of an Asian philosophy with the best parts of a Western philosophy, where 'respect for the individual' (Western view) is secured and protected within 'the support system of the group' (Asian view). Singapore's ideology focuses on hard work, thrift, honesty, education and self sacrifice. It also incorporates meritocracy which stresses that rewards, prestige, and advancements must go to those individuals within the group who are most able, enterprising, hard working and dynamic. In other words, success should be based on merit, and not birth or connections alone.

Singaporean behavioural patterns are found along the continuum between the two extremes of ego-centredness and group-centredness. Where any one human being is at any one time on that continuum depends on a multitude of things: exposure to international cultures, education, travel, insularism, repression, open personality, flexibility, conditioning, socialization, and so on.

Modern Singaporeans are adopting many Western ways and adapting them to suit their traditional Asian values. Following are some basic values which ground so much of their behaviour. These vignettes are only intended to give you a quick look through your cultural glasses and to increase your cultural awareness. Remember that these are very general patterns, and that there is much variety within all of the models discussed, and that there are many alternatives to the patterns of behaviour described. Expand your mind – take the cultural leap – and don't be afraid to think new thoughts and to explore new territory. Refrain from judging that which is different from your own as 'bad' simply because it is different. Hopefully, you will say 'Ah ha! I see it now'.

GROUP- AND EGO-CENTREDNESS

If you should ask a group of Singaporean sociology students what the basic unit of society is, they would reply that it is the group – the family. Of course, they would be correct – in Asia! The group comes first. The members support each other, help each other, and they rise and fall together as one whole. Loyalty is first to the family, then to the group, and then this extends out to the neighbourhood, the work place, the city and the nation. Loyalty to the group is at the highest point on the scale of human values. Individuals have duties and responsibilities to the group more than to the self.

If you should ask an American sociology student what the smallest unit of society is, he/she would say the ego – the individual. And that would be the correct answer – in the West! Much of the Western world, (especially cultures of the new world, like the United States, Canada, and Australia), is based on the value of the individual.

The Western societies stress the glory of the rugged individual, the dignity of the individual, the inalienable rights of the individual (even against the government, as for instance, in civil disobedience), the duties of the individual, and the responsibilities of the individual. Each individual must, in the end, stand alone and be responsible for his/her own actions and growth.

The West heartily believes in 'Number 1' (the ego). To those Westerners who have never lived in a group-centered society before, the concept of the group rather than the individual is a strange one indeed! It is a mind-boggling thought!

FAMILY AND KINSHIP PATTERNS

Traditionally in Singapore, the immediate family is made up of many people. Parents, children (adult and non-adult), mother's parents and siblings, and their children, and their children's children; and father's parents and siblings, and their children, and their children's children are all considered to be immediate family.

Living with in-laws or elderly parents, taking in orphaned nieces and nephews, supporting a brother who is out of work, etc., is nothing unusual. All of these people are considered to be a group! They all know each other intimately, and there are rights, duties, and responsibilities each has to the other, according to age, generation, sex, and relation.

However, with rising affluence and Westernization, many newly-married couples are moving away from the extended family to set up separate and individual households. Not only does the new family set up a new household, but it may also set up individual spaces for each individual. Each child may have a separate room for himself/herself.

Ties with the extended family may not be close. Some younger Westernized Singaporeans might grow up and pass relations and cousins on the street, never knowing who they are. They might see each other only at weddings and funerals when they are young, and later, perhaps not at all.

GROWING UP

In Singapore children are raised to stay. From early infancy on, children are conditioned to be a part of the group and to stay within the group. They are socialized to be dependent on the group, to make decisions that benefit the group, and to make choices for, and in support of, the group. Children are taught to assist, aid, and uphold the honour of the group, whether that group be the family, the school, the neighbourhood, or the nation. The person who places his/her own needs ahead of the needs of the group is considered to be amoral, almost a misfit, or even a social deviant.

The Singaporean child who becomes an adult belongs to a tightly-knit group. He/She is not expected to cut off previous relationships, nor to forsake family and friends. Children are trained to feel that they belong to the group. As infants, they might sleep in their mother's bed or room for a long time – perhaps for several years. They are carried close to the body, wrapped in a cloth, *sarung*, or modern infant sling. Today, they are also pushed along in baby carriages. Someone is usually holding them, cradling them, or carrying them. Decisions are made by the elders for the children. Dutiful children obey and respect their elders and care for them when they get older.

In addition to the pursuit of knowledge, the schools train the children to help each other, and to be part of a viable and caring group. The children call their teachers 'Sir', 'Madam' or 'Teacher'.

They eat together, sing together, and play together so well. They seem, to Western eyes, indeed to be like perfect children. If a child

The schools focus on the fine art of human relationships and values. Children are trained to be good citizens and people. Photo: Nicky Moey

refused to join in group activities, or if he/she disturbed the class group by asking and answering too many questions, or if the child insisted on doing things his/her own way instead of the group's way, the parents might be called in to try and solve the problem, even though these behaviours are considered normal and appropriate in many Western cultures.

STATUS INDICATORS

Unfortunately, personal gain, material wealth and status possessions are now becoming the status indicators of many Singaporeans, as in many Western societies. It is sad that so many of the traditional Asian values are being replaced by the anomy of Westernization.

Not so long ago, status — the Asian measure of a human being — was based not on external material and physical objects, but on the interior values of honour, integrity, and virtue. Today, these is a lot more of 'keeping up with the Joneses', or rather, 'keeping up with the Chans, or Ibrahims, or Rajus'. Cars, houses and the schools their children attend are now the most powerful status indicators. Even so, old Asian ethics die hard and citizens of good character, honesty and unselfishness are often honoured and given public recognition by the society.

EQUALITY AND RESPECT

Singaporeans believe in equality, everyone is treated equally 'regardless of race, language or religion'. Yet, they do not negate the fact that hierarchical relationships exist in their society, such as those between parents and children, teachers and students, employer and employee. Singaporeans pay special respect to people of higher status.

Westerners, on the other hand, often negate the fact that hierarchical relationships exist in their society. They see themselves as egalitarian and so they dislike being the subjects of open displays of honour, respect and deference. And yet, higher-status Westerners such as parents, teachers and bosses:

• are more likely to speak first, louder, and longer than lower-status

students, employees, etc.
- sit at the head of the table while lower-status people sit at the middle and towards the end.
- feel free to interrupt lower-status speakers more than lower-status speakers feel free to interrupt them.
- feel free to put a hand on the shoulder of the lower-status person — or even an equal status person.

HIERARCHICAL RELATIONSHIPS IN SINGAPORE

The working out of complex authority and status relationships has characterized Asian society for at least two thousand years. Singaporeans treat special groups of people with special respect and courtesy. Honoured guests, elders, parents, teachers, bosses and leaders are treated with deference. For instance:

Employer and employee The Asian boss is more-or-less on a pedestal. He/She is given the respect one would give to an honoured parent. First names are not used. The boss speaks to the next-highest in the hierarchical chain of command; he does not give orders directly to people further down the line. The boss does not socialize on a one-to-one and equal basis with workers. However, the Asian boss is expected to care about, and help with family, social, and personal problems, as well as work problems (much as a parent would).

The elderly The hierarchy is probably most humane when it comes to the treatment of elders. Unlike Westerners, elders receive more status, respect and deference than younger people. Elders are treated with special consideration, veneration, honour, and courtesy. It has been said that the measure of a society is the way that it treats its aged, its infirm, and its weak. Asian cultures have long cared for these people within the support system of the group.

Growing old in Singapore is not the tragic affair it is in a Western culture. Many elders live with their family, and if they live alone, it

is a shame, not to the individual, but to the family. Singaporean children believe that they owe their parents care and love for giving them the gift of life. They feel that since they were cared for as infants, they are indebted to their parents and they expect to care for them when they get older. In turn, they expect that their children will care for them. Well-mannered Singaporeans rise when elders come into a room; they ask elders to eat first and to enjoy the meal, and they do not cross their legs in front of elders.

Students and teachers Students show respect to teachers; they do not openly challenge them lest they cause a loss of face; they do not ordinarily ask and answer questions openly in class lest they cause loss of face (they wait until after class when they are alone to do this). Professors treat students as if they were in a parental role to them. Teachers treat the whole student, helping them with all types of problems: personal, social, and emotional, as well as academic. They do not socialize with them as equals.

Parents and children In the West, children criticize and contradict their parents in order to practise their 'independence' skills, in preparation for breaking away from them and setting up their own individual lives. They openly express their own ideas and they make their own decisions as much as possible, according to age and skill. Sometimes the young people deliberately take the opposite view of the parents (even if they agree with it) just to show their independence.

In Singapore, people generally do not criticize and contradict their parents in public; they show respect to them. They usually do not break away from them in order to lead their own individual lives. They prefer to be self-reliant, but they also stay within the support system of the group. They politely express their own ideas and make their own decisions – within the context of the group – through group consensus. This does not mean that the generation gap is non-existent in Singapore. Although young people tend to conform to their parents' wishes regarding course of study or career, in many instances, the parents' choices are in direct conflict with the young person's own interests and aspirations. Choice of marriage partner too is becoming a source of family conflict. The younger generation of Singaporeans want and insist on the freedom to choose their own marriage partners. Many rebel against the tradition of arranged marriages today. Many Westernized Singaporeans reject their parents' choices without a qualm.

Women and men Women are working for equality, but the woman in Singapore still has far to go. Males and females usually do not have equal-status friendships and relationships. Same-sex friendships are more common. When there is a relationship between a man and a woman, a romance might be assumed.

Terms of address as a reflection of respect The children of close friends may call you 'auntie' or 'uncle'. This is common courtesy for children in Singapore. These are terms of respect that Singaporeans use when addressing people. In very formal situations Mr, Mrs, Miss or Madam is used.

Formal titles and terms of address between people of unequal status are common in Singapore. It is difficult for Singaporeans to call people by their personal names, even if they are requested to do so. If a silver-haired professor, for instance, asked a young student to call him Tom, the student might feel very awkward as it is considered disrespectful to call one's teacher by a personal name; it is too familiar. However, some younger Singaporeans, being more exposed to the West, are beginning to get used to calling their teachers or elders by their personal names.

If some Singaporeans appear very Westernized, the Westerners should not automatically take this as an invitation to be informal and casual with everybody. Whether in a Singaporean home or at work, watch how the older and higher-status people are addressed and treated and what the older and higher-status people do, then follow their customs.

COMPETITION AND COOPERATION

Ego-centered Westerners believe that competition is what makes the world go round. There is an old saying that explains competition: 'The squeaky wheel gets the grease.' This means that the wheel that stands out from the group and that competes with the other wheels by making a bigger noise, gets the attention. The other individuals who remain silent go unnoticed, and unsung. All this, of course, means that Westerners believe that individuals must stand up alone, compete with others, and get away from the crowd, in order to be noticed, to get attention, and to obtain respect. While Westerners do not disparage the value of cooperative behaviour and teamwork, they find competition between individuals and even between groups, to be the appropriate, the most natural, and certainly the most productive way of doing things. Idealized capitalism, of course, has competition at its heart.

In contrast to the above, Asians emphasize cooperation, or group harmony, as a central value in their society. The Asians have a saying: 'The nail that sticks up gets hit on the head.' This means that the Asian who stands out in the crowd (like the squeaky wheel), who differs with, disagrees with, or questions the group, and who puts himself or herself above the needs and wants of the group, may find him/herself alienated from the group, and lose the respect of the group.

The ideal is that group harmony and cooperation are positive values which meld the group together. Certain kinds of behaviour can harm the group. For instance:

- Bragging and boasting about one's *individual* possessions and talents. This sort of competitive behaviour sets the person apart from the group and excites envy, so it is not acceptable.
- Praising an individual for work well done, or blaming an individual for work poorly done. This behaviour is designed to create competition, and to cause envy and jealousy; therefore it endangers the harmony of the group.

Singaporeans are urged to be both competitive and cooperative. Singaporeans work very hard; they want what is best for themselves and their family; at the same time they are reminded to strive for the overall good of the nation. The leadership has recognized that only through cooperative efforts on a grand scale, can Singapore meet the challenge of the decades ahead.

FACE

An old timer expat explained his idea of 'face': 'Show yourself to be a person of face, i.e., integrity and honour. Be honest but tactful; kind without being weak; and never lose your face or cause an Asian to lose face. Face cannot be underestimated! Asians have long memories and any loss of face (either yours or theirs) will be noted and long remembered. It may affect present and future business transactions.'

What is face? Face is the measure of one's internal quality, status, good name, and good character, but it is much more than personal pride; it involves the entire group (the family, the school, the neighbourhood, the work place, the city, and the country). Face keeps relationships intact. It preserves group harmony, and it promotes group solidarity. It measures the social standing of the person within the group – *and the social standing of the group too*. If one person loses face, the whole group loses face, so it is much deeper and stronger than a simple personal embarrassment. The concept of face allows the group to have social control over the behaviour of the individual! It is most noticeable in dealings between superiors and subordinates; i.e., in a hierarchical culture.

Do Westerners have face or privacy? Westerners revere the concept of privacy. It is the right of the individual not to have the group interfere in his/her business, and thus privacy helps the individual not to be under the social control of the group. Westerners sometimes refer to having a 'loss of face' as a form of minor embarrassment, but shame is usually not a large part of it. When a Westerner does something wrong, he/she feels more guilt than shame. If an individual does something to cause guilty feelings, 'the buck stops there' i.e., the group is not held responsible for the actions of the individual! Privacy is most noticeable when dealing with an individual; it is an important part of an egalitarian culture where every individual has his/her own personal rights.

This lack of Asian-type face is evident in the actions of many Westerners. They are not afraid to ask questions in the office, to speak up in class, to challenge their teachers, to say no frankly to their friends, to criticize their parents harshly, and so on, because the group does not share in the shame. Only the individual is responsible to him/herself, and the pro-active and admired individual should always express individual ideas and stand out and away from the group.

In Singapore face can be lost by:
- Doing or saying anything which could cause a member of the group to be left out of the group or expelled from the group, or doing anything which could cause the group to explode from within through anger, envy, jealousy, or criticism.
- Doing something to bring shame on the group. It is a form of social control. The group helps the individual to stay on the right path!
- Criticizing someone or pointing out mistakes or errors in public, especially if a junior points out errors of elders, parents, teachers, or bosses.

59

- Making someone feel embarrassed, insulted, humiliated, shamed, inferior, or ashamed. For instance, a young Singaporean student who went to study in Australia explained about the biggest culture shock he had there.

  He said: 'You know, the biggest thing that I noticed was that people don't worry about face the way we do. If you go to a party in Australia, you are expected to bring along *your own* bottle of spirits. Here, the Asian host would feel insulted (he would lose face) if someone did that. It might imply that this guest did not think that he could provide enough for him to drink.'

- Asking questions of a person in a superior position, or asking for clarification, especially if this was done in public. The person who was asked would lose face because it would be as if he/she had not explained properly; and the person who asked would lose face, because he/she did not understand the material, instructions, directions, etc.

- Answering questions in a class or office, especially easy ones, because it could make others in the group look foolish or stupid if they don't know the answers; or it could make the one who answered look foolish if he/she felt that the answer was not perfect! This is one of the reasons why many Singaporean students do not speak up in a class.

- Showing anger by shouting or swearing at someone, throwing temper tantrums, or losing your cool.

- Pointing or shaking a forefinger at someone, especially in their face.

- Saying no, or refusing someone outright.

- Open confrontation, conflict, or disagreement. If a subordinate argued or disagreed openly with a superior, the superior would suffer loss of face. This may explain why an Asian employee may publicly agree with the employer (but give signs of non-compliance: saying 'it will be difficult,' or hissing inwardly through the teeth, etc.) while privately continuing to do things his/her own way. The same action is seen as a courtesy by the Asian, but as a dishonesty by the Westerner.

Face can be saved in Singapore by:

- Pointing out errors or problems discretely and delicately; hintingly, and side-ways, and always finding a way to help the person to save face. 'Some people have been coming late,' instead of: 'Tan, you have been late twice this month.'
- Keeping calm, cool, and courteous. Never losing the temper. Never showing anger (a discrete disappointed look can be cultivated instead).
- Never shouting or swearing. Once, I saw two Asians have an accident. The police came. One man shouted, and gesticulated angrily. The other man was quiet, soft spoken, and dignified. The police paid little attention to the shouting man; but they paid attention to what the quiet man said. They looked at him with respect, and they believed what he said.

  In Asian eyes, it was obvious that he was the superior person. In the West, this behaviour may have the opposite effect! The quiet man might get put aside and the noisy man might get the attention!
- Never pointing to anything or anyone with a forefinger.
- Discussing the problem or difficulty without fault finding and without criticizing i.e., 'How can we solve this problem?' or 'What can we do to work together to solve this problem?'
- Saying no with the face or actions, but not with the mouth. An Asian friend said: 'When I do not want to hurt your feelings, I say yes with my mouth, but no with my face, body language, or actions.'
- Learning to tell the difference between an Asian yes and no.
- Always giving a person a way out of a bad situation without having to be humiliated.

TELLING THE TRUTH

Most Singaporeans are more implicit, subtle and indirect than Westerners. Singaporeans tend to hint at the point – never speaking it out in frank, outspoken and direct terms. To do so might cause someone to lose face. Many complaints are couched in parables, stories and indirect speech. Impossible demands made by superiors are answered by 'Yes, I'll try'; or 'We'll see what can be done' without outright protests that the demand is unreasonable. This kind of noncommital answer is a device for keeping harmony in the group, and for not allowing hurt feelings to disturb the equilibrium of a relationship.

Even so, this simple behaviour probably causes more cross-cultural problems between East and West than all of the other patterns of behaviour put together – except for that which causes a loss of face! For example, you ask your Singaporean friend to come for dinner on Thursday. She replies, 'Oh yes, I would love to, but it might be difficult.'

To the Westerner, this is a definite 'yes'. The Westerner believes firmly that the friend will overcome all problems and obstacles in order to come to the dinner. A place will be set for her, and the dinner will be held up waiting for her to arrive. She does not come. The friendship suffers a break which cannot be mended. The Westerner would understand only a very frank and direct 'yes' or 'no'. A direct 'no' would be appreciated. It would not be offensive because the friend may have accepted a previous engagement. All Westerners know that it is very impolite to break a previous date even if the second date is much more preferable. All that is necessary for a polite refusal is: 'I would love to come, but unfortunately, I have already told so-and-so that I would go to the lecture with her.' No hurt feelings at all by the very frank and outspoken Western-type of refusal!

Saying 'yes' The Singaporean 'yes' may or may not mean 'yes'. It may mean: 'I hear what you are saying', or 'I hear what you say but I don't understand' or 'maybe' or even 'no'. Some Asians say: 'It is better to say "yes" with the mouth when you mean "no" – and then let it die a slow death by not following it up with actions.'

Saying 'no' Singaporeans rarely say 'no'. To say 'no' is considered disrespectful and impolite. It may cause loss of face and hurt feelings. When Singaporeans do not wish to disappoint you or make you feel bad, they say 'yes' with the mouth, but 'no' with the face or actions. This behavior is not seen as dishonest; it is a courtesy!

How to tell the difference between 'yes' and 'no'

a. Saying 'yes'
    - A 'yes' answer shows respect, it may not be an actual fact.
    - A real 'yes' answer comes with some sort of document of understanding and is backed up with details of what is planned. 'Yes, I would love to come to your dinner. What time shall I arrive, and can I come early to help?'
    - 'Maybe' often means 'yes'.

b. Saying 'no'
    - An 'it is difficult' or 'not convenient' means 'no'. Note that the Asian friend who said 'it might be difficult' gave a very clear signal to her friend that she definitely could not come to her dinner, but the Western ear did not hear the message.
    - A 'yes, but there may be problems' usually means 'no'.
    - Any 'yes-but' usually means 'no'.
    - A sucking in of air through the teeth, means 'no'.
    - Instead of saying 'no', Asians often ignore the question or request, or talk around it. Don't press Asians when they pretend that they did not hear the request.

SMILES AND LAUGHTER

A smile or laugh which appears to be out of context can bewilder, upset or even anger an unwary Western person. In Asia, laughter serves many functions. People smile or laugh in response to funny and happy things, or when they are pleased, but a smile and a laugh need not always be an expression of joy or amusement.

A Singaporean may hide nervousness, shyness, embarrassment, loss of face, sadness, hurt feelings, bitterness, cynicism or irony behind a laugh.

Which smile/laugh is happy, which is not Close observation helps to tell the difference between a happy smile and a sad smile. Watch the eyes and the hands!

- If your friend drops a cup of hot tea in your lap, and then smiles, notice that the eyes do not laugh, the hand covers the mouth, and the laugh is not happy and light. The smile you see is the 'humiliation smile'. It means 'I am grievously sorry; I have inadvertently caused you pain. Please forgive me.'

- The policeman you are interviewing for a magazine article tells about his police dog who was killed in the line of action. He loved his dog; they had worked together for six years. As he tells about the tragedy, he smiles. The Westerner wrongly thinks: 'He has no feelings – he is a barbarian.' The sad smile was not humorous. It was intended to protect the listener from hurt. It was a very brave front to keep you from experiencing his pain.

- The pretty young nurses touch the strange shape of your handsome young football-player son's broken arm. They cover their mouth with their hands as they giggle softly. You notice that your son who is in deep pain, is about to explode with anger at the 'cruel' laughter. You pull him aside quickly and whisper: 'No Joe, they are not laughing because they think your broken arm is funny – they are giggling because it is not polite to touch people of the opposite sex in their culture, especially a handsome young man like yourself. Even though they must touch you in their work, they still feel shy about it.' You laugh to yourself at the quick change in your son as he smiles and holds out his offending arm and says: 'Here girls, you'd better come and have a closer look!'

SHOWING ANGER

Emotions are allowed open expression in the West. Anger, joy, excitement, and love can be voiced in public situations. People think that it is healthy to express emotions and to get their personal and individual feelings out into the air where they can be dealt with openly.

In Singapore and in the larger context of Asian society however, a show of anger (or other emotions) signals a person who is out of control and therefore, inferior. One who cannot control himself, and one who reveals innermost thoughts and feelings is not to be trusted.

DISCUSSIONS ON A PERSONAL OR EMOTIONAL LEVEL

In Singapore, topics which you should avoid are: emotions, love and affairs of the heart, personal and family relationships, feelings and sexual matters.

I once learned that my Chinese friend's father had had two wives when polygamy was legal in Singapore (1960s). I asked my friend

" TELL ME ABOUT YOUR WIFE ! "

65

many private and probing questions without realizing that I was invading his sacred and emotional realm: Did his father love both wives equally? How did he divide his time? Were the wives friendly? How did the children feel about each other? My friend was stunned and stricken! After some moments of silence, he said, 'You should never ask questions like these. These are things that we don't discuss, not even with our parents.'

This was the only time that I received such an open and frank caution from my Chinese friend. I learn many of my cultural lessons the hard way; I hope that it will be easier for you!

COMPLIMENTS

Compliments can invoke danger in Singapore. A man who praises the looks, dress, or charms of a woman is signalling a romantic interest in her. In the case of beautiful women, men should avoid complimenting them on their beauty to avoid being accused of making sexual innuendoes. Instead, it is wiser to praise a woman's skills, efficiency, cooking, etc.

In the case of children, do not praise the child's looks; nor say how chubby and healthy the baby is. The more traditional Singaporeans, especially the older generation, still believe that such compliments will bring the 'evil eye' upon the child. That is, some harm may come to the person. Some Chinese give their children nicknames such as 'little dog' or 'pig' to fool the malicious spirits into thinking that these children are not beautiful and healthy. Modern parents may scoff at such beliefs. When you praise their children, they may say 'No lah, they are so naughty' but today, it may be more out of a polite sense of modesty than fear of the evil eye. Secretly they may be proud and pleased at the compliment.

SILENCE

Silence is very important to Singaporeans and Asians in general. It has meaning, purpose, and value. When asked a question, it is polite to maintain a brief period of silence before answering to give honour to the one asking the question. It shows that one has given the question proper and considerate thought. To answer without this pause is to be thoughtless and impolite. This often causes problems between Western teachers and Singaporean students.

When asked a question, the Singaporean student waits for perhaps ten to fifteen seconds before answering. The Western teacher however, has moved on to another person after a typical four-second silence – wrongly believing the silent student to be unprepared, foolish, or stupid.

TOUCHING

Singaporeans freely touch people of the same sex, hold hands with them, and walk with their arms around each other. These gestures are not signs of homosexuality! They are signs of friendship and closeness as 'brothers or sisters'. On the other hand, there is no such thing as the social greeting and departure hugging and kissing between people of the opposite sex. It is seen as being too intimate. Even married couples do not make public displays of affection. However, the bolder, more Westernized courting couples of Singapore can be seen holding hands and embracing even in public, but this is not seen as appropriate behaviour.

Generally speaking, in Singapore, always aim for the most respectable behaviour. Do not publicly touch, kiss (even air-kiss), or hug people of the opposite sex. Otherwise you could be mistaken for making signals of amorous interest rather than social friendliness, and this could cause a public scandal to your friend!

CROWDS

In crowded food centres at peak periods, e.g., during lunch time, Singaporeans do not mind sharing tables with strangers. They would be suspicious however, if a stranger shared their table while there were many other tables available. In other crowded conditions, such as in the lift, in the bus or MRT, Singaporeans keep very much to themselves. If a man leaned too close against a lady, for example, she might suspect that he was trying to outrage her modesty. In packed conditions, Singaporeans normally do not hold their bodies as stiffly as Westerners do in order to maintain their bubble of 'individual space'. When forced to be close together, Singaporeans tend to be more 'relaxed' than Westerners who tend to stiffen their bodies. Do not mistake this 'relaxed' posture as an attempt to outrage your modesty!

Singaporeans often describe themselves as being *kiasu*, that is, being afraid of losing out, of not getting the best. This *kiasu* attitude is sometimes seen in crowded conditions: i.e., pushing and shoving to get on the bus or MRT instead of standing in line; queue jumping when buying tickets for a show; not waiting their turn to be served at the cashier's counter, etc. The government has had to mark lines at MRT stations to make people queue in an orderly manner. The fast pace of life and the need to survive in crowded conditions might have contributed to this type of disorderly conduct. Nationwide courtesy campaigns have been undertaken to educate the public to be more orderly and courteous.

Chapter Three

SUCCESS IN SINGAPORE: BUSINESS ETIQUETTE

SINGAPORE AND THE ASIAN PSYCHE

Due to the degree of rapid social change, modern high-rises, and other accompaniments of industrialization which have been a constant and ongoing factor in Singapore's development, the first-time visitor to Singapore, the Garden City of Asia, may feel as if he/she were dropped intact right into the middle of a Western country – rather than an Asian country – but that would be a fatal mistake!

Just because some of the younger and more modern Singaporeans are adopting some of the Western ways, dress and behaviour, the expatriate or the tourist may be tempted to believe that the Asian psyche has been replaced by the Western psyche – this is not true either!

Even if some of the Singaporeans who have given up their own ethnic culture, or who have lost touch with their own heritage, complain that the courtesies and habits on the following pages are old fashioned or out-of-date, the foreign guest in Singapore is advised to learn them, to understand them, and to work with them, because they are the everyday patterns of behaviour for the majority of the local people. In addition, an appreciation and an acceptance of Singaporean cultural customs and behaviour will ease the pain of culture shock and reduce the stress and strain accompanying it. It will also help to develop the traits necessary for business success in Singapore.

BUSINESS ETIQUETTE

Be courteous and professional at all times. 'One of the most acclaimed virtues in Asia is courtesy' stated one expat emphatically. 'Asians respect and admire the courteous person. Do take the time to be a professional; learn Asian-style courtesy because Western courtesy can have an opposite or contrary meaning in Singapore, and can signal rude and offensive behaviour rather than friendliness.'

Singaporean style of courtesy and ideas of professionalism are very different from Western styles. Following are some of these cross-cultural courtesies and their implications.

BUSINESS FRIENDSHIPS

Business friendships are based on honour, integrity and good character, not backslapping and jokes. Take time to show that you are reliable because you are seen as an extension of your group and your company. Take pains to establish and maintain contacts. Singaporeans highly regard warm and personal relationships. Be patient, time is needed to build a relationship, to build trust, and to work in Singapore.

NAMES

The people of the different ethnic groups have different ways of stating their names. See 'Names' under Chinese, Malay, and Indian chapters for more specific details. In general:

- Chinese place the surname (family name) first, then the personal name follows. Note that this is opposite to the Western way. Women often keep their own family name.
- Malays do not use a surname. They use their own personal name; add *bin* (son of) or *binti* (daughter of) then add the father's personal name.
- Indians use their own personal name followed by s/o (son of) or d/o (daughter of) and the father's name.

When first making introductions, and in formal meetings, if possible always use the person's title and the family or personal name (Vice President Wong, Dr Wahid). Later you can refer to the person as Mr Wong or Madam Wong. A good point to remember is that titles are ordinarily used for seniors or superiors; but not necessarily for peers; and juniors or subordinates would feel uncomfortable with them all the time.

In the West, the personal name comes first and the family name comes last. Women usually take the family name of their husband and drop their own family name, when they marry. The children carry the family name of the father. It is common for Westerners, especially those of the new world, to ask friends and acquaintances to call them by their personal name (James), or by a nickname (Jim). This is a sign of informal friendliness and equality. It does not signal romance.

Old World Westerners, like the British, are more formal and hierarchical; they may prefer not to be called by their personal name, but to be called by their family name (Smith - Jones). In this instance, they are more like Asians than Americans.

In Singapore, the best rule is never use personal names or nicknames unless invited to do so, or until a friendship has been established after a long time. If you are in doubt as what to call someone, just ask the person what he/she prefers. Also, be aware that it may be very difficult for Asians to call people (especially elders or superiors) by their personal names, even if they are requested to do so.

Some Westerners, i.e., the English and even some Americans are more formal; some professors, high ranking business people, and older and higher status people might certainly be offended by being called by their personal names unless they specifically request it.

INTRODUCTIONS

Where do you look? People in Singapore usually do not look directly into the eyes of the person they are meeting – it is a sign of disrespect, especially if the person they are being introduced to is older or has more status. The eyes are politely cast away or down. (To the Westerner, this is a sign of disinterest or dishonesty.) Westerners should be careful not to culturally misjudge this behaviour. When Westerners are introduced to each other, they look directly into the eyes of the person, shake hands firmly, and say: 'How do you do?' Some say: 'I am pleased to meet you.' Others say: 'It is my pleasure to meet you.' The answer is: 'How do you do' or 'It is my pleasure.'

Westerners are often informal. It is not seen as impolite to introduce oneself to another at a party or a social gathering.

What do you say? Singaporeans usually say: 'I am happy to meet you.' The answer is the same: 'I am happy to meet you.'

Singaporeans are more formal, and they rarely introduce themselves. They introduce each other, and they help each other to get to know one another. They often give some information that helps to break the ice and to set up a relationship quickly: 'Did you know that Raj went to Singapore University and read Sociology with our mutual friend, Michael Walter?' They also introduce each other in much the same way Westerners do, i.e., they say the name of the most important person first. The most important person is:

- The higher ranking before the lower ranking: 'Vice President Tan, this is my assistant, John Miller.'

- The older person before the younger person: 'Mr Smith, this is my son, Joe Craig.'
- The woman before the man: 'Ms Ong, I would like you to meet Mr Jim Johnson.'
- Among equals, either person can be named first. 'Wong Ah Keng, this is Joseph Smith.' Wong Ah Keng says: 'Just call me Wong' (Wong is his surname). If Wong Ah Keng has taken a Westernized name to help Westerners remember it more easily, he may say: 'Just call me Kenny.' (He will most likely choose a name which sounds close to his Chinese name). Joseph Smith says: 'Just call me Joe.' (Joe is the shortened form of the personal name Joseph).

To sit or stand? Both Asian and Western men stand to be introduced to men and women. Women stand when being introduced to older women. It is common to stand about the distance away that one can comfortably shake hands.

SHAKING HANDS

A brief handshake is appropriate between people of the same sex in the business world of Singapore. It is becoming more common for men and women to shake hands now, but because of the restrictions on cross-sex touching of some religious groups (Muslims) it is always better to err on the safe side by not offering your hand to a Muslim man if you are a woman. In cases where people of the opposite sex are introduced, the responsibility for initiating a handshake falls on the woman. It is she who is the one to offer her hand first if she wishes to shake hands. If she does not wish to shake hands, she simply smiles and nods as she is introduced. Children can either shake hands, or just smile and nod when being introduced to adults.

How firm the grip? Handshakes in Singapore are usually very soft and light to the touch; not like the bone-crushing one common to people from the West.

Westerners are supposed to give a firm, strong, and solid shake of equal strength. It signifies that one is offering his/her strength to the other, and that the two can work together for mutual gain. In the olden days, when knights in armour met each other on the fields, they took the heavy weapon out of the strong right hand, and transferred it to the left hand. Then they extended their weaponless right hands to each other, and grasped them firmly to show that they were capable of great strength, and that their strength was at the disposal of the other should a common enemy appear. Each had to offer equal strength or else the one who offered a lighter grip was thought to be weak, insincere, cowardly or lacking in fraternal spirit.

To this day, Westerners may not trust a person with a soft handshake, and they may not even realize why they feel this way since the origins of this custom has been lost in the mists of time!

Asians in general do not have a long cultural history of handshaking because traditionally they have used other courteous forms of saluting: bowing, salaaming, saluting, shaking their own clasped hands in front of them, and so on. Asians see the Western handshake, and they make use of it as a courtesy, but they are not aware of the Western cultural significance and meaning behind it, so they offer the alarming soft and gentle handshake without realizing that they are signalling a lack of cooperation, comradeship and fraternity to Westerners.

This simple cultural difference causes problems for both sides. Both Asians and Westerners enter the negotiating room with the vague feeling that something is wrong after being exposed to each other's 'peculiar' handshakes.

Many Westerners feel uncomfortable with the soft handshake which they call the 'dead-fish.' Some Asians traditionally touch hands instead of grip hands, and this can also signal a wrong message to people from another culture. Westerners wrongly think that their Asian counterparts are weak and ineffectual because of the soft touch or the soft handshake, and Asians think that Westerners are trying to lord it over them in a colonialistic way with the stronger and more powerful grip. Awareness is the key! Refrain from making judgements based on a handskake alone.

How long does the handshake last? In addition to being much softer and more gentle than the Western handshake, the Asian handshake is somewhat lingering. It lingers 'seconds too long' – sometimes for up to ten or twelve seconds in contrast to the typical three-second shake of the Western world. The Western shake is composed of about three one-second pumps, and then the two break hands cleanly.

In contrast, the Asian handshake may not really be a handshake; it can be more of a 'handhold' with the Asian clasping the other's hand between his two hands and holding it for a long time. This is often a gesture of respect. This extra long holding time makes Westerners nervous because if it is between men and men, or women and women, it may look like a homosexual advance; or if it is between men and women, it may look like an amorous advance.

These assumptions are not true across cultural lines however. Do not judge the Asian soft, lingering, and two-handed hand-holding or handshake by Western standards.

TRIGG.

When to shake hands Men shake hands with other men when being introduced, concluding a business deal, before and after negotiations, and at various other times. It is the same for women, but the handshaking should be only at the initial meeting, and not repeated or it could be taken as a romantic advance.

BUSINESS CARDS

Since the Chinese in Singapore make up 77.7% of the population, it might be a good idea for business cards to be printed in English on one side and Chinese on the other. It costs little to add gold Chinese simplified characters to the back of your own card. This can be done quite quickly and inexpensively in Singapore if you do not have them already made up. It is common to have the card printed on good quality paper, preferable embossed, with the company logo, and in one colour. Remember that the Chinese surname is always printed first on the Chinese business card. Always present your business card after introductions, making sure that you have one for each person in the group.

The polite way to give and accept cards In Singapore the polite way to present a card is to formally hold it in *both* hands, with the name facing the eyes of the receiver. The polite way to receive one is to accept it formally with *both* hands, looking carefully at it one or two times, each time looking at the face of the giver, smiling all the while, and showing that you have recognized and have noted well who the person is, and then to put the card away. This gives respect and recognizes and signals rank in the hierarchy.

Westerners traditionally present their business cards after an introduction, like Singaporeans do, but the manner of presenting and accepting is very different from the Singaporean way. The Western giver takes out a card (without checking to see if the name faces the eyes of the receiver) and offers it casually and informally with one hand to the receiver (usually the card is offered only to an individual, or a few individuals – and not to the whole group). The receiver takes it with one hand and casually and quickly glances at it, and then tucks it away in a pocket for closer study later. It is not polite to look closely at the card, or to study the card in front of the eyes of the giver; Westerners usually never do this because it is as if one is studying the other's status to see if he/she is an important person. The Western way gives the appearance of equality.

Can you see the humour in the scenario where the culturally sensitive Singaporean uses the Western forms of handshaking and handing business cards; and the culturally sensitive Westerner uses the Singaporean form and then they both begin to laugh? It would seem as if a business meeting would get off to a very good start with so much good heart in evidence.

GREETINGS

Some common greetings are: 'How are you?', 'Are you busy?' ('Very busy' is the answer), 'Good morning / afternoon / evening', 'How is your family?' and 'Long time no see.' Others include:

- 'Have you eaten?' The answer is always 'yes' – no one is really supposed to tell all about what they ate.
- 'How is your business?' The typical response is: 'My business is moderate.' No one is really supposed to tell all about how successful the business is.
- 'Where are you going?' The answer is 'For a stroll.' No one is really supposed to tell all about where they are going.

SMALL TALK

Good topics include: what Singapore is doing now, how it is progressively developing, wonderful food, beautiful scenery, lovely tourist sights, arts, music, enjoyable times, compliments to Singapore, mutual benefit, and mutual friendship.

Bad topics are: arguments about religion, sex, and politics; criticism of the government, the bureaucracy, or the food, and faults of Singapore.

Taboo talk for Singaporeans

1. Personal matters – Westerners especially should not talk about things which Asians feel are sacred and therefore secret: i.e., emotions, love and affairs of the heart, caring, affections, personal and family relationships, feelings, belonging, and sexual matters – all of which are of an invisible and spiritual nature and thus cannot be measured in physical and scientific terms. These relationships and feelings and emotions are the things which give meaning and purpose to their lives, and status to their existence. To the Singaporean, the one who discusses emotions and feelings for all the world to hear, is seen as a person of little worth – a weak person of inferior status. Those who openly talk about sacred things reveal secrets, and they cannot be trusted.

2. Jokes about sex – Westerners are also alerted not to tell the sexy joke; they are cautioned not to make sexual innuendoes, and they are warned not to discuss women in a sexual and casual manner. They should not do this even around young and lusty-looking Singaporean males. Most Asians know that only inferior persons (whether they be either Asian or Western) talk like this. Much face and trust will be lost, respect will be gone, and business will disappear like a cloud of smoke. No one wants to do busines with a 'lightweight'.

Taboo talk for Westerners

Singaporeans often ask about things which Westerners consider sacred – and therefore secret i.e., things to do with physical and material status indicators. Following are some things Westerners hate to talk about or hear:

1. Age – Westerners get more status from being young rather than old, so they do not like to talk about age, or to hear that they look older. Asians usually mean it as a compliment when they say: 'But you look much older' (meaning that you look wise, serious minded, and mature).

2. Weight – In the land of the fat, the thin are considered beautiful. In the West, people get more status from being thin than from

being fat. (Thinness is getting to be a status indicatior in Singapore too.) In the West it is an insult to be told that one is looking fatter! Asians (especially the more traditional ones) usually mean this as a compliment, intimating that you are looking especially prosperous. After visiting an old Singaporean friend again after a 13-year absence, I was devastated to hear him say: 'My, but you have filled out so nicely – you must be very happy' meaning that I was looking healthy and prosperous. Intellectually I understood, but emotionally, I swore to go on a diet immediately.

3. Money – The most sensitive subject of all is money because of what money stands for: one's status. Asking about money, salary and prices paid for things such as clothing, possessions, rent, homes, and so on, is considered not only to be very bad manners, but nosy and intrusive as well. This talk invades the Westerner's right to privacy. It would be like asking outright how much status one had, or how important one was! Americans, for instance, especially equate money, salaries, and the prices of expensive possessions with their own status. They do not discuss these things, not even with their parents!

4. Racism, Sexism, Homophobia – Westerners may not treat all people as equals, but they like to think that all people are equal. They believe that people who speak negatively about people of different ethnic backgrounds, who treat women as inferiors, who say unkind things about homosexuals, are ignorant and dense.

PUNCTUALITY

An important rule to remember: Polite Westerners should arrive for business meetings on time and together as a group, lined up in order of rank. Singaporeans however, still practice the ancient tradition of being late for a celebration or a wedding (so as not to appear greedy by arriving first).

If invited to a restaurant where a reservation has been made, one must be on time. If invited for dinner to a family home, however,

Singaporeans often arrive several minutes early if the host is a close family friend. This can be disconcerting to the Western hostess who may still have her apron on and the curlers in her hair when the Singaporean guests arrive!Singaporeans arrive a little late if they are invited to the home of someone they don't know well. This is to avoid appearing greedy. However, most modern Singaporeans arrive on time.

LUNCH-TIME TOLERANCE

Westerners often report that they have difficulty adjusting to the long lunch hours taken by their staff. Do remember that for many years, the noon-time rest period had been from noon to 2:00 p.m. This is changing now to a one-hour lunch break, from 1:00 p.m. to 2:00 p.m., but old habits die hard. Many people find it difficult to give up their rest time.

Some suggestions for those who find it a problem when they find their hard-working staff fast asleep over their computers:

- Make use of the lunch break to catch a few extra winks yourself. You will be surprised at how much more energy you have after a brief rest.
- Go back to the two-hour lunch break, and extend the working day by one hour.
- Do not try to do urgent business or locate people on the telephone between the traditional resting hours of 12 noon and 2:00 p.m.

SINGAPOREAN WOMEN IN BUSINESS

Westerners speak about working with Asian businesswomen in Singapore. More and more, women are attaining equal status and they occupy high positions in business and technology. Many of the engineers and professionals are women. When doing business with people of the opposite sex, be very careful to keep the level of discussion professional. Any sign of flirting could destroy the woman's career and your business deal.

An expatriate boss going over some documents with his secretary. Singaporeans tend to keep a respectful distance from their superiors. Photo: Munshi Ahmed

Some tips from expats:

- Do not compliment the businesswoman's appearance beauty, clothing, etc., as these are considered amorous advances.
- Do not say for example: 'You look pretty today' or 'What a nice dress.'
- It is appropriate to compliment her work, skills, job, performance, etc.
- Watch your body language when dealing with people of the opposite sex. Do not give too much eye contact, or follow with the eyes too much. Do not sit forward too much, or relax your posture too much with a woman colleague.
- Never touch, hug or kiss a person of the opposite sex in the casual social type greeting or departure gestures common in the West. These will be misread! One American businessman innocently, and socially, kissed a female Asian colleague upon his departure

81

from Singapore, and eighteen months later, it was still being talked about.
- To show respect: smile, use quiet speech, and do not use familiarity at all.
- Do not shake hands with a woman after the initial meeting. This type of behaviour sets a formal distance and makes the relationship businesslike.

DRESS

Singaporeans usually dress more informally than Western business people because of the tropical heat and humidity. In the more formal office, men often wear light-coloured long-sleeved shirts, ties, and dark trousers. Jackets are usually not worn for work. Conservative clothing is in good taste.

In the less formal office, it is common to see businessmen in short-sleeved shirts and no tie. More stripes and floral patterns are also seen in the less formal office.

Businesswomen here wear light-weight business suits which are generally more frilly and feminine than what Western business-women wear. Hose is worn in the more formal offices, but bare legs are often seen in the less formal offices.

Today, one can see young professionals with an executive brief case, a personal cordless phone, and a filofax. Even more impressive is the computerized personal organizer. Pocket pagers are not as status determining as one might think because they are too ostentatious for the socially correct modest and humble administrator/business person.

GIFTS

Singapore worries about bribery and corruption developing alongside of industrialization and modernization. There are directives aimed at preventing individuals from accepting great and grand gifts; however, some gifts may appropriately be given to the group.

Gifts can also be considered to be either public or private. Public gifts belong to the group, and they would be in the great and grand category. Private gifts are small things intended for a close friend, or for an individual. To the Westerner, small, personal, inexpensive, and token gifts are usually intended for a personal friend – for an individual. Private gifts are usually not intended for the group (but in Asia – they should be!).

Great or grand gifts: for the group These belong to the group. Instead of giving expensive gifts to individuals (which could signal corruption and a bribe), a presentation to the entire office or to the company as a whole can usually be given (group-centered gifts are not usually seen as graft). Of course, all gifts on a great or grand scale must be cleared with the authorities and Asian advisers. Appropriate gifts for the group can be instructional or educational materials, or anything which can be seen, used, and remembered by many people for a long time.

Always think 'group' when dealing with Asians. Appropriate gifts should be given on appropriate occasions, such as the final banquet concluding a deal. The gift, if it is large and grand, should be a formal presentation to the entire group, as a gesture of goodwill and friendship, from your group to their group.

Small and personal gifts: for individuals If the gift is small and is to be a token of remembrance, then it should be given to all persons in the group, perhaps wrapped in good luck colours and put beside each plate during the final banquet. The giving of small tokens of remembrance is preferred and they should be given modestly and simply.

If you must give a gift to an individual, give it in private, lest you offend the group. It is always better to give small things to everyone in the group, rather than to just single out one or two individuals. This could incite envy and disharmony and cause disruption of group morale.

At any rate, never give expensive things. A small token gift of fruit, sweets, or cakes is usually preferred – it is the Asian way! Also, some small item from your home town is more cherished than other things. Some small gifts to consider are: cups with the company logo, souvenirs of your home state, personalized pens or pencils, caps with the name of your company/city, small toys for the children, arm patches, badges, or musical tapes.

If giving sweets (very auspicious), they should be given with the words: 'they are for the children' (or for the grandmothers and grandfathers). This is a polite gesture and one that will tickle the Asian wit. Asians will appreciate your understanding of the delicacy of the matter. For instance, Asians, and especially the Chinese, love food, but they hate to appear greedy. By saying the sweets are for the children, the Chinese feel free to take them home and eat them up themselves, without losing face by appearing greedy.

Also, Chinese give gifts in sets of two, (even numbers) because happiness is born a twin. A gift of two bags of sweets, two bottles of wine, etc., signals that they are wishing you love and happiness in your life, in addition to the gift itself. On the other hand, Indians prefer uneven numbers. Check each ethnic group section in this book for more specific information on gifts.

Inappropriate gifts, symbols, logos Always ask Singaporeans for advice on designing the logo, and the use of colours, signs, and symbols on anything designed for Asians because you could inadvertently use a sign, symbol, or colour that is not auspicious in Asian cultures. For example, in the Chinese custom, red and gold are good-luck colours, but white and some shades of blue are associated with death and mourning. Also, turtles and turtle eggs, (a symbol of one who has no face; and a cuckold) and some other animals (like dogs) could carry negative connotations. For example, Chinese insult words using the word 'dog' are common: e.g., 'Running dog' 'dog-temper' 'dog-thing' and 'stinking dog faeces.'

Without Singaporean advice, company jackets, T-shirts, uniforms, and team sports clothing could certainly advertise the wrong message if one inadvertently used death colours instead of joyful colours and/or grossly inappropriate symbols! Anything expensive is inappropriate, also anything embarrassing, i.e., lingerie, clocks (associated with funerals), personal items, and flowers, which have long been associated with illness, death, or wastefulness would be inappropriate.

The polite response to a gift The polite Singaporean response is to disclaim: 'Oh no, you shouldn't, no need,' etc. Do not confuse traditional Asian courtesy, which requires at least two or three refusals, with actual unwillingness or dislike of your gift. It may be however, that the gift is not welcome because of the State ruling. Do not push or insist if it may cause embarrassment.

Opening the gift The polite Singaporean considers it bad manners to open a gift in front of the giver. Do not be offended if it is set aside until after you have left. Westerners normally tear open a gift immediately and show surprise, delight, happiness, and gratitude. This may be seen as greedy behaviour. If you receive a small token from a friend, try to show good manners by waiting until you go home to open it. Many Asians know however, that Westerners place much value on opening the gift before the eyes of the giver, so play it by cultural ear.

Giving a return gift Keep in mind the value and class of the gift and try not to outdo it. A gift usually infers an obligation and reciprocity (in all cultures – and that is why expensive gifts are frowned upon in Singapore!) Also, remember to wrap the gift corresponding to the value.

BUSINESS ENTERTAINING

Singaporeans often use the setting of food to achieve the objectives of impressing their business counterparts, to honour them, to determine their sincerity, to work out business points, and to make good relationships. Hence there are business breakfasts, business lunches, business cocktails, business dinners and business banquets.

Throughout these meals, you are seen not just as an individual, but as an extension of your company or corporation. If you are honourable, your company is honourable. If you are the host, remember the food taboos of your Singaporean business associates. Check with your guests first about the kinds of food which they cannot eat; Muslims cannot eat pork and some cannot eat flower crabs; Hindus and Buddhists do not eat beef and some are vegetarians. Singaporeans generally enjoy spicy food. You might have to tell the proprietor to use spices (especially chilli) in moderation if you can't take it yourself.

Ask Singaporean friends and associates to teach you the fine art of business banqueting. Be a good learner!

SOME COMMON PROBLEMS IN THE BUSINESS OFFICE

SPEECHES AND JOKES

Speeches are usually opened by addressing the honoured guests, followed by words of welcome. Jokes are seldom used to open a speech because they are not serious, formal nor respectful. Humour to warm up an audience has its place in a speech but remember that what is funny to you may not be amusing to a Singaporean. Be aware that jokes can backfire especially if they have sexual overtones.

MODESTY AND RESERVE VERSUS PRIDE AND BOASTFULNESS

Westerners speak positively and with pride about their possessions, skills and talents. If it is not overdone, it is not seen as bragging; it is a signal of a healthy self-esteem and a positive self-concept.

'Yes, I can write poetry, I have had two poems published' or, 'I really worked hard on that paper, I know I will get an "A" for it' are positive statements that are not thought of as excessive bragging. Self assurance, self assertiveness, aggressive and bold behaviour are admired traits designed to make the most of the individual in an ego-centered culture. These are traits which help people to get hired and promoted in the West. They help the individual to stand out from the group and be noticed.

Singaporean reserve In Singapore, the above traits and statements are seen as offensive. People look down upon fools 'who do not know their own limits.' Bragging, boasting, lack of modesty and humility are traits which can cause trouble and envy. Westerners are advised to behave in a humble, reserved and self-effacing manner when working in Singapore or else they may be seen as fools and braggarts.

Describing abilities Singaporeans tend to downplay their talents. They say that: 'Only a fool brags and boasts.' They believe that they should demonstrate competence while on the job rather than bragging about how well they might do the job. They prefer to let the boss see how good their work is; to let the work speak for itself.

They say: 'I can write poetry a little bit' (especially if they are an expert); or, 'Yes, I finished my research paper, but it is not very good' (especially if it is definitely an 'A' paper) or in the job interview: 'Yes, I have had a little experience on that computer, and I have had some experience as an office manager.' (Culturally translated, this could mean that the Singaporean is a highly qualified expert in the field, and has had extensive office experience, administrative and organizational skills).

The natural Western way is the tendency to enhance and exaggerate talents. To build them up; to stretch them and to find special words that make their talents look even better than they are.

Unfortunately, in Singapore, the Western-style forthright and 'boastful' behaviour will only be looked upon as another example of Western arrogance and foolishness. Westerners are advised not to exaggerate their abilities, but to learn to work with Asian modesty and humility.

In the Western world, modest and humble words will not win the Singaporean the job! Polite, modest and humble words may cause the Singaporean to be overlooked and thought of as being too passive. Many Singaporeans who are highly qualified are often denied promotions because they do not speak up positively about their abilities.

OPEN DISAGREEMENT AND CRITICISM

Open disagreement and criticism cause loss of face. If you wish to disagree or criticize, it must be done discreetly, delicately and subtlely; your point should be hinted at rather than stated blatantly, frankly and openly. Never single out an individual for criticism in public; always speak in general terms: 'Some people have been coming back late from lunch.'

Also, remember that it is bad form to openly criticize Singaporean ways, people, habits, behaviours or customs.Criticisms may be taken as a national insult, harking back to colonial and imperialistic treatment of Asians in Singapore by Westerners.

Cultural differences still exist in the office even though many Singaporeans have been trained in Western universities or they have been trained by Western business people. Photo: Munshi Ahmed

ASKING QUESTIONS, SPEAKING UP, SEEKING HELP

In egalitarian Western cultures it is important to ask questions and to give answers. There is no shame or loss of face involved if one asks questions or asks for clarification. On the contrary, a person who asks questions is thought to be quick-witted, intellectually curious, energetic and one who pays attention to the facts. In fact, if one does not understand the directions or instructions, or if one is not sure how to do the job, he/she is expected to ask questions. If questions are not asked, the employee is at fault if mistakes are made.

In hierarchical Asian cultures however, the polite employee, student, or child does not question a boss, a teacher, a parent, or anyone for that matter who is cast in a superior position. It would imply that the respected senior had not explained properly, or had not made himself/herself clear. It would also imply that the one who asked the question was foolish because he/she did not know what to do, and that a question had to be asked! Can you see the problems inherent in this cultural difference in Singapore? Still, ways must be found to work with the cultural behaviour. Some ideas follow:

- Be aware that questions are not a part of the Asian cultural way.
- Always be sure that instructions are clear.
- Write points out in a manual, with pictures, and clear instructions and directions.
- Provide a mentor during training.
- Encourage questions, and smile when questions are asked. Show how questions help the whole group to perform better.

WORKING IN A HIERARCHY

Show respect to all Singaporeans regardless of their position in the hierarchy. Showing respect means that you must:

- Never shout at, swear at or openly criticize anyone.
- Never make obscene gestures to anyone.
- Never say anything against another person's family.

In Singapore it is important to learn how to pay special honour to those in senior positions, to people in authority, and to higher-ups in the hierarchy. Some quotes from successful expats:

- 'Asians are very class conscious and always maintain status relationships. Americans have difficulty in knowing how to do this.'
- 'One must always maintain a degree of dignity to those in a higher position and to those in a lower position. A big mistake that we make is trying to socialize with the wrong people on a one-to-one basis.'

How to treat people in the hierarchy Some Asians interviewed on this topic gave some general advice on how to observe the protocol of hierarchy, i.e., how to show friendliness to people in different levels of the business/work structure.

Elders and seniors Always show deference and respect to them:

- Greet them first when entering a room, house or meeting room.
- Offer them the seat of honour.
- Stand when they enter a room.
- Invite them to eat first and wish them a hearty appetite.
- Treat them with courtesy, being careful to preserve their face.
- Do not criticize or contradict them (especially in public).
- Do not cross your legs when they are seated facing you and there is no table between you.
- Do not hug or kiss them unless you have a special relationship with them.
- Do not pat them on the shoulder or treat them in a familiar way.
- Sit to 'respect' attention with them.

Peers and equals Show friendship and equality as you would a friend of your same age and position. Never pat equals on the shoulder – it signals that the one patting is the superior.

Subordinates and juniors Show benevolence and care, as if you were treating your younger brother/sister with kindness. Help to bring them along, as in a mentoring relationship.

UNDERSTANDING SINGAPOREANS
Pertaining to the Chinese, Malay and Indian Sections

Singapore is modernized, industrialized, and, some might say, Westernized. The first-time visitor's first cultural shock may well be at just how Westernized this equatorial island in Southeast Asia has become. Arriving at the incredibly efficient Changi airport, being whisked away past the contemporary skyscraper skyline to the five-star hotel in a modern and air-conditioned taxi, driven by a courteous and well-spoken English-speaking driver, and dining later that evening on a truly gourmet meal with a sophisticated and high-tech Singaporean business associate, may convince the unwary business person, tourist or visitor that there is very little that is Asian about Singapore.

Airports, skyscrapers, taxicabs, hotels, and the other external trappings of industrialization, however, are only skin deep. To penetrate the surface, you need to look deeper and you need to look closer; you need to probe the internal nature of the culture. While it may be true that some of the younger and more modern Singaporeans are forsaking their own Asian heritage, and losing touch with their own customs and culture, a careful study reveals that there is still a very strong Asian heart beating vigorously beneath the hot and humid atmosphere of the concrete jungle that is modern Singapore.

Although Singaporeans may externally dress and behave in a Westernized way, the visitor would be wrong to assume that Singaporeans are like Westerners. They are not! Singapore is in a state of rapid social change and transition; many of the patterns explained in the next three chapters are also in the state of rapid social change! Some habits, customs, courtesies, and etiquette may be considered old-fashioned or out of date by some young and Westernized Singaporeans, or too modernistic and frivolous by some of the tradition-oriented elders.

The foreign guest in Singapore however, is advised to learn and understand the patterns of behaviours relating to the Chinese, the

Malay, and the Indians, because we have aimed for the behaviours which are considered acceptable and appropriate to the majority of respectable and ordinary host nationals.

The Western guest must overcome a tendency to judge Singapore as one would judge a Western culture. An appreciation and an acceptance of Asian cultural ways and behaviours can help visitors to enjoy and understand the people; it can help to ease the pain of culture shock, and it can help to develop the traits necessary for a successful cultural adjustment: empathy, tolerance, and a sense of humour.

Sometimes the cultural differences are so subtle, so almost invisible, that one is hardly aware that they are there. At other times the differences are glaringly bold and almost frightening, catching unwary Westerners by surprise; leaving them to wonder what is going on, and why they don't understand what has happened!

Explaining the social customs and courtesies of Singapore is not an easy task. The rules of etiquette and appropriate behaviour in any

Young Singaporeans having fun. Photo: Munshi Ahmed

culture are difficult to define, classify, and contrast. This is even more so in Singapore – where citizens come in every size, shape, colour, religious and ethnic group, economic system, and regional area. Behaviours vary from one group to another, from one social strata to another, and from one age group to another. The most which can be hoped for, is that a set of generalized rules and regulations can be explained and interpreted which can serve as a loose outline to guide your cultural footsteps while working, studying, or living in Singapore.

Exceptions are the norm! Some people adhere to cultural behaviour more than others. Some people deviate from expected patterns. For everyone who agrees with the interpretations given here, there are those who may not agree, or who agree with reservations. Use the information with which you are in doubt as a topic of conversation with Singaporeans. Ask for their advice and assistance in understanding. It is guaranteed to make for a lively and interesting dialogue. The healthy interchange of ideas which follows can open up cultural windows and let the light of friendship shine in.

The world was my oyster, but I used the wrong fork.
— Oscar Wilde

Chapter Four

THE CHINESE COMMUNITY

THE PEOPLE

The Chinese make up 77.7% of the population of Singapore. The cultures which the Chinese immigrants brought with them were highly ritualized. Rules regarding marriage rituals, appropriate care for the ancestors, filial piety, and saving and giving face, were strictly adhered to. This state of affairs was relatively stable in the early years of this century and remained so for well into the 1950s.

Teenagers of today talk of grandparents who had polygamous marriages (several wives at the same time), and of grandparents, and

The Malay influence is very strong in the dress, language and cuisine of the Straits Chinese. Photo: Munshi Ahmed

in a few cases, parents, whose marriages were arranged without them ever having laid eyes on their partner until the wedding day.

Converts to Christianity wonder how their parents will react to their new faith. Parents and grandparents steeped in traditional Chinese beliefs despair at the fact that their Christian descendants will no longer carry out the rituals which ensure their comfort in the afterlife.

Change, when it came, was sudden and radical. In one Chinese family for example, the grandfather in his eighties speaks only his own dialect, believes wholeheartedly in the rituals of ancestor veneration, visits the Chinese medicine shop for his cures, and has little access to the languages spoken on TV. His chief form of exercise is a half hour of *qigong* in the local park in the morning with his friends.

His son, now in his late fifties or early sixties, is more-or-less trilingual. He has a good grasp of his father's dialect; bazaar Malay, the one-time lingua franca of Singapore; and some English. He carries out the rituals of his religion in perhaps a slightly cynical way, hedging his bets as it were. He might, if he were health conscious, take a brisk walk round the East Coast Park or MacRitchie reservoir every now and then.

The grandson of the family might have received a university education in a Western country. In his late twenties, he is able to speak fluent English, as well as his own dialect, and Mandarin. He proudly calls himself a freethinker to his liberated yuppie girlfriend. If he is ill he goes to a Western doctor, although his mother might also thrust a traditional brew on him too. He plays squash or windsurfs and is planning a trip to Europe as soon as his job allows. He happily lives with his parents in their HDB flat, but will buy a condo when he is sure that he has found the right girl. Secretly, he is relieved that the family no longer lives in the *kampung* that grandfather often reminisces about. Countless variations exist on this theme.

Generalizations of this nature cannot cover the range of socio-economic, dialect, religious, and even political groups that make up the Chinese community in Singapore. For example, there are some Chinese who do not speak any Chinese, they are more comfortable with Malay and English instead. These are the Straits Chinese. They are Malayanized Chinese who are descendants from the old Chinese families of 16th-century Malacca in neighbouring Malaysia. However, such broad patterns do illustrate the differences in the range of life experience that has occurred in three generations of Singaporeans.

LEARNING TO SOCIALIZE

INTRODUCTIONS

Shaking hands Among the Chinese, shaking hands between people of the different sexes is acceptable. (This is not true for the Indians and Malays). The woman takes the lead here. If she wishes to shake hands with a man, she offers her hand first. If she doesn't, then a man should not offer his.

Although the Western-type handshake is acceptable among the modern Chinese, there is a cultural difference which communicates a different meaning if misread. Westerners traditionally offer their hand in a strong grasp of equal strength, pumping three times, and then releasing. Chinese, on the other hand offer a handshake which is soft, lingering, and sometimes two-handed. Chinese men often greet each other with a friendly pat on the arm. The elder pats the younger on the arm, not the other way around. Do not hug or kiss Chinese friends of the opposite sex unless you have a very close relationship.

Introducing according to rank What needs to be particularly stressed here is the respect shown to older people. An elder person should always be named first, even if a woman is present, or if a higher-ranking, but significantly younger person, is also present.

The Western practice of saying the name of the most important person first is good etiquette; generally speaking the most important person is:

- the older person before the younger: 'Mr Wong, this is my nephew, Mr Jones.'
- the higher-ranking before the lower-ranking: 'Mr Vice-President Wong, this is my assistant, Mr Tan.'
- the woman before the man: 'Miss Lim, this is Mr Liu.'

GREETINGS

1. ***In Business*** The polite Chinese says: 'Is your business prosperous?' The modest and humble and polite response is: 'My business is moderate.'

2. ***Socially*** The Chinese greet each other with 'Have you eaten your fill?' or 'Have you taken your food?' The response is: 'Yes, thank you.' (Even if you are starving!) This exchange of greetings is analogous to the Western: 'How are you?' 'Fine, thank you.'

   The Chinese also greet you with 'Where are you going?' and the reply 'Going out' would not be received as being evasive.

NAMES

In Chinese names the clan name comes first, followed by two words (or characters) which make up the personal name. Occasionally the personal name consists of only one word. The personal names all have meanings which can be translated into English. A girl might be called Little Swallow or Fragrant Blossom. A boy might be called Brave Warrior or Defender of Good.

Western			Chinese	
Joseph	Patrick	Craig	Tan	Hock Seng
Personal	Middle	Family	Clan	Personal

An explanation of Chinese names In the example given above, Tan is the clan name of the individual. He should be called Mr Tan. Hock is the name given to all the sons in that family. For instance, Tan Hock Seng's brother may be called Tan Hock Chye. (In some Chinese families, however, the third name is the common one for all the sons and the middle name is the one the individual is called by, as in Lim Seng Yew and Lim Beng Yew). Two generations of men (brothers) in the same family might be:

Tan Hock Seng	(brothers)	Tan Hock Chye	
(son)		(sons)	
Tan Eng Poh	(cousins)	Tan Eng Huat	Tan Eng Lok

All the males of one generation would have the same character (e.g., Hock) in their name. In the next generations both siblings and cousins of the same sex would share the same character (e.g., Eng).

Female names Chinese trace their descent through the male line. Traditionally, only the father's relations were considered important as a woman gave up membership in her own family on a marriage. Today, many modern Chinese women maintain very close ties with their mother's relations as well.

Chinese women long ago struck a note for women's rights because they do not change their family name on marriage. They retain their patrilineal name (their father's family name). A Westerner can refer to Tan Hock Seng's wife as Mrs Tan, but her friends call her Lee Poh Choo, or if they are very close, simply Poh Choo. Formally, she could also be addressed as Madam Lee.

What to call a Chinese? Always call a Chinese by Mr, Miss or Madam followed by the family name, or by the title and family name if it is a senior member of a business. However, if the relationship is on a more personal level, it is always best to ask what your friend wishes to be called. Sometimes, for instance:

- An individual may wish to use the personal name alone, Seng, as in the example given. However, it is usually not so polite to call an adult by a personal name, as that name is usually only used by family members.
- At other times he may prefer to be called Hock Seng.
- Or just Tan, this is usually a preferred form.
- Sometimes he will use a Westernized personal name like Danny Tan. Many Chinese have adopted Westernized names today because it is easier for their Western friends to remember.
- He may even prefer to be called by his initials, H.S. Tan.
- Or by a nickname or a shortened form of his name. This style is common in Singapore where a nickname may be based on some physical characteristic, such as Long Legs or Round Face.

What Chinese can call you It is a good idea to inform your Chinese friends what they can call you, because they are just as confused about foreign names as you are about Chinese names! Joseph Patrick Craig, the American in the example above, could well resent being referred to as Craig, but if he was English, he might prefer being called Craig.

It is good to remind Chinese friends that as soon as they call someone by the personalized name (Joe), it is seen as a step towards friendship, equality, and informality.

SOME COMMON COURTESIES AND CUSTOMS
The basic customs described in this chapter vary according to the religion, dialect group, clan and family of the people practising them.

TEMPLES

1. The right door is used for entry and the left door for exit (as in the Chinese operas). The polite guest follows this custom.
2. It is not necessary to remove the shoes in the outer temple area but inside it is required. It is a good idea for men to remove their hats.
3. Taking photographs is usually permitted, but it is a good idea to ask for permission first.

SHOPPING

1. ***The first customer of the day*** The local shopkeeper feels that it is a bad sign if the first customer of the day leaves without making a purchase. He makes a special effort to obtain a sale from his first customer, i.e. offering a discount, giving a special price, etc.

   If you are only window shopping it would be better to wait until later on in the day. If you find yourself inadvertently being a first customer, please buy something small so you won't ruin the whole day for him! A small item or a greeting card will do.
2. ***Washing away bad luck*** If the customer refuses to buy something, some older Chinese may fill a pail with water and toss it out onto the street to wash away the bad luck. The water is not aimed at the customer. It will be as if the impolite customer had never come by.
3. ***Debts: bad luck and good luck*** It is bad luck to *ask* for a payment of a debt early in the morning. You should wait until after 11.00 a.m. at least. It is a good luck to pay a debt early in the morning, it is a sign of good fortune for the creditor for the rest of the day.

FAVOURS

When the Chinese ask a favour of an important man, i.e. a letter of introduction, a business recommendation, etc., they usually accompany the request with two bottles of brandy tied together with a red ribbon, and some fruit. Be careful to distinguish between gifts, favours, and bribes! Bribes are definitely frowned upon.

INVITATIONS

When sending invitations to Chinese friends, use red or pink paper (as a sign of joy). White and blue are used in funerals. However, it is permissible to use a white card if the lettering is in red, pink or gold.

VISITING IN A CHINESE HOME

Always seek out the elders immediately and greet them with: 'Hello Aunty, hello Uncle — how is everything with you?'

1. *Wearing shoes* The Chinese do not have religious restrictions about wearing shoes in the home but they do get offended when visitors wear shoes into their house. Many of them have beautiful marble or polished wooden floors. They feel it is inconsiderate to wear shoes that may mar or soil them. Even if the floors are not beautiful, they would not like dust being tracked in!

   It is a good idea to quickly glance around to see if members of the family have removed their shoes, then follow suit. If you ask if you should remove your shoes, the polite answer may be 'no', but you might be considered uncouth if you don't take them off anyway. Chinese sometimes protest if you remove them, but you will still be thought of as having been raised properly.

2. *Bringing gifts* It is polite to bring a small gift of fruit, sweets or cakes when visiting Chinese friends. It is always appropriate to say that the sweets are 'for the children'. This is done to show that the giver does not assume that the receiver is greedy. The happy receivers can accept the gift without loss of face, and then feel free to eat up all the sweets himself. Always bring an even number: this is a sign of happiness and good luck. Bring six or eight oranges, two bags of sweets, etc. The host may return some of your gift, i.e. if you bring a bag of oranges, he may give two of them back to you

as you leave. This is to return some of the good luck.

3. ***Entertaining in the living room*** The Chinese entertain guests in their living room. They do not show visitors through the house, especially through the bedrooms. Even family members do not enter each other's rooms without permission. They think it is quite funny when a Westerner shows them the whole house (from the attic to the cellar, and even the closets)!

ON BEING A HOUSE GUEST

1. ***Meals*** In the morning, a knock on the door is a summons for breakfast. It is polite for the guest to join the family for meals. The guest should wait until the entire family is seated before taking the seat that will be provided for him/ her. (The same rule applies for lunch and dinner). The host seats the guest.

2. ***Unfinished food*** The Chinese family never wastes any food. It used to be common to leave unfinished food on the serving plates after meals and the next morning the left-over food would be cooked up with some vegetables and served for breakfast or lunch. This is the origin of Chop Suey. Today, you probably won't have Chop Suey for breakfast, but even so, your plate will be piled up with food, even if you politely refuse three times!

   Polite house guests should always leave some of the food on the plate at the end of the meal to signify that they are full and that the host has given more than enough food. An empty plate suggests that the guest is still hungry. Worse still it might suggest that the guest is greedy.

3. ***Washing personal items*** Traditionally, it was a social gaffe for a woman to wash frilly or lacy underclothing in the basin, and to hang it in plain sight for all the family to see. The reason for the blunder was that it would be an insult to the host to see unmentionables hanging up to dry. Only a wild and wanton woman would tempt a man with this display!

   Today, this may not cause undue concern in a modern Chinese

home, however, a courteous and thoughtful female guest asks the hostess for advice about washing out personal laundry items before she does it. The other alternative is to be sure to bring enough clean clothes to last for the duration of the visit.

4. ***The Chinese do not point out your errors*** The Chinese are very hospitable. They may never tell you if you are committing a faux pas. If you see a funny expression on the face of your host – an upturned eye movement and a slight twist of the neck – try to find out what you are doing wrong. You might ask a younger member of the family for advice.

GIFTS

To the Chinese, happiness is 'born a twin,' hence all gifts should come in pairs. This signifies the joy of being a couple. Single items and odd numbers are a sign of separation, loneliness, and death.

1. ***Accepting the gift*** 'Oh no, you shouldn't...no need,' etc. The Chinese accept a gift with at least three disclaimers so as not to appear greedy. This is the polite form for the recipient to follow. The giver should not be taken aback by this and think that this gift is not appreciated. The giver need only say 'I am pleased that you accept it.'

2. ***Opening the gift*** The Chinese consider it bad manners to open a gift in front of the giver. Chinese say that this is so the receiver will not betray with the eyes or face that the gift is not admired; or, as some others say, that the receiver will not appear to be a greedy person. In any case, do not be offended if it is set aside until after you have left. When you receive a gift from a Chinese friend, you should play it by cultural ear. Some Chinese know that Westerner courtesy expects one to open the gift right away, and that it is polite for the Westerner to show joy and excitement over the gift (whether it is liked or not)! You might ask if you could open it now rather than to wait!

3. ***Bread-and-butter gifts*** A thank-you note and a gift of food is

always appreciated by the Chinese. Some nice gifts to give are:
- A food hamper (a large basket of grocery delicacies, available from most supermarkets).
- Some fine cakes in reusable tins.
- A box of chocolates and a tin of cookies or biscuits. (Remember to give in pairs).

4. *Bad luck or taboo gifts* Some things carry an element of bad luck or can be taken as an ill or foreboding omen. The following should be avoided when buying gifts:
- Straw sandals – They are worn at funerals. A Chinese would have to make many offerings to the ancestors to avoid the bad luck associated with a present like this.
- A stork – For some older Chinese people, a stork on baby shower paper, or in a floral arrangement signifies death. The stork, or rather a crane, was and sometimes still is, carried on the hearse of a deceased woman to show that she has lived a long life. Young and modern Chinese people may not know about this custom today, and many asked about it did not understand the significance of it. To be on the safe side, do not unwittingly give a death symbol to a new baby lest the mother and grandparents are aware of the old tradition and become unsettled by it. As in the Western cultures where the stork is a symbol of the arrival of new life, (young children are often told that the stork brings babies) we can now see some birth congratulations cards in Singapore portraying pictures of a stork carrying a baby in its mouth.
- Clocks – The Cantonese word for clock can also mean 'to go to a funeral', so a clock as a gift can be taken for a bad omen. This would be especially true for a birthday or wedding gift.
- Colours – White, blue or black are associated with funerals. Red, pink and yellow are joyful colours; they are associated with good luck, good fortune, prosperity, and protection from evil. Many young Singaporeans may not be concerned about

the colour of a gift, but, to be on the safe side, stick with the happy colours.

- Sharp objects, knives, scissors – These objects symbolize the cutting off of a friendship.

- Handkerchiefs – The Chinese consider these a sign of sadness. They feel that they can cause grief or break off a friendship. Handkerchiefs are often given to mourners at a funeral.

- Flowers – Since the Chinese love food, and flowers cannot be eaten, they usually do not give them to each other as presents. As the nation becomes more Westernized though, flower shops abound and they are patronized by Chinese as well as Singaporeans from the other ethnic groups. On special days such as Valentine's Day and Mother's Day, the Chinese do give flowers to their loved ones.

Flowers can be sent to people who are sick in hospital. They can also be sent to funerals. Although the influence of Western-inspired advertisements is changing this, it is still the case that some young gentlemen would not bring or send flowers to a lady; that would be treating her as if she were ill.

It is the custom of many Westerners to send flowers to a hostess after a dinner party. In Singapore it would be better to send candy or a basket of fruit instead. The French and German custom of giving an uneven number of flowers as a gift, e.g., five roses, would be a double disaster. (Bad omens: flowers and uneven number.)

FOOD AND DRINK

Eating and drinking are the favourite pastimes of the Chinese. An old joke about Singaporeans is that they love seafood: when they see food – they love to eat it! A poor pun, but a poetic truth as far as the Chinese are concerned.

There is an ancient Chinese saying: 'anything which walks with its back to the sky can be eaten!' This is probably why no decent

Chinese would visit a friend at mealtimes without a gift of food; why most Chinese would not greet friends without inquiring as to whether or not they have eaten; why if a Chinese wishes to break off a meeting, he makes subtle hints about not having eaten yet; why they rarely give flowers as gifts, preferring to give food instead; why if a Chinese likes you, he/she may say: 'May I take you for lunch/dinner'; why if a taxi driver cannot pick you up, he signals that 'he has not eaten yet'.

1. *Meat:* The polite host always inquires if any of the guests are vegetarian, or if they have any food preferences or avoidances.

- Beef – Many Chinese (Buddhists and those from the South) do not eat beef. When serving dinner to Chinese friends, it is safer to serve chicken, seafood or pork. If serving beef, however, be careful not to have it too rare. American-style rare roast beef, for instance, may not be enthusiastically received. Traditionally, the Chinese do not like large slabs of meat, i.e., steaks, roasts and so on. They prefer their meat sliced, diced, or cut up into fine strips.

- White meat of chicken – In the Western culture, the white meat of the chicken is considered to be the choicest part. In the East, the opposite is true. The red or dark portions are the most desirable. When serving chicken, it is polite to offer the dark parts (wings and thighs especially) to the Chinese guests.

  A wonderful old Chinese gentleman of a very high diplomatic rank had been served chicken breasts at an official Western dinner party. It wasn't until we began discussing dining etiquette that he realized that he had not been slighted by the offering of the white parts.

- Mutton – The Chinese, especially those from the South, dislike mutton: 'too smelly, too heaty'. Chinese from the North however, and Mongolians prefer mutton and lamb because they are the most common animal protein foods in that area, and they also prefer the internal 'heaty' food necessary for comfort in colder climates.

2. ***Heaty and Cooling foods***
   - 'Heaty' is a term difficult to explain, for even Chinese friends differ in their interpretations. Some say that heaty foods make the body feel too hot, too full and too uncomfortable. Certain illnesses are caused by eating too much heaty food, e.g. a sore throat. Lamb, mutton, chocolate, almonds, fried foods, certain fruits like lychees, longans and mangoes, as well as granola are examples of heaty foods.
   - 'Cooling' foods are the opposite of heaty foods. They cause the body to cool down or to feel cold. Cooling foods can also cause or aggravate an illness, e.g., bring on a cold or a cough. They should be taken to counteract hot symptoms, such as fever and feelings of heat. More cooling foods should be eaten in summer. People with cold internal energy should avoid cooling foods. Some cooling foods are: melons, apples, yogurt, pork, celery, salt, bananas, tea, and watermelon

     I can't give an exhaustive list of heaty and cooling foods here, but draw any Chinese friends into a conversation about food and they will only be too glad to advise you!
3. ***Heads, tails and fins*** The Chinese prefer their fish, shrimp, etc. with the heads, tails and skin left on. These parts are often considered delicacies. Chicken might also be served complete with head, legs, and tail. Some Chinese eat every part of the animal – entrails and all.
4. ***Milk and dairy products*** Some Chinese do not take milk, yogurt, or dairy products. About 85% of Chinese are lactose-intolerant, i.e., milk and dairy products cause them stomach upsets. However, if Chinese are given milk at a very early age, it appears that they overcome this problem. The younger generation in Singapore seems not only to tolerate milk and dairy products, but to thrive on them. If you are giving a dinner for older Chinese friends however, it would be better to eliminate milk, cheese, butter, ice cream, whipping cream, etc.

5. *Fruit and dessert* Chinese usually prefer fresh fruits for dessert after meals. There are no fortune cookies in Singapore. Sweet desserts are usually reserved for company. Many local people salt their fruit because they believe that it brings out the natural sweetness by osmosis.

6. *Vegetables* Many Chinese do not like vegetables which are not cooked or stir-fried. Raw salads and vegetable dippers are, therefore, not likely to be enjoyed.

7. *Wheat products and rice* Chinese from the North of China may prefer flour, noodles, steamed bread and dumplings because the climate in the North is colder and more suitable to wheat production. Chinese from the South of China may prefer rice, where it is more commonly grown. Some Singaporean Chinese say that they cannot sleep at night if there is no rice in their stomach!

8. *Drinks: brandy, beer, iced drinks, wine, water, coffee* Alcohol is usually never served without food. The Western cocktail hour may not be agreeable to the Chinese taste unless there are plenty of snacks provided.

   - Brandy and beer – At a dinner party, the men would be pleased with straight brandy and beer served with their meals, not after! They also drink fine brandy with 7-Up, ginger ale, etc. They also like ice in their beer; don't be surprised when you see this.
   - Iced drinks – Many of the older Chinese do not like iced drinks. If you ask for a drink of water in some Chinese homes you may be given hot or warm water, the belief being that cold drinks are the cause of colds and bad throats and that they are bad for the stomach. Since many Chinese do not like iced drinks, the preference for iced beer is strange! Perhaps it is because of the heat of the tropics and their exposure to Westernization that they have developed the taste for iced beer.
   - Water and coffee – As a rule, Chinese do not enjoy water and coffee with dinner. In some cases, it is considered bad form to

ask for it; it is as if you 'had to wash the meal down' instead of savouring it! Water is thought to dilute the precious enzyme (ptyalin) in the saliva which starts the digestion process; they believe that drinking water with meals interferes with the natural digestive process and can slow down the metabolism. Indeed they may be right!

- Wine – Chinese enjoy a good Chinese wine, which is usually sweeter than Western wines, much like a Western sherry or port. They are not however, so fond of *dry* Western wines. Wine has been made in China for thousands of years. Traditionally, it is heavy and sweet.

9. *Chinese Tea* As the usual accompaniment to a Chinese meal, tea is usually served before and after meals, but not during meals, unless it is requested. It is served without milk, sugar or lemon.

When served tea by a Chinese, it is the height of rudeness to leave the cup untouched. At least two sips should be taken. It should also be sipped slowly. The host will be delighted if you praise the tea and accept another cup. (In the old days, business was always conducted with a pot of tea on a side table. After the business was concluded, the host would say, 'Let us take tea now,' and after drinking, it was the signal to depart. Today, this custom is only practised among members of the older generation.)

The Chinese believe that tea:

- *Prevents drunkenness* – The Chinese have a secret that enables them to drink large quantities of alcohol without getting noticeably drunk. They drink one or two glasses of Chinese tea before the festivities. They feel that it helps the absorption of alcohol.
- *Prevents fatness* – Tea washes away the fats which one ingests with the meal, so it counteracts the effects of animal fat, and therefore helps to keep one thin.
- *Aids digestion* – It helps digestion when taken after meals.

EATING IN A CHINESE HOME

Traditionally, the family style consisted of the entire extended family sitting around the table where each individual helped him/herself to the food from the communal dishes placed in the center of the table. Each member used his/her own chopsticks and took food from the communal plates. The only dish an individual used without sharing was the rice bowl. Today, in modernized Singapore, many Chinese eat in a Westernized fashion, using forks and spoons and individual plates – rather than chopsticks and bowls.

If eating a meal in a Chinese friend's home, you should always leave some of the food on the plate at the end of the meal to signal that you are full and that the host has provided more than enough food.

In a private home, the Chinese may not preface a dinner with a Western-style cocktail hour. Among themselves, they may serve tea (to prepare the stomach for the alcohol to be served with the meal) and then follow this with a game of mahjong while waiting for the rest of the guests to arrive.

EATING IN A RESTAURANT

Banquet-style dining most often occurs in restaurants, usually involves guests, is more formal, and typically may take place in a private room.

1. *The table setting* This consists of a pair of chopsticks for each guest; a bowl for rice; a bowl for soup; a small individual dish for the main courses; a dish for bones and other discarded parts; a small dish for soy sauce (a second small dish for preserved cut green chillies may be set); a glass for soda or beer; a cup for tea; and a porcelain spoon. A napkin will usually be folded into a clever shape.

2. *Seating* Chinese tables in restaurants are usually circular, the whole group can speak to and view each other equally. For good luck, the Chinese like to have an even number of guests at a dinner: six, eight, ten or twelve.

   Contrary to Western etiquette, the left side of the host has more honour attached to it than the right side. A woman guest sits to the left, and the man sits to the right of the host. A single guest of honour sits on the left side. The honoured guest usually sits so that he faces the front entrance. Younger guests sit with their back to the front entrance.

The reason for facing the door and for sitting at the left side of the host? In the old days, the guest was always allowed to keep his eye on the front entrance in case an enemy should try to sneak in to attack him. The guest sat to the left of the host, so that the host could protect him/her with his strong right 'weapon arm'.

If by chance the doors do not face south, look about the room. There will be a large painting on one wall. If there is no south facing doors, then the chief host and chief guest sit with their backs to the painting. Unlike Western etiquette where each individual chooses his/her own seat, guests at a Chinese banquet or restaurant do not seat themselves, they wait to be seated by the host who sits everyone, as much as possible, according to rank and protocol.

3. *The duties of the host* The host does not take his/her seat until he/she has seated everyone at the table. It is polite to apologize for the insignificant display and the inferior quality of the food (even if he has taken great pains to ensure that only the best is served). The host may have spent hours and even days discussing the menu with the chef. There is an art in choosing the courses in proper sequence. Spicy dishes must be set off with bland ones; delicate flavours with robust ones; and soft-textured foods should be complemented by crispy food.

4. *The duties of the guest* The perfect dinner guest stares in amazement as each course is brought in. The intelligent guest recognizes and responds to well-made choices. The gourmet guest celebrates dishes of exceptional quality. The enthusiastic guest even exclaims 'Wah!' at a particularly tempting dish! The astute guest praises all the subtle nuances and delicate flavours blended into each masterpiece. The curious and pleased guest tries to guess

the ingredients and expresses pleasure with each mouthful.

5. ***Planning the meal*** Ask for help from an experienced Chinese friend on how to plan a splendid menu. It is an art form. Some basic guidelines follow:

- Number of dishes – The host usually orders as many dishes as there are guests (with a few extra dishes thrown in for good measure). If there are only a small number of guests, then one or two extra dishes is a must! A good rule while ordering is to include at least one fowl, one fish and one meat dish.

- Cold dishes (appetizers) – Meals often begin with cold dishes. Unlike Western appetizers, which are served away from the table with cocktails, these cold dishes are often served as a first course. They consist of dried foods, sausages, dried fish, cold chicken, pickled eggs, etc.

- Soups – Soups can be served at any time during the course of a meal: at the beginning, the middle, and even towards the end, however soup is usually served near the end.

- Rice or noodles – These dishes are often served towards the end to make sure that everyone is filled up. (To serve it at the beginning might suggest a ploy on the part of the host to fill up his guests' stomachs inexpensively.)

- A prestigious menu – Such a menu consists of pork, chicken, Peking Duck (not regular duck), and fish dishes, as well as additional delicacies such as shrimp, crab, squid, sea cucumber, jelly fish, and the even more exotic treats of sharks fin or swallows' nest.

- A prestigious dish – Chicken, duck, or fish served whole. This shows respect and honour to the guest because the host has paid for a whole instead of pieces of a whole. The most prestigious foods are, of course, the ones which are the rarest and the costliest.

BEHAVIOUR AT A BANQUET

1. *Arriving* Guests do not always arrive on time for a banquet, dinner party, or especially a wedding. They often arrive thirty minutes to an hour or more late. They come late because they do not wish to appear greedy, as if they couldn't wait for the food; and because they do not wish to signal their importance by arriving before the more important people! Sometimes, people arrive earlier, but they wait outside until the most important people have gone in. Chinese are hierarchical people; they try to arrive in order of rank. If you arrive early, or on time, you may find yourself sitting alone advertising yourself as a greedy and pompous person.

   If you are meeting friends at a restaurant for dinner, promptness is appreciated because the restaurant people do not like to hold up reservations too long.

2. *Dress taboos* It is not a good idea to wear white, black or navy blue to a party, and especially to a wedding, as these are traditional colours for funerals. I once wore a lovely bleached off-white natural cotton long skirt and shirt to a wedding, and was startled when a Chinese lady said to me: 'Did your mommy die?'

3. *Speeches and toasts* In traditional Chinese practice, dinner speeches are given before the dinner, not after. Don't talk or leave during speeches. Applaud speakers and congratulate them if possible.

   • Before beginning to eat, the host invites the guests to drink. This is a form of greeting. The Chinese feel that once the drinking starts, fun and good conversation begins. If you do not wish to drink alcohol, simply ask for soda pop or apple juice or soda water. It is important that you join in on the toasting.

   • Do not drink until the host has performed the ceremonial

greeting. He raises the glass and says *ch'ing* (please). The guests raise their glasses with two hands, the left hand holding the glass, the fingers of the right hand under the bottom of the glass. Watch the other guests to see how they are holding theirs, and then do the same. When the host calls for everyone around him to drink together, a chorus of *'yam seng'* (bottoms up) is appreciated! Sometimes, after each new course is served, the ceremony is repeated. The Chinese sometimes have games during the meal to induce each other to drink. The losers usually end up by drinking the most!

- After the first drink, the host holds up his chopsticks, repeating *ch'ing*. This is the signal for the guest of honour to begin eating. After the guest of honour has been served (usually the host serves him/her), the other guests begin to eat. The host usually waits to serve himself last. The rule is each in his own turn, but it doesn't always happen!

4. ***The courses*** One course at a time is placed in a common serving dish in the centre of the table; there is usually a rotating circular platform on which food is placed. Be careful when turning it or the dish may land in someone's lap. Watch to see if the other guests have finished serving themselves before turning.

A serving spoon should accompany each new platter. The guests should use this to dish out the food. If there is no serving spoon, then use your own chopsticks.

The host may have a special pair of chopsticks that he can use to serve the guests of honour. The host takes great pains to watch the plates of the guests. As soon as a plate begins to look empty, the host begins to pile up food on it again. This is an honour the host shows to the guest. If you are the host, remember this courtesy. If you are the guest, you can also serve the host occasionally, or the persons seated on either side of you, or your spouse, as a special gesture of courtesy.

Do not lift up the whole serving plate. Leave it on the table while you dish a small portion onto the small plate in front of you. Your host or someone beside you may tilt the serving plate for you if you are trying to get some gravy.

A Chinese feast can consist of up to twelve courses. Pace yourself in the beginning or you may find yourself staggering through the last three or four dishes. The meal is rather like a buffet. Each guest eats just a little bit of all the dishes served. You should mentally divide the amount of food on the serving platter into the number of guests at the table; then take only your share, i.e. if eight people are seated, take one-eighth of the amount served.

Always take the piece or pieces closest to you on the serving platter, unless you are fishing for a special tidbit to place on an honoured person's plate. Don't worry, he/she will be looking for special tidbits to place on your plate too! You should never take the last piece as really polite guests always leave a little bit on the serving dish. You don't have to eat food that you don't like, but you must eat everything you dish out for yourself. No edible food should be left on your own plate.

- Soup – When drinking soup, use your chopsticks to eat the ingredients, but use the soup-spoon to take up the broth. The spoon should be dipped towards you, not away from you as in American etiquette. Unlike the drinking of Japanese soup, it is considered rude to pick up the bowl and drink directly from it. Slurping soup is considered acceptable. Chinese often inhale air with hot soup in order to cool it. Westerners do the opposite – they exhale air (blow on soup) to cool it.
- Meat or sweet buns – These should be eaten with chopsticks. The trick is to try and hold the bun on one side with the chopsticks. Take a small bite, then larger ones, until you have eaten your way through the whole thing. If this is too difficult just use your hands; no one is going to mind.
- A half-eaten fish – If any of the guests at the table are seamen,

fishermen, or even sailing-boat enthusiasts, a half-eaten fish should not be turned over on the platter. This is supposed to foretell the capsizing of his boat on his next sea trip. The bones are usually removed by the waiter/waitress and the fish eaten from the top down.

- Bones and shells – Remove bones or shells from your mouth with your chopsticks. Chicken thighs or wings can be eaten with the fingers. If there is a plate for refuse put the refuse on it. If not, leave them on your dish and the waiter will usually clear them off before the next course or two.

5. *Watch your chopsticks*
   - Don't reach across another person's chopsticks while choosing your tidbits.
   - Do not rest chopsticks on plates/bowls. Chopsticks are not rested on the dinner plate or rice bowl. They are never laid across them when not in use. They must be placed on a rest stand, the soy-sauce dish or a bone plate. The 'handle' portion of the chopsticks sits on the table and the 'mouth' portion sits on the rest stand or soy-sauce dish. (It would be embarrassing for the host if a guest laid his chopsticks across the individual plate or rice bowl at the end of the meal. It would be a sign that the guest is still hungry and that the host has not provided enough food.)
   - Do not stick chopsticks upright in a rice bowl, not even to chop up something in it. This is a bad omen, as a single chopstick is stuck upright in a bowl of rice at a Chinese funeral to show the separation of the person who has died. The single chopstick is a sign of heaven. It is symbolic of the single joss-stick that is burned for the deceased.
   - Do not wave chopsticks about. Waving chopsticks in the air or pointing with them is bad manners.
   - Do not make noise with chopsticks.
   - Do not always hold chopsticks in the hand. Rest the chopsticks

often. Put them down between eating and talking. The idea is to eat a little, talk a little, rest a little, and then repeat it all again and again!

- At the end of the meal, place your chopsticks neatly on the table, at the side of your dish. This is a sign that you have had enough.

6. **Second helpings** If the host asks you to have second helpings, it is polite to refuse: 'oh, no-no-no' (so as not to appear greedy). It is acceptable to take more after the host presses it on you. Even if you really don't want any more, it is polite to eat at least a few bites if the host urges you to.

- When 'no' means 'yes' – If you are the host, always press more food on the guests. If they really do want more food, the voice rises, 'no-no-no', the eyes track the food, and the hands are free floating, they are not crossed over the plate.

- When 'no' means 'no' – A real refusal is signalled when the voice drops: 'no-no-no'; the eyes look at your face; and the hands cross over the dish. When this happens, you can stop trying to put more food on their dish.

It is always polite to make a token refusal of second helpings even if you would like some more, this shows that you are not greedy.

If you really cannot eat the food, it is polite to give a reason (even if it is a little white lie). Say: 'Oh I am sorry, but I am allergic to sea slugs; I break out in hives when I eat them!' The Chinese much prefer to hear the polite excuse than the bitter truth that you hate the expensive and delicate sea slugs they have picked out especially for you! Never refuse food with a grimace. Never criticize the food or make negative comments about unfamiliar or unusual dishes.

7. **Burping** A gentle burp can be considered a sign of appreciation. Westerners should be aware of this custom so that they won't be taken by surprise.

8. ***Leaving the banquet*** At dinner parties or celebrations, all the talk and festivities take place around and during the meal. Guests do not stay around to chat  or drink after dinner and tea have been served. They leave immediately after the last bite or sip has been swallowed!

Do not be alarmed by the number of do's and don'ts listed here. The rules are easy to remember after you have read through them once. A kind heart is the most important attribute in Chinese courtesy. Chinese meals are good fun, relaxed and pleasurable. The host is mostly concerned that all the guests are enjoying the food and having a good time.

Be a good guest and learn to be a good host; delight in the people and in the food. Westerners may look at food with new cultural eyes after having had the experience of visiting or living in Singapore!

PUBERTY RITUALS

While the Chinese do not have a tradition of puberty rituals per se, they do have a tradition whereby young people become adults. This happens during the marriage ceremony. Traditionally, the hair-combing ceremony in front of the ancestor's altar on the day of the wedding signalled the attainment of adulthood for the bride and/or groom.

This ceremony, whereby the mother ritually and ceremonially combs the child's hair, notified the ancestors that the child is now grown up, and that he or she has become a man or a woman, and that he or she has taken a spouse. This ceremony is still seen in more traditional families in modern Singapore today!

In the past, unmarried people were not thought of as 'full-blown adults' by the family and the society, and even to this day, they may be given *hong bao* (red packets given to children by parents and elders) even if they are long past the age of childhood.

DATING AND COURTSHIP

Among the Chinese of Singapore, dating as it is known in the West, is a relatively recent concept. It has never been a part of Chinese cultural tradition. In the past, matchmakers arranged marriages and horoscopes readers and fortune-tellers were consulted to see if they would be successful. Aside from this, polygamous marriages (i.e., marriages where a man had more than one wife at the same time) and mistresses were common. The number of wives a man had were a good indication of his wealth and prestige.

In 1959, the People's Action Party promised marriage reform, and in 1961 the Women's Charter outlawed the old custom. Polygamy is no longer allowed (Muslims are still allowed to have more than one wife), and young Chinese feel that love and affection play an important part in marriages today. Young Chinese have also been influenced by Western practices through the mass media, television, movies, novels and magazines. The monogamous marriage, i.e., one partner at a time, if not for life, based on 'romantic love' is seen as the ideal. Young Chinese hopefuls wish to have more say in determining their marriage partners today, and indeed they do have!

Although dating in Singapore may superficially appear to be similar to the Western style, there are many major differences. Dating in Singapore is a courtship ritual that often involves more than the two individuals concerned. Family, friends, school chums, work mates, and even the government take it upon themselves to help young people to find suitable mates. This is especially true if the person is very shy. Indiscriminate multiple dating of even a handful of different partners, let alone the thirty to forty people as in the Western type, would be a serious blotch on the character of an unmarried person in Singapore, and it would cast doubts on the honour, dignity, and integrity of the individual.

When couples date in Singapore, it is not indiscriminate and casual, it is usually a prelude to a more serious step: engagement and marriage. Dating in Singapore today is more open to individual choice, but it is still very closely connected to group approval and support. When young people begin to date, they usually date in groups and only narrow down their choice to one special sweetheart after a long and happy friendship has developed within the group. The young people might meet in junior college at 17 or 18; at university at 19 or 20; and at work where they get to know each other in a casual environment. Dating is rare before 17, and even in university, the young people are apt to pay more attention to their studies even though they are acutely aware of the opposite sex.

Parents are less strict than they used to be, but they are conservative and still keep a very watchful eye on the young people. They expect the couple to be virtuous. Also, parents, family, and friends are expected to sanction and bless the choices their children make. If there is strong resistance to the choice, the child may not openly go against the group. Clan, dialect group, filial piety, social standing, and group pressure may prevail over individual choice in the crunch.

The Singapore government, as the avuncular head of the group, has set up an institution which is intended to help group members of higher education find partners. Traditionally, it has always been more difficult for highly educated women to find marriage partners. Men preferred to marry women who were educationally inferior to them, not equal or superior to them. Noticing this problem for unmarried graduate women, the government set up the Social Development Unit (SDU). It is open to unmarried graduates and it organizes social gatherings on a regular basis. It is responsible for many happy graduate marriages.

BOY-GIRL RELATIONSHIPS (SOME PATTERNS)

- Generally speaking, parents would be happier if their children did not date until they were about 17- or 18-years old.
- After a movie or social event it is common for a light snack at a hawker's stall.
- The boy 'sends her home' (which actually means he escorts her

home) at the time her parents have asked that she be in.

- Kissing is considered bad manners on a first, second or even third date. The couple may know each other several months before their first kiss; and reputable couples do not engage in public display of affection, unless they are away from the eyes and ears of their group.

- Girls are not expected to pay for a boy, nor to pay for their own way. In university where money is scarce, 'going Dutch' is not as rare as it once was.

- A blind date is always in a group. If a boy likes a girl in the group and asks her for a date, she must refuse if she doesn't wish to be thought of as 'easy'. After the group has gone out several more times, and a friendship has developed, he may be allowed to call at her home. Group dating is widely practised by young people in Singapore.

- It used to be understood that single girls did not go to clubs, discos, etc., without a male escort. They would earn a bad reputation if they did. This is beginning to change because in the last few years a number of entertainment places have opened up where it is acceptable for groups of single girls to visit. In Singapore some examples of these places are: *Yesterdays* in Thomson Square or *H2O* in Orchard Road.

Westerners should be aware of the serious nature of dating in Singapore. It is not the casual and light-hearted type of social relationship that it can often be in the West. Westerners are also cautioned not to date Singaporeans unless their intentions are serious, and they wish the relationship to lead to marriage!

ENGAGEMENTS

Matchmaking used to be common among the Chinese of Singapore, but today it is not common. Singaporean Chinese prefer to choose their own partners.

In traditional times When a matchmaker was used, (and sometimes she still is) she was generally an older woman and a friend of the family. The parents of a marriageable boy or girl engaged her to find a suitable partner or else they sent her to approach someone whom they considered suitable. She was given a nice *hong bao* for a successful match. In some cases, a successful match meant that eighteen hams were presented to the matchmaker. I was once a matchmaker for some dear Chinese friends, but I am still waiting for my eighteen hams!

The matchmaker knew both the families involved and both families generally came from the same dialect group and had equal social standing. In seeking information about the girl, the matchmaker was not above bribing the maid of the girl's family. If everything went well, photographs were exchanged and the young man's mother was taken to meet the girl. Often a meeting between the boy and the girl was also arranged. A fortune-teller or astrologer was consulted, and magic tests were carried out to see if the match would be a successful and harmonious one. Horoscopes were important; a girl born in the year of the tiger was considered a dangerous match for a boy born in the year of the goat; she might devour him. A girl born in the years of the tiger, monkey or snake might have to resort to falsifying her birth year, or else end up a spinster.

Betrothals today Matchmakers are still used today, but more as a formality. They act as a go-between and they help with the wedding arrangements; they are especially deft at negotiating the bride price and gifts. The Chinese do not feel that it is proper for the parents on both sides to engage in direct confrontation over these monetary details; they wish to prevent potential strain and tension. Three things take place during a betrothal today.

1. The couple exchange rings (or other jewellery).
2. The young man buys special cakes or sweets (a type of peanut brittle or toffee) which are wrapped up in red paper and taken or sent to the friends and relatives of the couple. (In the past, they were only taken to the bride-to-be's relatives.)When the sweets

are received, the friends know that a wedding will soon be on its way. Presents are not sent for the engagement as the wedding will take place shortly. Gifts are taken to the wedding reception.

3. A marriage gift (bride-price) is arranged. This is a symbolic transfer of money from the groom to the bride's parents. It traditionally signified the transfer of the parents' rights and duties over the girl to her husband. It gave the husband sexual, domestic and procreative rights over his wife. It ensured that the children could bear his clan name. It was also a symbolic payment to the girl's parents for bringing her up, washing her nappies, and providing her with day-to-day care because as a daughter she, and her services, were both lost to the family; she became a member of the boy's group. It was never a dowry and it did not buy a wife. This bride-price is still given today, and it must be paid up before the actual ceremony takes place. It usually helps to buy the bride's trousseau and bridal furnishings. Today, this custom is residually seen in the responsibility of the boy's side to pay for the wedding (in the West, it is the girl's side who pays for the wedding), and in the boy's 'requirements' for marriage. He should have an income of S$3000-plus, own property, a car and status indicators such as household appliances.

WEDDINGS

Marriages take many forms in modern Singapore: a church wedding in white for Christians; a civil ceremony or 'registry marriage,' required by law, but which many Chinese do not feel is as important as the traditional Chinese tea ceremony marriage and the new phenomenon of mass weddings. At a mass wedding, up to 100 couples marry at the same time; there are group rates on the receptions, banquets, and even on the honeymoon.

Yesterday's traditions In the old days before the 1960s, the wedding would last three days, with certain rituals ascribed to each day. Traditionally (and even sometimes today the following rituals can still be seen), a bridal bed was set up before the wedding. In order to ensure its power of fertility, a little boy was made to sit or roll on it. Everything in the bridal chamber was new and bright. Red and pink colours adorned the walls, windows, and bedding. The bride's possessions were brought in and everything was made ready. Just before the ceremony, there was a combing of the hair ritual in which the boy and girl, each in their own homes, had their hair ritually combed. The combing was usually done by the mother. This symbolized the attainment of maturity.

In theory, the marriage was consummated on the first night. The bride was not expected to put up a show of resistance. In the not-too-old days, a specially-prepared piece of cloth was laid on the marriage bed and the bride's mother-in-law would inspect it later for signs of virginity. She might test any stains she finds by rubbing lemon juice on it. (If the stain turns yellow after washing, it is genuine.) If the signs were not favourable, the girl might be sent packing with the words: 'You are not a good girl, go back home to your mother.' The marriage would then be terminated by a divorce rather than an annulment. The Cantonese used to be more specific. It used to be the custom for the groom's family to send a pig to the bride's mother after the consummation. If the bride was found lacking, the pig's ear or tail would be cut off and the mutilated pig paraded to the bride's home – for all the neighbours to see. This is hardly seen in Singapore today.

Today's traditions Unlike a Western marriage, which is a union between two individuals, the Chinese marriage is a union between two groups. The rituals and ceremonies are designed to highlight the union of the two groups. Today, the entire ceremony is telescoped into one day. The bride ordinarily wears a white Western-style wedding dress for the day-time festivities, and changes in the evening to a red or pink evening gown for the banquet. She has a professional hairstylist and make-up artist attend to her hair and face. The groom wears a smart suit, Western-style, with a shirt and tie.

The groom fetches the bride in a gaily decorated car, festooned with red, pink or gold ribbons and a bride doll or bouquet of flowers attached to the front end. He may bring ceremonial gifts in beauti-fully-decorated baskets to the bride's family: some pork, two chick-ens, two bottles of brandy, red wedding candles, the remainder of the bride-price (if it has not already been paid), clothing, etc. The bride's family returns half of the food and drink to symbolize the unity of the couple and the closeness of the two groups.

When the couple reaches the groom's house, the young man aims a well-placed kick at the car door; this is a carry over from the days when the groom would kick the sedan chair in which the bride was traditionally carried to his house. It symbolizes the authority he is assuming over his wife. At the threshold, the bride steps over a pot of smoking charcoal to cleanse her from evil.

Now, the most important part of the ceremony takes place. On entering the home, the couple pay their respects to the household gods and to the ancestors. They bow three times before the altar to inform the ancestors of the wedding. The tea ceremony follows. This cer-emony traditionally formalizes the marriage! Two chairs are set up, and the parents of the groom sit on them. The couple offers each parent a cup of tea. The bride and groom are supposed to kneel while offering the tea, but today some couples prefer to remain standing. The father is offered tea first, then the mother. If they take even one sip, it is a sign of acceptance of the bride; they take her as their own. She 'marries the whole family' so to speak. If they refuse, it is a sign of rejection and trouble can be expected. This does not happen very often, but if the mother is hesitant, her relatives and friends urge her to drink it up.

The parents replace the tea-cups on the tray that is held by a friend or maid, along with a *hong bao* for the bride. The *hong bao* may contain gold jewellery instead of money. It is rare for guests to witness this part of the ritual as usually only the family is present. After the parents have been served tea, the senior aunts and uncles, in order of age, status, and rank, come and take their places and continue the ritual.

The couple then pay a visit to the bride's home to perform the tea

The Tea Ceremony is the most important part of a Chinese wedding. The bride is formally accepted into the family when her parents-in-law accept the tea. Photo: MITA

ceremony there. The couple is presented with gifts of sugarcane to symbolize sweetness in their life. They may also receive a cock and a hen, given to them by the bride's mother. These are placed under the bridal bed to foretell the sex of their first-born child. (If the cock sticks its head out first, they believe the first-born will be a boy. If the husband hears the cock crow during the night, it means he will have many children.) Many young people leave this ritual out of their ceremonies today. In the old days, the couple was actually supposed to keep the fowls until they died a natural death. In the afternoon, it is traditional for modern urban couples to visit public parks to pose for photographs. If you visit the Botanic Gardens, especially at weekends, you can usually see wedding groups being photographed.

In the evening, a large banquet is held for all the friends and relatives. It is a festive occasion with hundreds of people in attendance. The bride and groom move from table to table inviting the guests to drink with them. The guests at each table rise to toast the couple, often singing out '*Y-a-m S-e-n-g!*' They hold the notes for as long as possible. Guests from different tables often compete to see which group can sing the loudest and the longest. There is merrymaking, drinking and eating...eating...and more eating.

Today, there is a new alternative to banquets. At a banquet, all of the festivities take place during the eating. As soon as the dinner is finished, all the guests go home. As an alternative to this, some couples are choosing to have buffet receptions in the day. They cost less, they are more informal, and they prevent food waste, and they have some advantages which the banquet is lacking, such as permitting dancing, karaoke, skits, and choir performances after the eating.

Many Chinese couples today still make their home with the husband's parents, but many prefer to set up housekeeping on their own.

WEDDING GIFTS

1. **Hong Bao** It is customary to give a *hong bao* to the bride and groom. These red packets are presented at the door. The groom stands at the door to receive guests while the bride stays in a room until the dinner has started.

   Hong bao packets can be purchased at any of the Chinese Emporiums. Be sure to get the one with a 'Double Happiness' sign on the front as there are red packets available for many occasions.

   The amount given depends on how well you know the couple getting married. It should always be enough to cover the cost of the meal that you and your partner are eating. Sixty dollars is an average amount. Whatever you give, it must be given in an even number, in new crisp bills, and in an even amount of bills.

2. **Gift Voucher** An alternative is to purchase a gift voucher from a department store. If you don't know the couple too well, it might be better to offer the voucher rather than cold, hard cash. The amount, though, should still be an even one.

THE WEDDING FEAST

1. *Dress* Whatever type of dress women wear, colour is important. White, black or navy-blue should be avoided. Unbleached muslin signals bad luck for it is often worn to mourn a dead parent. Red, pink or gold are auspicious colours and mean good luck for weddings.

   - Less formal wedding – dressy short dresses or pantsuits for the women and short-sleeved shirts for the men.
   - More formal wedding – if the dinner is being held in an up-scale restaurant or hotel, then the guests should dress more formally: tie and jacket for the men and more formal outfits for the women.

2. *Arrival* In the past, people always arrived late, sometimes an hour or two after the designated time. Today this practice is frowned upon more and more, especially by modernized Chinese. Some Chinese make a point of being punctual just to make a point of rebelling against the traditional late starts! A safe thing to do would be to come just a little bit late; aim for the middle path. If the invitation states 7.30 p.m. sharp, then 7.45 p.m. would be about right.

3. *Dancing* There may be a lively band and singers to entertain the guests, but unlike a Western wedding where all the guest drink and dance after the eating, there is usually no dancing at a Chinese wedding. This may be why the buffet is becoming an attractive alternative to the sit-down banquet.

4. *Departure* Guests leave as soon as the dinner is finished and the last drink has been taken. To the Westerner, this seems an abrupt ending to such a festive occasion, but to the Chinese all the festivities occur during the meal.

BIRTHS

Traditionally a child is considered one-year old at birth, and a subsequent year is added at each Chinese New Year. Thus a baby girl born one month before the Chinese New Year celebration would be considered two-years old at the age of four weeks.

1. *The 'First Month' celebration* The most important occasion on the birth of a baby is the 'First Month' celebration. A party is held and friends are invited. Good food is served and hard-boiled eggs, with red-stained shells, are distributed; the red eggs are an ancient symbol of new life. Gifts are given to the baby. This celebration is of great importance for the first son and the first daughter only. Subsequent children will have some ritual, but not the elaborate affair accorded to the first-born. (Sometimes, instead of a party, cakes and red eggs are distributed to friends and relatives at their homes.)

2. *Traditions for the mother* After the birth of her child a mother went into confinement for a period of 30 days. She did not touch cold water, wash her hair, bathe, nor have any male visitors. She was encouraged to eat ginger and to take tonic wines.

   Today, the modern mum, especially if she is living away from traditional parents, is likely to forego these rituals.

GIFTS

1. For a mother in hospital – A gift of food is most appreciated: a basket of fruit, sweets, cakes, or cookies. Bring in pairs.

2. For a new mother at home – A gift of food would also be appropriate: a basket of nourishing delicacies containing chicken essence, biscuits, milk, fruit, tonic wines, etc. She may be on a special diet after childbirth.

3. Flowers are not appropriate – Flowers are usually given to sick people or sent to funerals. Some Westernized Chinese might not be upset by a gift of flowers, but to be on the safe side, stick with the gift all Chinese love and appreciate: food!

4. A gift for the new baby – An outfit with matching top and bottom; a baby dress along with small items like a small rattle and toy, or a packaged gift set containing a nightie and a blanket, or a sleep

set is always appreciated and appropriate. A more elaborate baby gift: could be a gold bracelet or necklace, or a piece of jade, accompanied by a small gift (always give in pairs).

5. Colours – Remember that the most joyful colours are red, pink, yellow, gold, and orange.

6. Storks and bad omens – Do not give a woman a gift that has a stork or pictures of a stork on it. Young modernized Chinese may not be aware of the symbolism of the stork, but by the time they grow up and have a baby, their parents and grandparents might tell them about the taboos. Storks are a symbol of a woman's death.

I remember a woman who had been a classmate at Singapore University. She was intelligent and modernized. When she had a baby, a good-hearted Westerner gave her a flower arrangement that set her into a fit of uncontrollable weeping. The unwitting expat had made a flower arrangement herself which consisted of a pretty white basket, decorated with three blue bows, and filled with five flowers (In the Western culture, blue is associated with boys, and pink is associated with girls) arranged around the centerpiece of a tall ceramic stork. How many ill omens and taboo objects can you find in the arrangement! Yes: 'too many to be a coincidence,' thought my friend! A bomoh had to be called in to give her some peace of mind! The bad omens were:

- White basket – the colour is a symbol of death.
- Blue colours in the ribbons and bows; all symbols of death.
- Uneven numbers (3 bows or 5 flowers) – all symbols of sorrow and separation and loneliness. There is one happy couple in the three bows, but one bow is left lonely without a partner; there are two happy couples in the number five, but one is left alone without a happy partner.
- The stork – a symbol of death; it is carried on top of a hearse to show that a woman had died.
- Flowers – traditionally not given to healthy people; only given to sick people or sent to funerals.

131

RELIGIOUS AND PHILOSOPHICAL SYSTEMS

The Chinese have a rich mix of religious and philosophical systems. Some Chinese incorporate all of them into their own personal belief system, or else they mix and match bits and pieces from all of them. If you ask a Chinese friend what his religion is, he may look puzzled and say: 'I am a freethinker' meaning that he might embrace a rich mélange of beliefs and behaviours. Elements of all of the following can be seen in death and funeral rites, rituals, and ceremonies. I would like to thank my dear friend Chris Treichler for many of the ideas expressed in the following vignettes:

Taoism in its folk religion aspect, is a magical, mystical, occult belief system concerned with longevity, immortality, and preserving sexual powers and youth. It uses a mixture of medical science, healthy life-style, vegetarian and healing foods, and superstitions and elixirs to accomplish these things. Taoism is the basis for many of the ritual Chinese behaviours. In its higher form, it is the concept of the 'Way' which is the rational and natural order of things. The ideal is that which is simple, unadorned, plain, and based on limiting desires and strengthening the spirit.

Confucianism is an ethical code of personal conduct, a philoso-phy of life, a political doctrine, and a folk religion with deities, temples, and rituals. It has been one of the greatest forces for social stability in the history of the world. It is humanistic in its thrust; not speaking about god or heaven, because, as Confucius said: 'How can I speak to you of god, when you do not yet know how to live with humans; and how can I speak to you about heaven, when you do not yet know how to live on earth!' It places everyone in a social hierarchy and instructs on the roles to be played within the structure.

Buddhism embraces the concepts of reincarnation and ancestor-veneration, both of which play a very important part in death rituals. It stresses the importance of meditation and the release from physical desires. In reincarnation, life does not end with death, it goes on through life after life until it completes the cycles necessary for purification and enlightenment in Nirvana!

Ancestor veneration is of great importance in maintaining family solidarity and the ties between the living and the dead. Reciprocal obligations are set up between the Chinese and their deceased relatives. Obeisance can only be performed by a junior for a senior and thus a young unmarried boy would be committing an unfilial act if he died before his parents did. After death he would not be venerated at the family alter. A boy who dies young is held to be the reincarnated soul of someone to whom the parents owed a debt; when he dies, the debt is considered paid in full.

The prime concern in ancestor veneration is with the duties of children in the support and care of their parents, both living and dead. The worst thing a child can do is to neglect his parents by not providing them with food, clothing, shelter and happiness while alive, and ritual veneration and care after death.

This is a paper car that will be burnt for the deceased. This ensures that the deceased will have transportation in his life in the other world. Photo: Munshi Ahmed

133

FUNERALS

After a death, the body is ceremoniously washed, usually by the chief mourner. If the deceased was a man, it would be the man's oldest son. The body is dressed in an odd number of suits of clothing: three, five, seven or even more. This is to keep warm on the long journey to the King of Hades. In the HDB flats, the body is carried all the way down via the staircase to the void deck on the ground floor. All ceremonies usually take place there. Lifts are not used and coffins are not brought up to the flat. Embalming is done by casket companies. The deceased is laid out behind a screen; paper money is burned and offerings placed close by. A chair is also set close by and the deceased's favourite clothing are placed on it.

Two candles must be kept burning throughout the period so that the spirit of the dead one can view the surroundings. The priest talks to the body as if it were still alive: 'Look, your friends are here to say farewell.' Weeping and wailing starts at a specified time, when it is believed that the spirit of the dead person has returned. This weeping on cue provides a sympathetic welcome to the spirit. The amount and duration of the wailing lets the King of Hades know how much the spirit was loved or hated during his lifetime. Rich families can employ professional mourners to add to the din so the noise will reach the ears of the King of Hades. Members of the family keep a constant vigil until the body is buried, sometimes not for three, five or seven days. This vigil ensures that a pregnant cat or rat will not jump over the dead body, thus turning it into a zombie. Also, since many wakes are held in the open void decks of the HDB flats it insures that animals will not disturb it.

Friends come to pay their respects and they are given food and soft drinks. They sit around and play mahjong with the bereaved to keep them company and to help them stay awake. Loud music is played to ward off the evil spirits. Priests light fires and jump through the flames to beat off the evil spirits who lie in wait to capture the soul of the deceased. On the morning of the funeral, the bereaved come together for one last gathering. In some funerals stilt-dancers may perform. After the final rites are finished, the mourners accompany the coffin to the graveyard or crematorium. It is an ill omen if the coffin bumps any door posts on the way out. The carriers crowd around it closely and inch it carefully past poles and posts. It is often no easy matter as some coffins can weigh hundreds of pounds.

A brightly decorated open-sided truck will be waiting and the coffin is placed in it, surrounded by flowers. On top of it there will be a picture of the deceased and a figure of a heron for a lady, or a tiger for a man. A procession forms: first comes the band, wearing colourful costumes; the band is usually provided by the clan association of which the deceased was a member, then the priest, the hearse and the mourners.

The bereaved wear sackcloth over their clothes: the men wear sackcloth headbands and the women and children wear sackcloth hoods. They all wear straw sandals or only white socks. Grandchildren wear dark blue. Great grandchildren wear pale green or they might be wearing clothes containing traces of red to signify that the deceased has lived to a ripe old age but this depends very much on the dialect group of the family.

The mourners start off on foot. Automobiles follow to pick up the mourners after they have walked about half a mile. Once the coffin is unloaded at the graveyard or crematorium, several rituals are performed. Today, many Singaporeans are cremated rather than buried as the country is running out of land for cemeteries. After the funeral (usually three to seven days after the death), the family burns an elaborate paper and bamboo house complete with paper hand phones, fax machines, television sets, automobiles, clothes, jet aeroplanes, and paper money. All these ensure that the deceased has everything needed in the afterlife. They are 'air mailed' to the deceased through the ritual burning; the essence of the gifts passes through to the spirit world in the flames and smoke.

For a specified time after the funeral, the members of the family wear a little patch of coloured cloth on their sleeve to show that there has been a death in the family. The patches may be white, black or blue depending on the relationship to the deceased. Sons-in-law of the deceased as well as offspring of the daughters of the deceased wear patches with a strip of red to indicate that they are 'outside' the family (they do not have the same surname). This means that they have their own sets of parents and paternal grandparents who may still be alive.

For the first seven days after death, the soul is thought to be hovering between the two worlds. Meals are ritually placed on the altar for the spirit, and on the seventh day it is thought to pay its last visit to its earthly home. During the night, a bed will be made up and a meal set out for it; in the morning, the family looks for signs of the ghostly visit: was the blanket disturbed and were any grains of rice scattered about? On this day, a graveside visit is paid and all things associated with the dead are burned – the final act of separating the dead from the living. The ancestral tablet is set up, and, from then on, rites will be periodically performed to serve the deceased's needs and gratify his demands. The total period of mourning for parents used to

The bereaved wear white clothes and sackcloth. Various rituals are performed at the wake. Photo: Munshi Ahmed

be three years. Today, it is one year. Traditionally, sexual relations and earthly pleasures were forbidden during the period of mourning and a marriage could not be contracted during this time.

MOURNING ETIQUETTE

1. Visitors usually come in the evening, around 7.00 p.m..
2. They first pay their respects to the bereaved and offer sympathy. One of the bereaved relatives takes the visitor behind the screen where the coffin is placed.
3. The family member kneels and burns joss-sticks. The visitor should stand at the foot of the coffin and bow three times towards it. He/She need not kneel unless the deceased is a close friend. If a visitor kneels, the bereaved lights joss-sticks for him/her.
4. It is traditional for the visitor to take some food and drink later. In conversation, a mention can be made of how peaceful the deceased looks, etc.
5. Visitors should wear sober colours or white. Red, pink, gold and other light or bright colours should be avoided.
6. On the final day, after the burial or cremation, a large meal is served to the mourners who have accompanied the body to the graveside or crematorium.
7. When a visitor leaves, the family gives him two pieces of red thread or string to keep away any bad luck associated with the death. Just wrap them around a button and discard them after you get home.
8. The visitor may also be given a *hong bao* containing a single coin – a five- or ten-cent piece. This should be used to buy a sweet on the way home. It will dissociate you immediately from the dead and break any bad luck surrounding the death. Throw away the money if you do not buy the sweet. It should not be taken home. Sometimes sweets are already placed on the table for visitors. A handkerchief may also be given to mourners who come on the final day.

GIFTS

1. It is common to give a gift of money to the family. It helps to defray the cost of the funeral and the traditional food and drink. The money should be put in white or brown envelopes and handed to the person in charge of gifts or to one of the bereaved.

    For a death, money is usually given in odd amounts to symbolize the separation of the loved one. An odd number of bills should also be given; if the offering is $35, give three $5 bills and two $10 bills, not an even number for example, of three $10 bills and five $1 bills.

2. Some Chinese prefer not to receive packets of money. Wealthy families may ask a charitable organization to set up a table on the premises to receive money from the mourners. They prefer a donation to be given to charity.

3. Flowers and wreaths can be sent to a funeral.

Clearing the graves of deceased family members during Qing Ming. It is a time where the ethic of filial piety is reinforced. Photo: MITA

CHINESE NEW YEAR

Unlike Western celebrations, Chinese New Year celebrations do not last for one night and a hangover. It goes on for fifteen days, but it is longer if you count the preparation that goes on beforehand which is part of the fun and festive activity. The Chinese New Year begins on the first day of the lunar calendar and falls anywhere between 21 January and 19 February. It is the most joyous time of the year for the Chinese. In China, it heralds the beginning of Spring; in Singapore it represents a new beginning. It is the time when all debts are paid up, when all new clothes and shoes must be worn, when the entire house must be cleaned and renewed, when old arguments are forgotten and peace restored between family and friends and when the gods and ancestors are worshipped, venerated and propitiated.

All manner of sweets and delicacies must be prepared or bought: waxed ducks, melon seeds, groundnuts, sausages, mandarin oranges and many other tasty things. Christian Chinese may not partake of the rituals which focus on reincarnation, charms, deities, and spirits, but they still celebrate and enjoy the food and festivities. Charm papers and red banners inscribed with lucky words written in gold paint are fastened to the doorframes of the house to ward off evil spirits.

Seven days before New Year's Eve, the Kitchen God of each household sets off to visit the Jade Emperor in heaven. It is his duty to report on all the good and evil deeds of the family. (A Chinese husband can always find respite from a nagging wife by going into the kitchen where the picture of the Kitchen God resides. She does not dare nag her husband in front of the eyes and ears of the Kitchen God!)

On New Year's Eve candles are kept burning all night long; sugar-cane is placed behind a door to make sure that each member of the family has a life that is sweet to the end. Those whose parents are still alive stay up all night long in the belief that this will add long years to their life. A grand reunion dinner is held in almost every house, and family members come from near and far to pay their respects to their parents and demonstrate their filial piety and devotion. The reunion

Shopping for decorations in preparation for Chinese New Year. Red and gold are the most auspicious colours. Photo: MITA

Mandarin oranges represent good luck and prosperity. Photo: MITA

dinner is a very important ritual which keeps the extended family together. The reunion dinner reinforces the ties of solidarity. It is an occasion for members to gather in the family home, share in a communal meal, re-affirm kinship, pay respects to the elders, and to venerate the ancestors. It is a celebration of family togetherness for the Chinese!

At 11.00 p.m. (the start of the new morning, according to the Chinese) each member of the family pays homage to the ancestors at the family altar. After this, the children offer tea to their parents, and the parents offer *hong bao* to the children. Around midnight, a great deal of noise (it used to be firecrackers before they were banned) is made to scare off any evil spirit that might be lurking about. All the doors and windows are thrown open to usher in the New Year and to greet the benevolent spirits that will bring good luck with them.

On the first, second and fourth days, relatives and friends visit each other to eat, drink and wish each other good luck and prosperity. In many families, the third day is reserved for praying to ancestors at the family altar. Some sadness may be felt, so as a custom, people usually do not visit friends on this day. The fourth day is a traditional day for businessmen; they usually host a big feast for their employees. On this day, any employee whose services must be terminated will be given notice. Various festivities go on until the fifteenth day, at which time the New Year celebrations are officially over.

HONG BAO

Hong bao is a gift of money in a red packet to bring good luck. The Chinese consider red a symbol of good luck, protection, good fortune, life, and happiness. The packets are usually given by parents and grandparents to children and children of relatives and friends. Most Chinese give about $2.00 to children of not-so-close friends. For their own children, the rich give from $10.00 to $60.00.

It is especially auspicious to give brand new bills in even numbers and in even amounts: $2, $4, $8, etc. The new bills prevents anyone from muttering: 'old', 'dirty' or 'no-good looking' money. These words are unlucky and should not be mentioned during the New Year. They can inadvertently bring on misfortune. It is customary to give your Chinese amah or employee a *hong bao*. The red packets can be purchased at any of the Chinese Emporiums. Some employers give the equivalent of one month's salary if the employee has worked for a year or more.

In Chinese families, the *hong bao* is given to children, unmarried people, members of the family who are younger than the giver, i.e. the grandfather gives to the son and the grandchildren; the son gives to the children - his own and nephews and nieces, etc.

A *hong bao* should not be given to any government servant, i.e. the postman, the garbage collector, the road sweeper, etc. Even though the government frowns on this habit, people still do give them as an act of goodwill and as a small token of appreciation for services during the year. A *hong bao* is ordinarily given to a hairdresser, barber, etc. at this time.

CHINESE NEW YEAR ETIQUETTE

During the New Year celebrations, everyone (the expatriates as well as the Indians, Malay and other local communities) is affected by the festive spirit. This festival has been included in this book because it is the time of the year when most Westerners come into contact with their Chinese neighbours.

1. It is important to pay all debts by New Year's Eve. Make sure that you have paid your amah, grocer, driver, newspaper delivery man, etc.

2. It is customary procedure to give your Chinese employee four days off during this time. The holiday should begin on New Year's Eve and last through the third day.

3. If giving a present to someone during this time, remember to give in happy pairs. Brandy is a favourite gift but make sure that it is accompanied by something else, i.e. a box of sweets, a brandy

miniature, etc. Another favourite gift is a food hamper.

If invited to someone's home for tea, etc., it is good manners to bring six mandarin oranges, which are the colour of gold, for luck and prosperity. They may give two oranges to you in order to return some of the good luck. Before leaving, the visitor could leave a *hong bao* for the maid.

5. When visiting a Chinese friend during the New Year do not wear black or dark colours; now is the time for your brightest and reddest dress or shirt!

6. If you cannot visit Chinese friends or business associates during the first fifteen days, be sure to ring them to wish them *Gong Xi Fa Chai* (Good Luck and Prosperity). Cards can also be sent.

SPECIAL CHINESE NEW YEAR FOOD

1. *Nian Gao* A 'Year Cake' made from glutinous rice flour and sugar. It is the king of cakes for the New Year. The word *gao* has the same sound as the word 'high' in Chinese. It gives those who eat it a higher status. It can be eaten steamed or fried.

2. *Mandarin oranges* The fruit symbolizes gold. They are called *kam* in Cantonese, which is how gold is pronounced in the same dialect. Bring them in even numbers when visiting friends.

3. *Raw-fish salad* This salad (*yu sheng*) is eaten during the new year period. It is eaten for a longer life or for extra wealth. The fish is thinly sliced and tossed together with a mixture of shredded vegetables in a sweet and piquant sauce.

5. *Other kinds of festive food*
   - Peanuts – they are the nut of longevity.
   - Oysters – called *ho see* in Cantonese, means 'fortunate situation'.
   - Sea moss – or *fa cai*, sounds like 'to prosper'.
   - Shitake mushrooms – called *dong gu*, means wishes fulfilled from East to West.
   - Red dates – called *hong zao*, means 'prosperity comes early'.

TABOOS AND SUPERSTITIONS

1. No unlucky words must be spoken during the New Year festivities.
2. Brooms must not be visible or used on the first day or else good luck will be swept away.
3. Nothing in the home should be broken. Be very careful when handling cups, glasses, and especially mirrors. If anything, especially a mirror, is broken, it means the family will split up or a death will occur in the family.
4. Traditionally, all family members have new clothes for the New Year.
5. Needles and scissors should not be used for they are believed to bring bad luck.
6. Children may not be punished or scolded on New Year's Day.
7. Washing the hair is considered unlucky during this time. It washes away good luck.
8. Rain on New Year's Day foretells a year without drought.
9. A gambling win foretells good fortune for the coming year.

Chapter Five

THE MALAY COMMUNITY

I would like to acknowledge my gratitude to my dear friend, Cikgu Ehsan Haji Ali for his assistance with this material. I learned most of the information in this chapter at his cultural knee. This chapter rightly belongs to him. Thank you, Cikgu.

THE PEOPLE

About 14.1% of the population of Singapore are Malays. Social change has touched the Malay community and changed much of their traditional way of life, more so perhaps, than any of the other people in Singapore. It has put considerable stress on their spiritual and social customs and values, but even today, the spirit of the Malay people remains essentially the same. They are a courteous people; etiquette, kindness, generosity, and hospitality are core values for them. These values are reflected in the way they treat each other and in the way they treat strangers – with respect and compassion. Few people can visit a Malay family without being overwhelmed by the kindness that is shown to them. Malays have a deep sense of community; friends, relatives, and neighbours feel a responsibility to help each other (with time, food, money, support, etc.) in times of joy, need, and sorrow.

MALAYS ARE MUSLIMS

It is their religion which shapes the foundation of the everyday lives of the Malay Singaporeans. Being Muslims, the Malays are expected to recite the creed: 'There is no God but Allah, and Muhammad is the Messenger of God'; pray five times a day and worship Allah as the one true God; practise charity and help the needy; fast during the month of Ramadan; and make an effort to go on a pilgrimage to Mecca at one time during their lifetime.

By religious law, certain things are *haram* (forbidden); hence Malays must abstain from pork and alcohol and some other foods, and they must not come into contact with the nose, wet hair or lick of a dog. It is also *haram* for men and women to casually touch members of the opposite sex, and for women to sit together with men in the mosque, and to wear immodest clothing (many Malay women cover their entire bodies, leaving only the face, hands and feet exposed). There are also certain things which are *makruh* (allowed, but not encouraged), for example: smoking and the eating of raw onions and raw garlic.

THE CONCEPT OF BUDI

According to Dr. Tham Seong Chee of the Singapore University, the ethical system of the Malay people revolves around the concept of *budi*. *Budi* is the ideal behaviour expected of them. It reflects the degree of character and good breeding of the individual. The rules of *budi* are: respect and courtesy to all, especially elders; affection and love for parents; a pleasant disposition; and peace and harmony in the family, neighbourhood and society as a whole.

Dr. Tham Seong Chee defines *budi* as: 'The internalization of the social conscience of the individual. It is the measure of the nobility of his character. One's name and status in society is concomitant with one's *budi*.' There are two forms of *budi*:

- *Adab* – This is on the individual level. Each person has a responsibility to show courtesy in word, deed, and action to all people at all times.
- *Rukun* – This is on the social level. The individual must act to obtain harmony, whether it be in the family, community or society.

While Malays, on the whole, do not value the pursuit of wealth, power, materialism, and conspicuous consumption for their own sake (believing that human care and compassion are more important than self-centered egoism and materialism), they do firmly believe in industry, hard work, and self-reliance. They feel that responsibility to family, friends and the community should not be sacrificed for such things as the profit motive or the accumulation of personal and acquisitive wealth. In other words: 'People are more important than possessions!'

MALAYS IN TRANSITION

Nearly all Malays in Singapore are Muslims (99%); their official language is Malay, and they practise the Malay culture. They are the largest minority community (14.1%) in Singapore; they are better educated than they have ever been; and they are quickly emerging as a solid middle class group. A person is classified as middle class if he/she:

- earns a personal income of $2,500 and above.

- has post-secondary education and above.
- holds a job that is regarded with some prestige.
- owns at least a five-room flat.
- owns a family car.

While urbanization and modernization have changed the life-styles of many of the Malay people in Singapore, (many of them have never lived in a *kampung*, being born and raised their whole lives in HDB flats instead), the community as a whole has tried very hard to preserve its values and traditions. Many of the younger generation, while better educated, more up-to-date, and in more professional occupations than their parents, still adhere to many of the age-old traditions of courtesy, hospitality, and etiquette that form an essential part of the Malay culture.

In Singapore today, the Malay *kampung* communities have largely disappeared as the ethnically integrated HDB flats have replaced much of the old physical structures of yesterday's Singapore. In 1982,

A Malay family in their newly renovated HDB apartment. Photo: MITA

Yayasan Mendaki (Council for the Development of the Singapore Muslim Community) was set up to encourage and perpetuate Malay values which were, and still are, in danger of being threatened by the Westernization, urbanization, modernization, and industrialization of Singapore.

A Malay leader spoke of the poignant loss he felt with the demise of the *kampung* communities: 'We have lost the sense of belonging that we had in the *kampung*,' he said. 'Perhaps our children will find a new sense of belonging playing in the void decks of the blocks, for they will develop a sense of place together with other children. This is impossible for us to appreciate, and it is impossible for them to explain to us.'

Of all of the ethnic communities in Singapore, the Malays seem to be hit the hardest by the effects of Westernization but according to Professor Willmott, of the University of Canterbury in New Zealand

Dressed in Western-style shirts and blue jeans, a group of Malay girls attend Swing Singapore – a street party organized by the government where people of all races and ages come for some good, clean fun. Photo: Munshi Ahmed

who wrote in 1990: 'There is hope that the multi-ethnic experiences of the Malay children in Singapore will give them different but comparable feelings of communion of the type that their parents experienced in the close communities of the *kampung*. It will produce its own identity quite different from that of their parents, and it will be a national communion rather than an ethnic one.'

MALAY CHILDREN, FATHERS AND WOMEN

Malays love children. They raise them gently and tenderly. Parents may be more inclined to *cium* their children than to kiss them, i.e., they place the side of their nose against the child's cheek and give a little sniff! Ideally, the Malay culture teaches that a child is taught by example and praise; traditionally, physical punishment has always been frowned upon and the standard to be looked up to, if not always realistically followed, has been the model of explanation and clarification. Respect between parents and children is touching and tender.

The Malay father assumes a much larger role in raising the children than fathers of many other cultures. The Malay father and grandfather and uncle spend a great deal of time holding the children, playing with them, carrying them about, and rocking them to sleep. If a Malay father or grandfather sits down for a moment, a little child will surely find his/her way into his lap.

Malay women dress in a style which allows them to obey the laws of Islam and at the same time to keep relatively cool in a tropically hot and humid climate. Most women wear a traditional *baju kurung*: a long-sleeved and loose overblouse that reaches just below the knees, over a floor length *sarung* (the word *sarung* literally means a covering or an envelope, and indeed, the *sarung* is much like an envelope; it is a skirt-like garment wrapped around the waist and tucked in at the waist band – like an envelope).

Women in business tend to wear Western-styled clothes which are designed to cover their arms and legs. Most schoolgirls wear regular school uniforms. In recent years the Dakwah (missionary) movement

A female telephone operator in traditional Malay headdress – traditional ways and modern technology go hand in hand. Photo: Munshi Ahmed

has dictated that women also wear a *tudung* (headdress which covers the head, neck and hair, leaving only the face exposed). The trend of wearing the headdress began in Singapore in the mid-1970s, as part of global Islamic revivalism, but it only gained wider acceptance among Muslim women in the past few years.

Many people tend to think that Malay women are downtrodden just because they must sit apart from the men in the main portion of the mosque, and they are not allowed to mix casually with them, nor to eat with them, and they must keep the major parts of their bodies covered. This is a major error in thinking! In fact, the older a Malay woman gets the more self-possessed she becomes. Malay women enjoy being women. They are strong and reliable and have no fear of hard work. They are often thought of as the upholders of sound Muslim behaviour and they are a valuable standard for the younger generation to model themselves after.

LEARNING TO SOCIALIZE

INTRODUCTIONS

Salaaming or shaking hands It is not traditional for men and women to shake hands with each other. Malay women may *salaam* with men if they cover their hands with a cloth. The reason for this is that Muslims ablute (purify themselves with water) before praying and if a man came into contact with a woman after ablutions, he would have to ablute again.

The traditional Malay greeting between Muslims is similar to the Western handshake without the grip. Malays offer both hands to the person they are greeting, lightly touching the outstretched hands of the other, then either one or both hands are brought back to the heart. The greeting simply means: 'I keep your greeting in my heart.'

- Elders or seniors – Older people use only one hand in the greeting gesture because they have more status. People of higher status may use only one hand.
- Juniors or subordinates – Juniors use two hands in the greeting gesture to show more respect to the elders.

1. Men either *salaam* or shake hands with each other. Old intimate friends shake each other's hand in this manner: they grasp each other's right hand in a firm and solid grasp, they shake once, and then release. Men who are not old friends, give a *salaam* with a head nod.

2. Women also use the above form, but they have a slightly different version. The women may stand, but often they sit down first, knees to one side, both feet tucked under the body, away from view. They lightly touch the hands of their friend between their two hands, then bring their hands up to their faces, covering the nose and mouth in a gesture that could be analogous to the prayer position of the hands. Then they touch the heart with their right hand. This means: 'I kiss the greeting and put it into my heart'!

3. Younger people lightly *cium* the hand of their elders, i.e., they

'I greet you from my heart.' After softly touching hands, the women bring their hands to the breast. The younger woman uses both hands as a sign of respect.

bring their face down to lightly touch and sniff the hand of their elders. This is a request for a blessing of the elder. The young Malay repeats this *cium* whenever leaving the home or preparing for a journey.

4. In Westernized and business settings Malays may offer to shake hands with both men and women if they feel that the person is not aware of the Muslim custom. They are more concerned about not hurting the feelings of the other than they are about their own personal feelings. Some modern Malays freely shake hands with people of either sex without worrying about it at all.

The polite woman however, (Western or otherwise) does not offer her hand to a Malay gentleman, and the polite gentleman (Western or otherwise) does not offer his hand to a Malay woman. The Westernized custom of offering a social greeting or departure hug or kiss to members of both sexes should be avoided.

- Between men and women – A nod of the head and a bright smile is a polite greeting form between people of the opposite sex.
- Between people of the same sex – If the Westerner or non-Muslim knows the Muslim greeting gesture, he/she can use it, because it shows honour to Malays, and respect for their culture and customs.

    If the Westerner or non-Muslim does not know the Malay greeting *salaam*, then of course a standard handshake is appropriate. However, be aware that the Muslim handshake is apt to be a very light touch of the hand (because of their own cultural tradition of lightly touching hands); do not wrongly judge this light touch from the Western cultural standpoint, where a handshake must be of a firm and solid equal strength to show sincerity and an offering of strength and cooperation.

Introduce according to rank The basic rules are the same as for the Chinese, i.e., the elder's name should be mentioned before the younger, the more important before the less important, the woman before the man, etc. In entering a Malay home or community, always first seek out the elders to pay your respect to them.

GREETINGS

Traditional greetings often reflect values or cultural concerns which are dear to the heart of the people. Malays value spiritual and religious qualities, so among themselves, they say:

- 'I wish you peace and tranquility' (*Selamat sejahtera ke atas anda*).
- 'Peace be to you.' (*Assalam alaikum*). The response is ' And peace be to you.' (*Waalaikum salam*).
- 'Where are you going?' The polite reply is 'No where in particular' or 'For a stroll.'
- 'May you walk in peace and tranquility' combines both the religious and the secular values.

When non-Muslims greet Muslim friends, the informal: 'Hello, how are are?' is acceptable, but it may be more courteous to greet them in English in one of their own greeting forms: 'Peace be to you.' It is a sign of respect for their culture and ways. In addition, it is important to greet Muslim friends with the polite: 'How is your family?' or 'How are your children?' and so on.

NAMES

Most Malays trace their descent through the male line, but they do not have family names as they are known in the West (i.e., the family name placed last after their own personal name); or as they are known to the Chinese (i.e., the clan/family name placed first with their own group and personal names placed last).

Some Malays trace their descent through the female line (eg., the Minangkabau people) but this is not common in Singapore.

Male names Malay men generally attach their father's name to the end of their own name, and they use the word *bin* which means 'son of' to show that the male is the son of (father's name) Thus the name only lasts for one generation. For example:

> Grandfather : Isa bin Aman
> Father : Osman bin Isa
> Son : Ali bin Osman

The grandfather is named Isa bin Aman. His friends call him Isa. Malays call him Encik Isa (the equivalent of Mr). Westerners call him Mr Isa. He is (or was) the son of Aman. Some Malays drop the *bin*, thus, Isa bin Aman may be simply called: Mr Isa Aman. If you call him Mr Aman (as in the West), you would be addressing him by his father's name.

Female names There is a difference between women's and men's names. For example:

> Zaitun binti Abdullah, the wife of Isa bin Aman

The woman's name is Zaitun binti Abdullah. She is called Zaitun by her friends. Malays call her Puan (Mrs) Zaitun. Non-Malays call her Mrs Zaitun. The word *binti* means 'daughter of'. She is the daughter of the man Abdullah. She does not traditionally take the name of her husband when she marries; she retains her father's name.

Some Malay women however, do adopt a Westernized form of address, i.e., they may attach the name of their husband to the end of their own name: Mrs Zaitun Aman. Thus, in the business world, etc., she may be called: Mrs Aman. However, on the legal documents, her name would still be: Zaitun binti Adbullah. If Zaitun is unmarried, she is called: Cik (Miss) Zaitun

Honorific titles When you see the title: Haji (feminine: Hajjah) placed before someone's name, it means that the person has made a pilgrimage to Mecca.

The name Syed (feminine: Sharifah) somewhere in the name indicates that the person may consider him/herself to be a direct descendant of the Prophet Muhammad.

SOME COMMON COURTESIES AND CUSTOMS
Following are some general descriptions of some basic Malay customs. Of course, these customs vary according to the personal practice of the people involved.

CLOTHING
Like their fellow Chinese and Indian Singaporeans, the Malays have grown accustomed to seeing scantily clad Westerners and tourists on the beaches and streets of Singapore. They themselves dress very modestly however, according to their religious customs and traditions.

When visiting a Malay home, or when invited to a Malay festivity, *do not wear skimpy clothes* of any kind. Malays take their religion very seriously, and modest dress is part of their religious culture. Guests and visitors to their homes and functions should respect their beliefs and not be a cause of embarrassment to them by exposing parts of the body which should be covered in polite Malay society.

Clothes that should not be worn by women while visiting with

Malays are: anything which exposes the armpits, legs, neck, cleavage of breasts, stomach, and back. Do not wear shorts, cut-offs, mini-skirts, bikinis, halters, shirts and dresses without bras, and tight-fitting skirts. You might not be expected to cover your hair, but it depends upon the orthodoxy of the people involved. To be safe, ask for advice from your Malay friend.

DOGS

Muslims are not allowed to come into contact with the wet nose, hair, tongue, or saliva of a dog. They especially do not like to have a dog leap or jump on them! This is a religious restriction. If a Muslim visits you in your home, keep your dog in a separate room.

GAMBLING

In Singapore, betting and gambling for money is forbidden by Malay religious law. The actual element of gambling that is forbidden is the winning or losing of money.

GESTURES AND TOUCHING

1. *Pointing* It is not polite to point to a place, object, or person with the forefinger. That finger points out animals. The entire open palm is used to point out humans, or the thumb may be used, with the four fingers folded under.

2. *Gesturing to 'Come Here'* Never use the forefinger crooked and waving; this is the way a human commands an animal. Instead, use the four fingers of the right hand, fingers together, with the palm facing downward – in a waving motion. It is sort of like shovelling money off a table into the left hand.

3. *Australian drinking gesture* The Australian 'drinking up' gesture where the first three fingers of the hand are folded to touch the palm, and the thumb and little finger are extended straight up could be offensive.

    The thumb is a symbol of good and the little finger is a symbol of evil. It could theoretically mean 'Good is evil' and therefore, it could be very offensive.

4. ***The head*** Your friend has a beautiful child with soft brown eyes and a dimpled smile. Restrain your impulse to pat her on the head. The head is considered to be the seat of intellectual and spiritual powers; it is sacred and should not be touched. It is permissible to pat her on the chin with the right hand though.

   Your friend has a bee alight on his head. Restrain your instinctive gesture to brush it away. Warn him instead. The head is sacred, it should not be touched.

5. ***Public display of affection*** Any touching in public, whether it is casual or romantic, between members of the opposite sex who are not closely related by blood, is strictly taboo for Muslims. This applies to sweethearts, friends, the waiter in your hotel, shop assistants, colleagues at work, or any Muslim with whom you have contact. Even married couples are careful to observe this

It is polite to point with the thumb of the right hand, with the other fingers curled in to form a fist. Photo: Courtesy of Jamilah Mohd Hassan

religious rule. If you are visiting with Muslims or joining them for a festival, please do not hug, kiss, or walk arm in arm with anyone, not even your sweetheart while you are the guest of a Muslim.

MOSQUES

Some mosques do not allow visitors into the main prayer hall, and some do not allow them to visit during prayers.

1. Non-Muslims may visit mosques but they must be quiet and respectful. One can visit when prayers are not taking place. The best time to go is from 9.00 a.m. to 12 noon.
2. All shoes must be removed. Muslims wash their feet before entering. Muslims step over the threshold with their right foot first. Do not cross in front of people who are praying at any time.
3. Women should have their arms, legs and head covered when they visit, and they should be modestly dressed.
4. Women, even non-Muslim ones should not enter the mosque while menstruating.
5. The Quran should not be touched. At home, Muslims cleanse themselves before touching their own copies. If the book is a translation, such as the ones used in schools, then it is considered to be an ordinary book and it can be touched.
6. One end of the mosque is called the Mehrab. Only the *imam* (leader of communal prayer) can enter there, so do not go in.
7. Ask permission to take photographs.

RIGHT HAND / LEFT HAND

1. Use only the right hand while eating!
2. The left hand is the supporting hand. Traditionally, the left hand is used for cleansing (hygienic purposes), after using the toilet. It is therefore, only used as a supporting hand. It is never used to hand anything to anyone. It would be very rude to do this.
3. Give or receive objects, food, plates, money, gifts, etc., only with the right hand. The polite way to do this is to give the object with

The polite way of handing an object to someone is to hold it in the right hand while lightly touching the right wrist or forearm with the left.

the right hand, while lightly touching the right wrist with the left hand. If the object is heavy the left hand can be used to help support the right hand at the wrist.

ON BEING A HOUSE GUEST

1. *Smoking* While Muslims do not have religious restrictions against smoking, it is considered commendable for them to refrain from it (*makruh*). Ask for permission before smoking in a Malay home, especially if elders are present

2. *Adab of host and guest* According to Malay *adab*, hosts assume responsibility for the well-being of guests. They make every effort to show hospitality for it is a reflection of their good name and character.

   But the courtesy is more than hospitality, much more! Hosts, in fact, take on the welfare, health, security, feeding, and care of the guest, as if the guest was under the host's special protection and light.

3. ***Responsibility of the guest*** Since the guests put themselves entirely into the hands of the Malay host for the duration of the visit, it is polite for the guest to inform the host before doing anything independently, such as leaving the house or going shopping. If you are going to be out late, if you are going to miss a meal, or if you need assistance, you should inform the host.

4. ***Shoes*** Always remove your shoes before entering a Malay home. This has to do with ritual taboos. Malays may pray in their living room, so shoes which might have come into contact with something unclean, dog excreta, for example, would soil the floor, thus making it unfit for prayer.

   If the home has a porch, the shoes should be removed before stepping on the porch. In a flat, leave the shoes outside the door, placed neatly to the right or left of the door, do not block the entrance. If the host suggests that you keep your shoes on, look to see what the family members are wearing, and do as they do. The family might be wearing special house slippers in the home, in which case you should certainly remove your shoes.

5. ***Feet*** While the head is sacred, the feet are the least important – they come into contact with unclean things! The soles of the feet should never be exposed. It is particularly impolite to put the feet up on a desk exposing the soles of the feet for all to see! This causes grave insult to Malays. Also, be careful about using a foot as a pointer. Never point out someone or something with your feet as one would point a finger!

6. ***Sitting*** When sitting on a chair or sofa, do not cross your legs if older or respected people are present. Most Malay homes have Western-type furniture, but on some festive occasions people sit on colourful mats on the floor. Do not sit down at the first available place, wait until the host invites you to sit and indicates a place for you. Do not step over anyone who is seated on the floor.

It may be that men and women are seated apart, the women at one end of the room and the men at the other. This may be especially true at ritual or festive occasions, such as weddings, funerals, etc. In more ordinary circumstances, this might only be done when seniors are present.

Since heads are sacred, do not sit on a pillow or cushion which is meant for the head! Malays jokingly say that this raises a pimple on the bum. Chinese and Indians also do not sit on anything meant for the head.

Sitting on the floor:

- When elders are present – When sitting on the floor men sit cross-legged and women sit with the knees to one side and the feet tucked under them, *away from view*. Do not point the feet at anyone. Women can keep their feet neatly out of sight by tucking them under the hem of their dress.

- When younger people of equal status are present – If at a friend's home, and elders and respected seniors are not present, then it is permissible to sit with the knees up, down, or sideways; watch your host and hostess for cues.

7. *Conversation* Risque talk or jokes about sex are not acceptable. A younger person should not correct an older one. Malay children do not disagree with or correct their parents or elders in public. If a parent makes a statement which the child thinks is incorrect, he/she is courteous in asking for clarification. 'Do you think that it was Tuesday when the guests were here, not Wednesday? What is your opinion Father?' Younger people are careful not to embarrass their elders in public, and they are especially careful to protect their 'face'. Young people tend to keep silent and listen respectfully when elders are speaking.

Malays speak quietly and they have gentle ways. In more formal situations, they do not laugh loudly nor speak harshly. They do not gesture wildly nor wave their arms about while speaking. Westerners, when being a guest in a Malay home, should restrain themselves, and pay particular attention to their own body language so they will not appear to be coarse.

Of course, juniors are more uninhibited than seniors, and when family and friends are gathered, there is plenty of happy laughter and noise.

8. *Bathrooms and toilets* Bathrooms are likely to be fairly similar to Western ones, especially in the more recent HDB flats. Malays believe that it is best to wash in running water, so their cleansing and purifying ablutions are always performed with running water.

It is considered cleaner to wash with water than to use toilet paper. It is also a religious obligation. In any case, toilet paper may not be available. A bucket of water and a scoop is usually available for cleansing. In some of the older buildings, there may be a squat toilet; in the newer buildings, the toilets are of the Western type.

9. *On leaving* Remember that the host assumes responsibility for the health, happiness, and wellbeing of the guest as long as the guest remains under the family roof. The guest literally 'gives himself/ herself into the safe keeping of the host'. The polite guest remembers then, when the visit is over, to ask the host for permission to take himself/herself back again! In Malay, the guest literally says: 'May I take back myself now?'

10. *Bread and butter gifts* The thoughtful house guest asks to help with the shopping: 'Can we shop together?' This is a polite way of asking if you can make a contribution to the cooking pot! Even if you are refused, press on. Ask to be considered a part of the group – as one of the family.

Do not offer money. Money as a gift is suitable at weddings or funerals, but not when one is an honoured guest in a Malay household. It is insulting to offer money to a Malay host.

Gifts should be given on departure rather than on arrival.

- Bring gifts from your home country – If gifts are for the family, it is better to bring something from your home country, as a memento or as a souvenir, or as a token of remembrance, rather than to buy something which is readily available in Singapore.

- Food is a good gift – A suitable gift, of course, is always food (make sure that it is *halal*). If you bring food, remember to bring enough for all the family and guests that will be present.
- Household items – Other acceptable gifts are household items: colourful serving trays and bowls, and pretty kitchenware, etc. If you bring food, you can use the trays and bowls as part of the gift.
- For the children – For the children, some toys are nice, or some pretty dresses or shirts. Children are especially loved and petted. Any consideration for them endears you to the Malay heart.
- Unsuitable gifts – Items to be avoided are of course pork, pigskin items, liquor, perfumes which contain alcohol, ashtrays or other smoking paraphernalia, knives, personal items such as underwear, and toy dogs, or items with pictures of dogs on them (for example, children's clothing with dogs on them). Avoid dark and sombre colours and white, which is associated with funerals.

11. *The etiquette of gift giving* Malays accept gifts with pleasure and may give one in return. If the hostess gives you something of her own it is an honour. You are being told that you are one of the family. Malays do not feel it is polite to open a gift in front of the giver. The Malay accepts the gift, expresses delight and pleasure, shows the package to the family members, and then sets it aside until the family is alone. Even children are careful not to open a gift in front of the company.

SOME GENERAL GUIDELINES

1. The prayer rug – A guest in a Malay home should never sit or stand on a prayer rug. Usually they are kept rolled up except when in use.
2. The Quran – A guest should not touch, or ask to touch, the holy book. Muslims ablute before they touch it.

3. Household chores – It is good manners for a female guest to offer to help with some of the household chores.
4. On rising – The Malay family appreciates it if the guest get up with the family and does not sleep in late.
5. Crossing in front of another – The polite guest is always careful when crossing in front of another person. There is a proper way to do this; bend over slightly from the waist, extend the right hand in front of you, touch the right wrist with the fingers of the left hand, then say: 'May I please pass?' It is impolite to cross in front of another person without using these courteous words and gestures.
6. Dressing modestly – Men and women should always dress modestly while visiting or staying in a Malay home.

FOOD AND DRINK

Always offer a Malay visitor refreshments; some tea, fruits, or biscuits. The polite host invites the guest to eat with the request: 'Please eat' or something similar. It is the custom for the Malay to wait for this invitation before he/she begins to eat. If you simply place the food out, but do not issue the invitation to eat, the Malay will not begin to eat.

1. *Forbidden (haram) food*
   - Pork – It is absolutely forbidden (*haram*) to eat pork as it is considered unclean. It will never knowingly be touched, served, or eaten. A Malay amah (maid) should not be expected to handle it, or to cook bacon, ham, etc.
   - Meat and chicken not slaughtered by a Muslim – There are religious restrictions against eating any meat which has not been slaughtered by a Muslim according to very strict dietary laws. When serving meals to Muslim friends and guests, inform them that the meat has been specially purchased and conforms to their standards. Properly prepared meats and chicken are called *halal*. Meat (mutton or beef) and chicken can be purchased in most supermarkets. The package has the

word *Halal* clearly printed on it, and a green crescent and star are visibly displayed. A provisioner can also supply you with meat and chicken which conforms to Muslim standards if you make a special request.

- Other forbidden foods – Jelly, if the animal from which the gelatin was extracted is not known; amphibians such as frog; carnivorous animals and birds such as tiger, bear and eagle; creeping, crawling animals like snakes and lizards, and squirrels and guinea-pigs.

- Alcohol – Alcoholic drinks are also *haram*. Have soft drinks available for your Muslim guests. Do not expect to be served alcohol in a Muslim home.

2. ***Frowned-on (makruh) foods*** Foods which come under this category are flower (or rock) crabs, shrimps, prawns, abalone, or any shellfish. Why? It is because they do not fit into a single category, i.e., they can live in two worlds – on land and in the water. Muslims can eat only those birds, fish or animals which fit into one category – they either live on land, or in the water. If they live in both worlds, then they are *makruh*.

Shi'ah Muslims do not eat crabs and other shelled seafood, but most of the Singapore Muslims are Sunni, so crabs, prawns and shrimp are usually not a problem for them. Since seafood is such a popular food in Singapore, ask the advice of your Muslim friends before purchasing the food for any meal you prepare for them.

3. ***Preferred food*** The foods which Malays generally like are foods with a shrimp-paste (belacan) flavouring or anchovy flavouring. They are especially fond of spicy or curried foods, lots of red chillies, coconut milk, lemon grass, green cooked vegetables, chicken (chicken seems to be a favourite!), mutton and beef. Plain white unsalted rice is served with most meals. Fresh fruits are a favourite dessert.

4. ***Not-preferred food*** Malays are generally not fond of Western cheeses and Western-type sweets after a meal. However, the *adab*

of Malays is such that they will try to adapt themselves to any food the host offers, as long as it does not contradict religious obligations. Polite Malays always try at least a little bit of what is offered – it is part of their courtesy.

INVITATIONS

1. *Personal invitation* An invitation to dinner or a celebration in a Malay home will be given in person if at all possible. It is rude to refuse an invitation made by a personal call. Refusing a written invitation does not give as much offence.
2. *When to arrive* Guests arrive on time or ten to fifteen minutes early. If you know the family well, it is polite to ask if you can help in the preparations.
3. *Malay time* Traditional Malays consider the new day to begin at about 6.30 p.m. Thus Saturday really starts at about 6.30 p.m. on Friday evening. Always be sure that you come on the correct evening. Check the day carefully with your Malay host.

TABLE ETIQUETTE

1. *The table setting*
   - Plate and utensils – A plate of rice is set before each person. Forks and spoons may be placed at the side of a plate of rice, but there will be no knives. Knives are considered by Malays to be weapons, and hence they are never used at table. Another explanation for the absence of knives at the table is that they are unnecessary since the meat is already cut into bite-size pieces before cooking.
   - Drinks – A glass of water, soft drink or fruit juice is set at the left side of each plate of rice. The left hand may be used to handle the glass as the right hand is normally soiled from eating.
   - Serving platters – Serving platters or bowls are set in the centre of the table.

- A dish of salt – A dish of salt on a Malay table is more than a dish of seasoning. It is a symbol of friendship. If the host offers you salt from the dish, dip the  forefinger of the right hand in and taste it. It cements your friendship.

2. *Seating* Many of the following patterns discussed, i.e., sitting on the floor to eat, separating men from women, the host not eating with the guest, etc., are traditional and more formal ways of courtesy. These may only be seen during more traditional and formal occasions, but it may not be uncommon to see them as part of the everyday patterns of living either. At any rate, it is good to be aware of traditional Malay customs and courtesy so that you can show respect and honour for their ways. It is a sign of a good heart to learn the Malay way.

- During festive occasions – Often refreshments or meals are served to guests while they sit on colourful mats on the floor. This custom is more often seen during festive and more formal occasions, such as wedding parties. For these family gatherings, it is common for men and women to be seated separately.
- During regular occasions – The guests sit at a dining table. The guest of honour may be seated at the head of the table, or alternately, at the right side of the host.

  Even in Singapore, it is sometimes the case that men and women may not only be seated separately, but they may also be served at different times. On some occasions the women serve the men first, and eat after the men have finished. If Western guests are present, it is common to invite both men and women to eat at the table at the same time, the women usually on the left of the host, and the men on the right.

- The duties of the host – In traditional homes, the host or hostess might not join the guest for the meal or refreshments. This enables the host to give his full attention to the guest while the hostess is free to serve the needs of the guest better.

  The manner in which the host gives his full attention to the guests is worthy of note. The host sits forward, in a very alert manner, watching the faces of his guests closely. He gives one the impression that what is being said is of the utmost importance and deserving of quiet and considerate respect and attention. In modern Malay homes, the host and hostess may both join the guest for meals and snacks.

METHODS AND MANNERS IN SERVING AND EATING

Many of the customs given below are traditional and more formal ones, closely followed in the pattern of dining in the more traditional families. In more Westernized families, some of the behaviours listed below may be modified or modernized. It is wise however, to understand the traditional cultural customs so that you can join any type of family with courtesy and ease. When the occasion is more formal, you can be an adept, when the occasion is less formal, you can adapt.

Your Malay friends will be genuinely pleased if you take the time to learn Malay customs and courtesy; many mistakes are forgiven the considerate guest and the compassionate heart.

1. *Showing hospitality* Malays are quick to show hospitality to a guest by offering food and drink. The guest should not absolutely refuse any food or drink that is offered. Only a little need be taken if one is not hungry. Refusal to eat or drink is a sign of bad manners.

2. *Explain if you cannot eat something* If it is absolutely necessary to refuse food (because of illness, allergy, special diet, or vegetarian proclivity, etc.) you should explain the reason. If possible, just

169

break off a small piece of cake, etc., and nibble at it. The Malays have a saying that goes 'Never refuse food with your face; refuse with your mouth.' This means that you should never make a face or grimace when refusing what is offered. To refuse food and drink is to refuse the Malay hospitality. It is an unkindness. It could also suggest suspicion that the offering is not good in some way. In the old days, when people had to refuse some food or drink, they could do so without offending by simply touching the plate, bowl or glass which held the food or drink, with the forefinger or thumb of the right hand. This was to appease the spirit of the food offered. Without this appeasement, the spirit might take offence and cause some misfortune to befall the offender. Today, to use this polite gesture is a sign that you understand the Malay culture, and that you respect and honour it.

3. *Finger bowls* The Malay hostess may offer a small finger bowl of water and a towel. This is a courtesy intended for the guest to use for washing the hands. It may be offered before, during, and after the meal. It is not soup, so do not drink it! Once, in an effort to be extremely polite when I was doing field work in a Malay village, I drank the finger-bowl water! The hosts tried, but found it very difficult to restrain their impulse to gasp and giggle.

    Another more common variation is the *cerek tangan*, a pot of water on a stand. It resembles a teapot. It is used before the meal, between the main and dessert course, and at the end of the meal. To use it the pot is held in the left hand while the right hand is held over the stand. Water is poured over the right hand so that the water drips into the stand. The pot is passed round from guest to guest – with perhaps one guest holding the pot as the next person uses it to wash.

4. *Eating with the fingers of the right hand* Traditionally, Malays eat with the fingers of the right hand. Forks and spoons may be provided for Western guests, but it is polite, and also good fun, to join the family and to eat as they eat.

- Polite way of eating with fingers – A small amount of food is scooped up into the hollow created by holding and bending the fingers of the right hand together. Bend over the dish slightly and using the thumb, push the food into the mouth. The tongue should be sticking out slightly to receive the food.

- Impolite way of eating with fingers – Do not get the palm soiled. Do not suck food into your mouth, or make sucking noises. Sucking or licking of fingers is considered to be very bad manners.

5. *Using a fork and spoon* Sometimes cutlery is used instead of the traditional fingers of the right hand. When it is used, it is not used as Western cutlery is used. No knife is offered. A fork and spoon are placed next to the rice plate. The fork is held in the left hand and it is used to push the food onto the spoon. The spoon, which looks more like a dessert spoon than a soup spoon, is held in the right hand and it is used to convey the food to the mouth.

6. *Serving and passing food* Food is passed around the table from right to left. The food is usually placed on serving dishes. Each person helps himself/herself to a little, using the serving spoon.

- Using the left hand for passing, serving – The left hand may be used for serving and scooping food from dishes with a spoon, passing dishes of food, and for holding a glass. This is allowed because the right hand will be soiled from eating. If you are using fork and spoon, then use the customary right hand for passing, serving, holding glass, and eating.

- Be polite: say '*minta maaf*' – Before using the left hand to pass food dishes, to serve with the serving spoon, or to drink with, it is good manners to say: '*Minta maaf*' (excuse me).
- When passing – When passing a serving dish that is too heavy, hold it in the left hand and support it with the back of the right hand.
- When serving – Serving spoons are placed by all the dishes. When serving, do not let the spoon come into contact with the plate; and be careful not to touch the food on your plate with the serving spoon. Drop or pour the food onto your rice or dish. One should never hear the clank of spoon against dish or the squish of spoon against food.

7. *When the host/hostess serves* The host/hostess may serve the guest and they love to dish out generous portions! If they put too much rice on your plate at the start of the meal, it is preferable to ask to have some put back before you add other foods to your plate.

   Leaving unwanted food on a plate is bad manners, so only take or accept what you can eat. It is good manners to try a little bit of everything.

8. *The signal to begin eating* Before eating or drinking, it is polite to wait until the host asks you to accept it, even if is it set before you. It is then customary for the guest to ask the host to join him/her. Raise the cup or dish (put the plate on the flat of the left palm, and hold it out with the right hand), gesture towards the host and say: 'Will you please join me?' The host then asks the guest to carry on. This is the signal for the guest to begin to eat.

9. *Asking for/accepting second helpings* The host and hostess are always pleased when a guest asks for seconds, it is a sign of good faith, trust, and appreciation for the good food. It is polite to eat seconds. You do not need to say 'NO-NO' if you really wish to have more. Simply smile broadly and say 'Yes please, it is very delicious!' When refusing more food, spread your hand over your own plate and say 'No thank you – my stomach is very full!'

10. *Do not waste food* Malays, like most Asians, do not like to waste food. Dropping food or rice on the floor or table is like throwing away one's livelihood. Be careful not to do this. At the end of the meal, the plate should be clean to show that one has had enough. Tradition has it that if rice is wasted the spirit of the rice cries.
11. *Burping* A quiet burp after the meal is a sign of appreciation.
12. *Taboo* Do not spit, blow your nose, or clear your throat while in the presence of other diners.

EATING IN RESTAURANTS

An invitation to a Malay home for a meal shows special honour to a guest. Today, many Malays, especially those who are younger and/or involved in the business world, may take guests out to a restaurant to eat. Much depends on the type of guest, the length of stay, the occasion, and so on.

CIRCUMCISION / PUBERTY RITUALS

Circumcision The Malays consider it essential for personal health and hygiene. Anthropologist feel that it is a rite that celebrates the passage of a boy from childhood to young manhood. Boys are usually circumcised when they reach puberty, although this operation can be undergone soon after birth or between eight and twelve years of age.

There is also a tradition of circumcising females. Circumcision for girls (clitoridectomy) is often performed by the midwife or by a Muslim doctor at a clinic. Not all Muslims think that this is a religious obligation, and the ceremony is not universally observed. Many however, believe that this is a symbolic gesture and a religious obligation. A tiny piece of the skin of the clitoris is removed. (A Malay woman demonstrated the amount by rolling a minuscule piece of paper tissue and indicating the tip of it with her fingernail). No feast is given, but neighbours and relatives might come in for refreshments.

The circumcision of yesterday In the past, (and in rural areas of Malaysia today), whole families of boys, brothers and cousins, were circumcised together in a public ceremony by a *mudim*, a man who specializes in circumcision. The traditional ceremony that went hand in hand with the circumcision varied from place to place, but it went something like this: A large feast would be held in the afternoon. Friends and relatives came to support and congratulate the boys. The boys wore traditional Malay costume, sometimes looking almost like miniature grooms, or they dressed in Arab dress, showing the Arab influence in this ritual. Though they sat at the feast, they rarely had an appetite! At about 3.00 p.m., they bathed at the well, carefully cleansing themselves.

A brave boy might volunteer to go first. (It was said that he would be the first to marry)! The boys were circumcised one at a time. Each boy sat on a banana stem or stool while his father's friend sat behind him to hearten and to hold him. Some of the young men I interviewed about this ritual jokingly said that they were held like this so that they wouldn't try to run away and climb a tree. The *mudim* reassured the boy by quietly talking to him. The foreskin would be stretched with a peg and quickly cut off with a razor-sharp knife. Some medication was applied and the boy was bandaged and limpingly led away to a ceremonial mat. A *sarung* was strung tent-like from the ceiling to cover him. His wound was dressed every day and he was given a special diet of grilled fish and rice. In ten or twelve days, he was completely healed and he rejoiced that he had 'passed the test' and taken his first step into the world of manhood.

Etiquette for the circumcision of today Today, the circumcision is usually performed at a clinic, using sterile circumstances and blessed anesthetics. The event is private and is commonly announced afterwards.

- If a celebration is held it will be on a grand scale and guests observe the correct dress for weddings.
- Ordinarily money is given to the boy to cheer him up. The amount depends on how well you know him. Any amount is acceptable but the most important thing is the sincerity of the giver. A warm heart is the best gift.

DATING AND COURTSHIP

In Singapore, many young people of working or university age mix with friends of both sexes, but dating as it is known in the West is not common. If a young man takes a girl out several times, her parents expect an engagement to be forthcoming. Most of the mixing between young people takes place in school, at work, at university, or at social functions, like weddings and Hari Raya, or through the efforts of friends and family.

As in all groups, a range of behaviours exists today among young Malays, ranging from the complete absence of dating by highly devout young Malays committed to their internalized values and ethics, to casual and indiscriminate dating, such as is done in the Western world, by young people who have lost touch with their own culture and values.

There is pressure exerted however, on young men and women to preserve their good reputation because random dating can almost make a young person unmarriageable. Previously, close family friends arranged engagements for their children when they were still infants (the marriage to take place when they came of age), but that is indeed rare in this day and age. While Malays still do arrange marriages, especially in cases where the young people are very shy, it is more common for the young people to have met and become friends in the setting of school, university, or work and then go to the family for help in arranging the marriage.

In cases where the family helps the young people, the boy's mother, or one of her friends, approaches the girl's mother. Being very careful to make the suggestion as delicately as possible, she says something like: 'You have a beautiful flower in your garden. We have seen it grow and flourish, and therefore, we would like to pluck it.' The girl's mother takes one or two weeks to discuss it with her daughter and the family. If there is some problem, the girl's parents are very tactful in their refusal; there is no desire to hurt feelings or to cause loss of face. A negative answer will be given as gently as possible: 'My daughter is very young, she is not yet ready for marriage.'

Since Malays do not have the Western tradition of casual and indiscriminate dating, and because dating today is seen as a preliminary step to an engagement, do not date Malays if you do not wish to get married.

MALAY MARRIAGE AND DIVORCE

Traditionally, marriage was seen as an alliance between two families. The young couple formed a partnership based on contractual obligations. Romantic love and infatuation were thought of as unnecessary (or indeed, even a hindrance to a marriage). They felt that if the couple fell out of love the marriage would have nothing left to sustain it. Romantic love was seen as a form of temporary insanity. (Modern science appears to agree with this view today. Marriage psychologists agree that there must be much more than infatuation to make for a successful marriage!) If a man and his wife were too emotionally involved, they were seen as a bit strange, maybe even bewitched.

Today this concept has changed. Affection, love and respect are recognized as necessary to the maintenance of a stable relationship. Hence young people have more to say in the choice of a marriage partner. In modern times, a respectable girl or boy from the same community whose parents are well known to the family is a preferred partner.

Malay divorce In the past, divorce was easily obtained by men. If there was disharmony and conflict in a relationship, the Muslim husband could formally divorce his wife by pronouncing *talak*: 'I divorce thee' three times before reliable witnesses. Although one pronouncement is enough, *talak* can be pronoundced in three stages:
1. The one-talak divorce – The first, the one talak divorce is where the man says the word only once; the couple are then separated but not fully divorced and can be reconciled.

2. The two-talak divorce – Should trouble begin again the man cannot resort to the one-talak divorce a second time; he must pronounce the two-talak divorce. Still the two can be reconciled. The two-*talak* divorce, like the one-*talak* divorce, can only be pronounced once.

3. The three-talak divorce – The final step is the three-*talak* divorce. After this, if the couple wishes to be reconciled and remarry, the woman will first have to be married to another man and then divorced by him before she and her first husband can remarry. This is commonly called: *Cinta Buta* – Love is blind!

Today, things are slightly different. Malays themselves are quick to point out the disadvantages of divorce, polygamy, and easy remarriage. Also a woman can now file a complaint, and in some cases, she can institute divorce proceedings if she has good reason to do so (adultery, lack of maintenance or sterility). Easy divorce is disapproved of and the Syariah courts provide special services to help with marriage counselling and reconciliation. Early marriage is discouraged; mutual consent by both marriage partners is required before a marriage can take place; it does not grant divorce easily; and it does not allow polygamy except in extreme cases (insanity or barrenness). The husband must give valid reasons for taking another wife and he must show that he has enough finances to support more than one wife with equal distribution of wealth.

When polygamy was first decreed in the religion, it was a humanitarian concern. It was intended to take in the widows and children of the men who had been killed in war. It was a form of social welfare.

ENGAGEMENT

Once a proposal has been accepted, the boy's family sends some elderly representatives (the father's brother or others) to make the arrangements with the girl's family. The parents do not engage in negotiations as it is considered indelicate for them to talk face to face about financial matters. At the meeting they decide on a date for the wedding, a bride price which will probably go towards paying for the wedding, and they bring gifts of fruit, cakes, jewellery and clothing. A ring is given to the girl and she gives a ring to the boy in return.

The meeting is held in a specially decorated room and the girl is dressed beautifully for the occasion. The boy's delegations present the gifts to her and feast their eyes on the future member of their family.

The date of the wedding is often set for a year or two in advance. During this time the two may be allowed to date (it depends on the family) but decorum and propriety are expected from both of them. This extended time gives them an opportunity to grow close to each other and allows the boy's family time to accumulate the bride price. The boy also gives the girl a monthly gift of money to show that he is assuming responsibility for his future bride. (His relatives who are helping to arrange the wedding, delicately hint to the boy's parents: 'Don't let the flower fade. It is better to freshen it with water all the time.') The sum is about $50; it is normally saved for her trousseau or for their future.

Many parents prefer to see their older daughters married before the younger. If this happens, the young man must bring gifts to the older sisters in compensation 'for stepping over the obstacle' (*langkah bendul*). They do not mind if the girl marries before her elder brothers.

A *kenduri* (prayers followed by a feast) is usually given at the time of the engagement. The *kenduri* for a wedding is called *walimah*. Friends and family are invited. Gifts are not expected. Dress should be modest; long skirts and long-sleeved blouses for women; the men wear casual clothing, a batik or dressy Malay shirt, but no tie!

THE WEDDING

A Malay wedding is full of music, colour, excitement and splendour. It used to go on for days, but now in modern Singapore, a Malay wedding ordinarily lasts for only two days: on Saturday, the marriage is legalized at a private ceremony, and on Sunday, the public ceremony or *bersanding* takes place. Sometimes everything is done on one day, Sunday!

Before the ceremonies begin, the bride is attended to by a woman called the *mak andam*. She is a professional wedding arranger who helps with the wedding protocol. The groom's family pays for her special skills. Today the *mak andam* may have her own beauty salon where the bride-to-be goes for her beautifying treatment. The *mak andam* shaves the girl's forehead, trims the eyebrows, and cuts off any unruly hair from around the hairline. It used to be the custom that she would also file the front teeth, but this is no longer done. All this ensures that the bride has a fresh and radiant appearance.

It also has another purpose! By observing the way the three strands of hair at the centre of the forehead fall after cutting, the *mak andam* is able to tell whether the girl is a maiden or not. The information is available to the couple's parents on request. Although this is still done, it is now more of a formality and it is no longer considered to be significant. This is an ancient custom which predates the Muslim ceremonies. It was also once the job of the *mak andam* to instruct the girl on the physical side of marriage but this is no longer a custom either. Traditionally, the bride was expected to put up a show of resistance to her husband on their first night together. It showed that she was pure and modest, and that she had been brought up properly. The girl's mother could take comfort in the length of time her daughter took in avoiding her husband! The *mak andam* then bathed the girl with water and limes to symbolically purify her. All of these rituals and ceremonies are still observed to some extent, but they are becoming less and less serious and common.

On Saturday evening the legal wedding ceremony, *akad nikah*, takes place. The bride sits in a room in her home made out to be a bridal chamber. It is decorated like a page out of the *Arabian Nights*. Silks, satins, sequins, fine curtains and canopies beautify the room. Women love this part of the festivities; they can't wait to see how skillfully the family has adorned the room! The groom waits in the hall outside with his relatives and friends. The *kathi*, a man versed in Syariah law who is authorized to perform Muslin weddings speaks to the bride and groom separately. Then they sign the marriage certificate. After the signing the groom pays a marriage gift (*mas kahwin*) to the bride, usually S$50.00 (In the old days it used to be S$22.50). They then *salaam* together. In the old days if this was an arranged marriage, this would have been the bride's and groom's first meeting. Even though they are legally married the two do not 'stay together' until after the next stage of the marriage, the *bersanding*.

The *bersanding* is held the following day, in many cases on the void deck (the ground floor of the girl's family's HDB flat). On one end of the void deck, a raised platform (*pelamin*) is set up with thrones on it; tables and chairs are set out in front of the platform. The family employs one of the many companies which hire out tents and other paraphernalia for such receptions.

As soon as the groom arrives, the bride appears. While the groom

The groom signs the marriage certificate. Photo: Norah Mohd Hassan

bargains with the bride's male relatives to gain entry to the platform, the bride takes her seat on the left side of the *pelamin*. The *mak andam* holds a fan before the bride's face and the groom must bargain again to be allowed to see the bride's face. He then takes his seat next to her. Both are splendidly dressed in bridal costumes (often rented from the *mak andam*; they are very expensive, often costing about $850.00 or more for the day). The two sit like the king and queen for the day, holding court over their wedding guests.

The guests all take part in a Blessing Ceremony. Rice, scented leaves and petals are laid out beside the thrones. Each guest then

The bride and groom on the pelamin. *Photo: Norah Mohd Hassan*

approaches the couple, and begins to scatter the leaves and petals on their open palms, beginning with the groom's right palm, and ending with the bride's left palm. Then a small bouquet of leaves is dipped into a paste-like liquid and sprinkled over their palms. Lastly the saffron rice is sprinkled in the same manner. An attendant standing by the side of the pelamin, gives each guest a gift, traditionally a hard-boiled egg encased in gold or silver thread (*bunga telur*). Today the guests may be given chocolates or cake in a glass. The gift symbolizes fertility.

During these rituals, the bride must keep her eyes downcast and assume a shy and modest appearance. She is not to laugh, smile or look around. This is the ideal behaviour expected of her. It indicates her state of modesty and purity. Her friends try to tease her and to cause a giggle or two with remarks like: 'Be Patient' 'Happy Landing,' and so on, but her face remains motionless. After an hour or so on the throne, they step down, and the guests are served traditional food. Because many weddings take place on Sundays, some of the guests may have to attend two or three weddings.

There are many variations on this public ceremony depending on the wealth of the families, time constraints, and other factors. Some people hold the Bersanding ceremony very briefly at the Syariah Court on a Saturday, while others may include even a third event, such as a modern Western-style reception at a hotel.

ETIQUETTE AT WEDDINGS

1. *Gifts*
   - A gift for the home (the kitchen) – Traditionally, a bride must be able to set up a fully-equipped kitchen when she marries, so kitchen utensils, dishes, pots, teapots, serving dishes, fruit bowls, and cake dishes make lovely gifts.
   - Inappropriate gifts – Knives, ashtrays, wine glasses, or very personal things such as underwear or night gowns.
   - Money – Although money can be given, a personally-chosen

gift is more appreciated. If money is given, it should be given discreetly. It is usually wadded up into a small packet and handed to the father of the bride or to his trusted friend (who acts as his representative) in the midst of a *salaam*. You can say: 'A small gift for the young couple – to help them out with their new home.'

- The wrapping – The present can be wrapped in traditional wedding paper, or red (symbol of love), or green (symbol of religion).

2. *The wedding banquet* It is usually 'open house' on the day of the wedding feast. People generally come between 11.00 a.m. and 5.00 p.m. The bersanding is usually held around 3.00 p.m. towards the end of the banquet. Guests do not stay the whole time, they come and go as they wish.

3. *Seating* When you arrive, notice how the other guests are seated. In void decks, the whole affair is fairly casual with people sitting with their families, but at more formal occasions men and women may sit separately.

4. *Eat with fingers of the right hand* Guests eat with the fingers of the right hand. Follow Malay custom rather than add to the chores of the servers by asking for forks and spoons. However, if Malays see that you are foreigners, they may courteously offer you forks and spoons.

5. *An evening reception too?* Some Malays also have an evening reception at home or in a hotel. Western-style wedding dress for bride and groom might be worn for these affairs. These evening receptions are usually meant for work colleagues. They might include a meal which begins at a specified time, and maybe also a disco.

6. *Dress* Women should wear modest clothing: no revealing, plunging necklines, or backless, strapless gowns. Even the arms and legs should be covered. A pretty long skirt and a long-sleeved blouse is in good taste. Malay women take this opportunity to wear

all their gold jewellery. If you want to get into the spirit of things, you might wear a *baju kurung* (a loose overblouse over a *sarung*) or *a sarung kebaya* (a close-fitting overblouse worn over a *sarung* – usually worn by a married woman.) An appreciative Malay says: 'She has a shape like a guitar!'

Men dress casually. Sports shirts with open collars or batik shirts are common. Malay men often wear their national dress, the *baju Melayu*, known also as the *baju kurung*. Do not wear shorts.

7. *Behaviour*
   - Restrain your exuberant ways – Have fun but be restrained: no loud laughter, wild gestures, shrill voices.
   - Congratulating the bride – Men should watch other men to see how they greet or congratulate the bride. If they *salaam* with her or shake hands it is fairly safe to follow suit. If the bride is wearing gloves it is all right to shake hands with her.
   - Photographs – Ask permission before taking photographs.

BIRTHS

A Malay baby is a lucky baby. He/She is born into a warm and loving community. Parents bring up their children with considerable gentleness and tenderness. There will be no lack of physical affection or cuddling for the child. Malays recognize the importance of close physical contact for babies, and the whole family makes sure that the child has full emotional support.

There used to be many restrictions regarding the birth of children. These still remain in the memories of the elders, but in Singapore today, they are rarely practised. For instance, a pregnant woman would not sew any seamed articles for fear that the child's anus would be closed at birth; she would not sleep during the prayer hour for fear that the child might be born lazy; and neither parent would be cruel to any living creature for fear of a deformity in their child.

Today, many Malays, like their Chinese and Indian counterparts, go to hospital to deliver their babies, and as a result, many of their traditional practices have been set aside. The most important rituals were those in which the father played a crucial role soon after the birth of his child. There were three rituals performed, only one of which is still common. These rituals established a very close bond between father and child from the very first moments of the child's life.

1. ***Washing the birth cloth*** It was the custom for the husband to wash the sheet on which the mother had given birth. This was symbolic of the responsibility he assumed as husband to his wife and as father to his child.

2. ***Burying the placenta*** The placenta is seen as a 'twin' of the newborn. Soon after delivery, the father placed the placenta in a clay pot with a cover. Some rock salt was added. It was kept for forty days, then the father buried it under the house (traditional Malay houses were built on stilts). The salt was a sign of friendship between the child and the father. The placenta was buried as if it were the 'twin' who had 'died'.

3. ***Muslim rituals for the newborn*** Every child is a carrier of the 'light'. This light should be seen to burn firstly in its own home. Malays believe that the child's first cry should also be heard first in its own home, as it is 'a cry of loyalty to and respect for the parents'.

   After the first cry, the father takes a clean white cloth that has been dipped in boiled water. He rubs the child's mouth to open it wide. This is a symbolic act to indicate that the child will always speak the truth. He then rubs the eyelids gently with his thumbs, starting from the inside and working towards the outer corners. This symbolizes that the child should see nothing but good in the world.

   Next the father softly sings or calls the Muslim prayer into his child's ear so that it is the first thing that the infant hears and will therefore always remember the greatness of Allah. This last ritual (Muslim rituals for the newborn) is the only one now that the father can still perform in urbanized Singapore.

BREASTFEEDING

Most Malay women breastfeed their babies. They believe that breastfeeding cultivates a respect and closeness between mother and child that lasts throughout life. Today, modern Malay women also believe that besides the benefits of close spiritual and psychological bonding breastfeeding has scientific benefits as well: the nutrition is superior and the benefits of immunization are very important.

THE CHILD'S NAME

The child is given a name within one week of birth so that the name can be placed on the birth certificate. Forty-four days after the birth, a religious ceremony, *habis hari*, is held at home and the child's name is formally bestowed on him. A large *kenduri* may follow or just a token of thanks may be sent to the mosque. The Malay child's name usually has some religious significance, for instance one can see the spiritual qualities wished for the child in the following names: Faridah – Strong; Zuraidah – Bright; Kamal – Firm; Shaharuddin – Surrender and Sincere.

ETIQUETTE

1. *Visiting the new mother* Friends can visit the mother at any time during her confinement. Traditionally the mother was confined to the home for a certain period of time after the baby's birth, during which time she was fed a special enriching diet, and she was given a daily massage to help return her figure to its normal state. Today, these rituals are not so common.

   However, it is best to avoid visiting in the early morning hours in case she has access to the above services. It is in the early morning that the midwife (a Muslim lady experienced in post-natal care) comes to clean the baby and to give the massage.

2. *Gifts* It is not common to give gifts to the mother, but a small gift of fruits is suitable. When visiting the new baby at home, gifts are usually brought for the child.

Any baby gifts are welcome: clothing, baby blankets, soft cuddly toys (not dogs), books, etc. There is no taboo about numbers or colours, but bright and cheerful colours are favourites of babies. A gift of cash can be put into an envelope with the note that it is for the child's savings or education.

3. *Ceremonies* If you are invited to any of the ceremonies following the birth, remember that they are religious in nature. Also, dress appropriately and modestly, and in loose enough clothing so that you can sit on the floor comfortably. Pants suits are appropriate.

Some ceremonies include:

- *Naik buaian* – This is when the child is introduced to the cradle.
- *Cukur rambut* – At this ceremony, the child's head is shaved to cleanse the child for life outside the mother's womb.
- *Jejak tanah* – Here the child's feet are introduced to the soil for the first time.

FUNERALS

Muslims are buried within twelve hours of their death so as not to delay the burial unnecessarily. When a Malay dies a *bilal* (the man who summons Muslims to prayer from the mosque) or an *imam* (leader of prayer in a group) is called to the house. They both know how to carry out the proper rituals. The deceased person's children or relatives wash the body and fold the arms over the chest, then cover it with a white cloth. The head will already have been placed in a position facing Mecca.

Someone always stays with the body and verses from the Quran are read. Muslims believe that the physical body dies, but the soul lives forever. When the soul is emancipated from the body in death, it goes either to heaven or to hell. Both are described in great detail in the Quran. The human's conduct when the body is alive determines the fate in the life hereafter.

The *imam* ritually purifies the body with pure water and then with camphor water. The body is wrapped in three layers of white cloth. The last layer is arranged to look like clothes, but there will be no stitches in the material. Herbs are sprinkled on the body. Before the face is wrapped the family comes in and the *imam* says a few words. Prayers are said and then the body is taken to the mosque or directly to the graveyard.

Muslims do not fear a natural death. They have a saying that goes: 'When you think that tomorrow you will die, you will live forever.' They do fear a disastrous death: accident, suicide or murder. They feel that in these cases they will not be able to fulfill the purpose in their lives and their duties to Allah and their family. Good Muslims pray for a peaceful death, one where they have had the opportunity to make their peace with Allah and to say their prayers before dying.

ETIQUETTE AT A FUNERAL

1. *Paying respects* Friends and neighbours come to the house and they are allowed to see the face of the deceased for one last time. Guests pay their respects by standing quietly while viewing the body, bowing the head and making a silent prayer. Muslims make an appeal that the soul of the deceased will be forgiven.

2. *Refreshments* There may be no refreshments served at all due to the sorrow of the occasion.

3. *Mourning* Muslims do not mourn visibly; they try to restrain their grief. There should be no loud talking or excessive noise. Weeping and wailing will not be seen in public. A mourning wife will not expose herself to men who are not her relatives for 100 days; some take a longer time – a year or more.

4. *Gifts*
   - Flowers can be sent to the home; they will be strewn over the grave. Wreaths are not customary.
   - Money is often given to the family; it is put in a white envelope and handed to the chief mourners. Any amount is acceptable. It depends upon the relationship, about $10–$20 is average.

5. *Colour*s The traditional colour for funerals is white, but sombre colours are also acceptable.

HARI RAYA PUASA

Malays celebrate three major festivals, all of which are associated with their religion, Islam. The three are: Hari Raya Puasa (*Aidil Fitri*), Hari Raya Haji (*Aidil Ad-ha*), and the birthday of the Prophet Muhammad. Hari Raya Puasa and Hari Raya Haji are public holidays in Singapore.

I discuss the Hari Raya Puasa festival here, and I am grateful to *Festivals of Malaya*, edited by Joy Manson, for the background information on Hari Raya Puasa, and I wish to thank Esah Binti Susman for helping me with the etiquette.

THE SIGNIFICANCE OF HARI RAYA PUASA (AIDIL FITRI)

Hari Raya Puasa is the day marking *the end* of the month of fasting. We remember the five principles of Islamic practices:

1. That there is no God but Allah; the Prophet Muhammad is the messenger of Allah.
2. To pray five times a day.
3. To fast during the month of Ramadan.
4. To tithe (*fitrah*) during Hari Raya Puasa and give alms (*zakat*) any time within the cycle of a year.
5. To go on a pilgrimage to Mecca.

As we can see, the third and fourth principles are reflected in the Hari Raya Puasa.

Fasting In the Quran (sura II.183), the ninth month of the Muslim lunar calendar is set aside for a compulsory fast. It says: 'The month of Ramadan is that in which the Quran was passed down.' Muslims abstain from food and drink from dawn to dusk every day; they eat before dawn and after the sun has set. It is a time of self-discipline and cleansing.

Tithing A tithe is also a principle obligation of Islam. It was ordered by Allah.

Alms Muslims give 2.5% of one year's total savings if the savings is more than approximately $2,400; if the year's total savings is less than $2,400, there is no need to give alms.

The tithes and alms are channelled to MUIS (Majlis Ugama Islam Singapura) which is the Islamic Council of Singapore. The collected tithes and alms are then distributed to the needy.

A DAY OF THANKSGIVING

The holiday is set by the sighting of the new moon which ends the month of fasting (Ramadan). The first day of Shawal (the tenth month of the Muslim calendar) is Hari Raya Puasa. Muslims give thanks to Allah after their completion of the gruelling month of fasting.

The Malays joyfully prepare for this holiday by giving their homes a fresh spring cleaning, perhaps even a new coat of paint as well. On the 20th day of the fasting month (the day when the Quran was passed down) the houses and mosques of the Malays are brightly lit up with coloured lights and/or oil lamps; it is considered a religious virtue to do this. And also on this night, the Malay women prepare cakes and sweetmeats for the guests which will arrive on Hari Raya day. Also, about three days before Hari Raya, they prepare much more food.

On the day of Hari Raya Puasa new clothes are laid out for every family member. Families go to the mosque to pray. Later, the children shake and *cium* the hands of their elders and ask for pardon for all their misdeeds of the previous year. The whole family partakes in this ritual of forgiveness and of asking for forgiveness. Asking for pardon is done in order of seniority. The young ask the elders; the wives ask the husbands; the husbands do the same. Everyone starts off Hari Raya Puasa with a fresh new spirit ritually purified from anger and resentment.

The rest of the day is spent in fun and merrymaking; family and

The shops are well-stocked with things that Muslims will need in preparation for Hari Raya Puasa. Photo: MITA

Buying food at the Hari Raya Puasa Fair organized by the government. Photo: MITA

friends come to visit and to share in the festive foods which have been prepared. Everyone looks splendid. Adults give alms to the poor, they visit the graves of their relatives, and they make up old quarrels with old friends and family members. This day is a day of much goodwill and sweetness. The month-long fasting has purified the body and the spirit, and the Muslims rejoice in the end of the fast and in the beginning of a fresh, new, clean slate.

ETIQUETTE

1. *What to wear?* Wear long sleeves and long pants or skirt. Dress modestly.
2. *What to bring?* It is not necessary to bring anything to a Hari Raya Puasa festivity, but if you wish to bring something small, then bring some sweets for the children, or some cookies, chocolate biscuits, etc., for the family. It is a nice idea to bring sweets and cookies from your own country. The Cold Storage supermarkets stock many items like this from many foreign countries.
3. *When to come?* Any time after twelve noon is a good time to come. People say that it is alright to come right up until about eleven o'clock at night!
4. *How long to stay?* You can stay as long or as short as you like. About one-half hour to two hours is about right.
5. *What to say?* Always greet all the members of the family with: 'Selamat Hari Raya.'
6. *What to expect?* Take off your shoes and enter the house. Sit down where the hostess indicates a place for you. Make cheerful conversation: 'Hello, how are you, good to see you.' The host/hostess will give you food and drink. Don't start drinking or gobbling up the food right away; wait until the host/hostess invites you to eat. Eat heartily; if you do not, your host/hostess will be very disappointed.

Chapter Six

THE INDIAN COMMUNITY

THE PEOPLE

Indians make up 7.1% of the population of Singapore. The Indians of Singapore are a diverse group. They come from India, Pakistan, Bangladesh, Sri Lanka, and even from some parts of Africa. The term Indian is very loose indeed; it encompasses culturally, linguistically, religiously, and even geographically diverse peoples. In addition, they range from the modern and the liberal to the conservative and the traditional.

VARIETY AND DIVERSITY

Religiously speaking, the largest group is Hindu: 56.5%. But there are also Indian Muslims (22% of the Muslims in Singapore are Indian), some Indian Christian and Catholics, and even smaller sects such as Zoroastrians, Jains, Sikhs, Blue-belt Sikhs, etc.

Indians in Singapore are mostly Tamil speakers, (63.9% of the Indians in Singapore are Tamils) but altogether there are more than ten language groups with different scripts. In 1978, even though Tamil is one of the official languages of Singapore, it was found that more Indians understood Malay than Tamil or English! Today, in 1992, Tamil, Hindi, Urdu, Punjabi, Bengali, and Gujerati are all offered as second language choices for Indian children in school.

There are Indians in every strata of Singapore society. Indians have always been prominent in politics, business, and the professions, and especially in the law. There are also doctors, businessmen, trade unionists, political leaders, police and army personnel, as well as stall keepers and labourers.

BRIEF BACKGROUND

The first Indians in Singapore were merchants and traders from the South Indian coast dating back to AD 100. They traded cloth, iron tools, magic amulets, and precious stones for spices, tin, gold, and ivory. The Indian influence was so strong that even the name of Singapore was derived from the Sanskrit words *singha* (lion) and *pura* (port).

When Sir Stamford Raffles established a trading post in Singapore for the British East India Company in 1819, Indians came with him. Narayana Pillai was one who helped him draw other Indians from Penang to build the island's infrastructure. Indian merchants followed from Malacca to set up markets and bazaars. Raffles also drew on convict labour from India to help in the developing of the infrastructure.

THE INDIAN COMMUNITY

Those who have Indian friends attest to their warm and vibrant personalities and their lively sense of humour. Indians come from so many different educational and social backgrounds that it is difficult to speak of a universal pattern of etiquette and customs for the Indian community. The majority of the Indians come from Southern India and are Tamils, so most of the habits and customs in this chapter draw on Tamil traditions. The Indian settlement can still be seen in parts of High Street and Serangoon Road.

Singapore Indians who are of the Muslim religion own most of the shops in and around Arab Street. Many of them have families in India. They come here and lead a bachelor-like existence while sending money home to their families. They usually sell textiles, perfumes, and jewellery. They are pleasant salespeople; they don't seem to mind if a customer browses around before buying. The perfume man can mix special exotic fragrances for you alone! He will let you sniff every perfume in the shop and show you the most expensive oils in the world.

To get the feel of the Indian community, one should visit Serangoon Road (Little India). Although not as grand today as when it was in its former glory, Serangoon Road is still the centre for Indian life and most Indians shop there: saris, slippers, men's dhotis, heavy steel cooking utensils, brass stands and lamps for prayer, spices, herbal medicines, betel nuts, jewellery, etc., can be found in the small shops that line the streets.

Also along Serangoon Road are many little flower stands and shops which sell garlands for weddings and other Indian ceremonies, and for offerings in the temple. Scented fresh flowers are available for the family altar. It is also the custom for Indian women to wear flowers in their hair to celebrate joy in their marriage, to enhance their beauty, and to complement their beautiful saris.

A husband often stops on his way home from work to buy a flower for his wife's hair. An Indian woman is at her loveliest when she has bright bangles on her arms, flowers in her hair, and when she knows that she is loved sweetly by her husband. If her husband dies, she will never again wear flowers in her hair or bangles on her arm.

Indians have a deep faith which is woven into the pattern of their everyday lives. Every morning, in more traditional families, the Hindu mother offers prayers and burns incense at the family altar to greet her god and the new day. She may do this at sunset too.

Friday is a special day. Hindus flock to the temples to offer prayers. They make several different kinds of offerings. A banana and a half-coconut offering is the most typical. For a donation of $1.50 the devotee buys a banana and half a coconut which symbolize *vasanas* (human desires). The fruit is then offered to the gods as a petition to help them to put aside *vasanas* –because the wise in heart try to live their temporal lives not controlled by their physical desires nor swayed by the deception of their senses. The putting aside of *vasanas* is an essential step on the long, long path leading towards nirvana (where the human soul is joined with the world soul forever and is released from the chain of rebirths in reincarnation).

The petitioners write their names on small slips of papers and the priest reads them out during the formal prayers. The devotees are given holy ash or vermillion to put on their foreheads, and betel nuts which can be chewed by the elders, or else placed on the altar. The fruits are blessed and then taken home where they can be eaten or placed on the family altar. If the offerings are not eaten they will not be thrown away after they have become rotten. Instead, they will be placed under a tree, or released into a river to return to nature.

You often see an Indian woman with a red dot on her forehead: it is a symbol of her marriage. A North Indian women wears a red streak on the parting of her hair. An unmarried woman sometimes wears a black dot on her forehead.

This black colour is used to counteract the effect of the evil eye! If a lovely young girl gets too many compliments, Indians feel that some kind of harm may come to her, so this dot repels evil influences.

Modern young misses match the dots on their foreheads with the colour of their saris today. This is not traditional – only fashionable.

LEARNING TO SOCIALIZE

INTRODUCTIONS
1. *Shaking hands with people of the same sex* Indian men shake hands with one another and Indian women shake hands with one another, but they do not usually shake hands with people of the opposite sex.
2. *Shaking hands with people of the opposite sex* In a Westernized or business setting, men and women might shake hands across the sex line, but it is not considered to be very polite, so Westerners are advised to just nod their heads and smile when being introduced to people of the opposite sex.
3. *Introduce according to rank* As a courtesy, always introduce the oldest person first! When introductions are made it is polite to say the name of the elder before the younger, the senior in importance before the junior, and the woman before the man.

GREETINGS
In modern Singapore today, many young people do not use the traditional Indian greeting among their own peer group, but the polite young person always uses it when greeting an elder person. The greeting is made with palms together in the prayer position, hands raised to the front of the face, and head bowed slightly. They say: *'Vanakkam'*. Western-type greetings are acceptable: 'Hello, how are you?' 'Long time no see!' or 'How is your family?' These are all common greetings in Singapore.

NAMES
Most Indians in Singapore trace their descent through their fathers although some Malayalee Indians are matrilineal; i.e., they trace their

Many young people do not use the traditional Indian greeting among their peers; however, the polite young person always uses it when greeting an older person. Photo: MITA

descent through their mothers and even inherit from them. The name 'Nair', for instance, is a clan name signifying that the family is matrilineal.

Male names The majority of Indians in Singapore do not use family names. They use the initial of their father's name, placed before their own name. For example:

M. Thiruselvan

'M' is the initial of the father's name (Manickavasagam). Thiruselvan is the personal name of the man. Because the name may be difficult to pronounce, he may shorten it to either:

Thiru or Selvan.

Friends call him Thiru, and business associates call him Mr Thiru. He might instead, wish to be called by the last part of his name: Selvan. In this case, his business associates call him Mr Selvan.

The man's full name includes his father's name after his own name. For example: Thiruselvan s/o Manickavasagam

               Man's name   Father's name

Sometimes, the man may choose to use s/o (son of) in the shortened name: Selvan s/o Manick

Female names Kamala, the daughter of Selvan uses d/o (daughter of) to show that she is the daughter of Selvan: Kamala d/o Selvan. Or she uses the initial of her father Selvan before her own name S. Kamala. When Kamala marries, she normally drops her father's initial or name, and uses her husband's name after her own: Kamala Selvan (or Kamala Thiruselvan). Friends call her Kamala, and her business associates call her: Mrs Selvan or Mrs Thiruselvan.

Family names Some Indians have adopted family names which are kept from generation to generation. Christian Indians often follow this custom. Some names taken by Syrian Christians or Roman Catholics are: Jacob, John, Thomas, Pereira, Fernando.

SIKH NAMES

Indians of the Sikh faith are recognized by their distinguished physiques and their turbans. They have traditionally been regarded as warriors. Their religion is a blend of Hinduism and Islam, and it does not recognize a caste system. They trace their descent through their fathers, but they identify themselves in a different way from Hindus.

Male names All male Sikhs adopt the name of Singh. It is not a family name. It is a name which is given to all Sikh men; it identifies them as belonging to the brotherhood of Sikhs.

  For example: Bhopinder Singh s/o Joginder Singh

Bhopinder is the man's personal name. Joginder Singh is his father's name. His friends call him Bhopinder. In business he is called Mr Bhopinder Singh. Some Sikhs add another name to their list, which is the name of their birthplace or clan. So if Bhopinder was from the Gil clan he might call himself Bhopinder Singh Gil s/o Joginder Singh Gil, or B.S. Gil for short.

Female names An example of a Sikh woman's name is:

Kamaljeet Kaur d/o Gurdev Singh

Kamaljeet is her personal name. Kaur is not a family name; it is the name given to all Sikh women to signify their sisterhood. Gurdev Singh is her father's name. When she marries Bhopinder Singh, she is called Kamaljeet by her friends. In business, she is called Mrs Bhopinder Singh.

SOME COMMON COURTESIES AND CUSTOMS

Indian Muslims in Singapore observe the same religious rituals as Malay Muslims. For instance, they do not eat *haram* foods, they do not drink alcohol, they cannot touch dogs, etc. Find out if your Indian friends are Muslims before you cook a meal for them. The following customs are generally speaking, Hindu customs.

BOOKS

Books are almost sacred to Indians. They would never sit on a book or throw it about, or generally handle it in a disrespectful manner. This feeling for books probably began years ago when holy books were the only printed works in existence. Also, books are visible symbols of knowledge and learning – priceless possessions in the East where Chinese and Malays also have this reverence for books.

CLOTHING

1. *Men* Indian men wear Western dress in the business office, although at home they might prefer traditional Indian dress.
2. *Young girls and women* Young girls wear Western dress; in school they wear school uniforms. At puberty the girl changes to traditional Indian dress, wearing a sari or a Punjabi suit (a long overblouse and trousers) made of silk, cotton or cotton/polyester. Though the Punjabi suit is traditionally worn by North Indians, it is seen as more comfortable and convenient than the sari, and recently it seems to be worn more and more by women of all ethnic groups. Today, more modern Indian women wear Western-style

clothing – jeans, dresses, skirts and blouses. A lot depends on the educational and religious background of the women.

3. *Attending Indian functions* When attending an Indian affair, or when visiting an Indian home, erotic zones must be covered. Modest dress is in good taste and clothes intended to attract attention should be avoided. No shorts, mini-skirts, plunging, strapless, backless or braless dresses.

GESTURES AND TOUCHING

1. *Pointing and beckoning* Do not point at a person with either the left or right forefinger or with two fingers. You can gesture towards them using the whole right hand, palm upwards. Do not use the typical Western beckoning gesture of a crooked and wagging finger to call a person to you; use the whole hand, palm downwards; the hand makes nearly a complete circle.

2. *The head* Do not pat a Hindu child on the head. Most Indians, even grown-ups, do not like to be touched on the head. They believe that the head is the most spiritual and sacred part of the body — it is the area of direct access to God. Noe one should touch the head or defile it.

   You can pat a child on the cheek, or gently pinch a child's cheek without causing offence. Indians often use this gesture with children as a token of affection.

3. *Touching of the opposite sex* As with Chinese and Malays, avoid casual or romantic touching of members of the opposite sex in public. Men can touch other men, and women can touch other women, but men and women should not touch each other. Do not touch shopkeepers on the arm, or waiters or waitresses to catch their attention, etc., least you unwittingly signal an amorous advance! Public decorum must be shown, even between husband and wife. Do not hug, kiss, hold hands, etc. when attending an Indian social gathering.

4. *Social distance* Indians usually maintain a social distance with members of the opposite sex (about an arm's length away). The

older generation respects this 'body buffer zone' more than the younger generation does. If you observe a step backward when you stand too close to Indian friends, it probably does not mean that you have bad breath, it may mean that you have invaded their personal space.

Traditionally, people usually stand about as far away as their traditional greeting gesture. Westerners, for instance, stand about the distance of a common handshake, so the social distance is quite close, probably about two feet. Indians stand about the distance it takes for two people to engage in the polite Indian greeting gesture of hands being raised to the front of the face and folded in front, probably about three feet or a bit more.

5. *Traditional Indian head toss* When speaking with Indian friends, you may notice a certain kind of gesture made with the head. They toss it quickly from side to side as only Indians can. It means consent or agreement. It is different from the Western shake of the head which means no, but close enough for one to mistake it for no if you are not aware.

6. *The right hand* Indians, like Malays, do not use the left hand for social purposes – ever! Be careful when handing gifts, food, money in shops, etc. Do not receive change, merchandise, etc., from an Indian shopkeeper with the left hand! Of course, if you are handing a heavy object with the right hand, then the left hand can help. Use the back of the left hand to support the object.

SHOPPING

1. *The first customer* As with the Chinese, it is a good omen if the first customer of the day buys something, however small. It is bad omen if the first customer of the day buys oil (not auspicious). Sugar, sweets, fruits and flowers are all auspicious thing to buy first thing in the morning.

2. *Bargaining* Indians appreciate a customer who bargains well. (Bargaining tactics are given on page 24.)

SMOKING

1. Do not offer Indian women cigarettes. Most of them don't smoke.
2. Ask for permission to smoke in an Indian home. In the presence of elders, it is better to refrain from smoking. It would not be respectful. If you ask for permission to smoke, you may be given a positive answer out of courtesy, even if they do not wish you to smoke. Singaporeans do not like to refuse their guests anything if possible.
3. Sikhs may not allow smoking in their homes at all because smoking is prohibited in their religion.

TEMPLES

1. Shoes should always be removed before entering a temple. Leave them to the right or left side of the door so as not to block the doorway.
2. Indians step over the threshold, not on it.
3. Indians ordinarily bathe before going to the temple. Once they are there, they wash their feet, face and eyes before entering. To be polite, Westerners can wash their feet before entering too as a gesture of respect for their religion. There are sinks in the outer courtyard for this purpose.
4. Statues and pictures inside the temple should not be touched.
5. It is permissible to speak quietly and to wander about, but keep silent if there are services going on.
6. Inside the temple there are several small shrines or Sanctum Sanctorums. They are small rooms with a screen or gate across the entrance. The screen is removed just before daily worship. Only priests are allowed to enter these places.

   Visitors should not go further than the steps in front of the screen. Inside the Sanctum Sanctorum you can see a statue of one of the deities (various manifestations of God). This is where the offerings of banana and coconut are made.
7. Women should not enter a Hindu temple while menstruating.

8. Women can wear pantsuits, slacks, etc., Ideally, legs should be covered (at the very least beyond the knee!) Wear modest dress; show respect.

In a Western church, men show respect by removing their hat and putting on their shoes. At a Tamil church service, everyone takes off their shoes. In a Muslim mosque men show respect by putting on their hats and removing their shoes. In a Hindu temple, men show respect by removing their hats and removing their shoes. In a Sikh temple, everyone puts on a head covering and removes their shoes. Though the habits are different the object is the same: Showing respect!

9. Ask permission before taking photographs.
10. If you ask a priest for a prayer, leave some money as an offering, perhaps $3 or $5. Indians prefer odd numbers, they are luckier.

VISITING IN AN INDIAN HOME

1. *Invitations*
   - Informal invitation preferred – Indians extend an invitation to a dinner or a gathering as informally as possible; a personal telephone call or a personal visit is much preferred to a card or note. More formal occasions, such as weddings, require a written invitation.
   - Arrange a specific time – If you are invited over in the

'evening' – remember that the Indian evening can mean anything after 4 p.m. In the Western style, 'evening' usually means anything after 7.00 p.m. Be sure to clarify the time with your friend.

- A specific invitation – Indians prefer an invitation which includes a definite time and place. Do not say vaguely, as is sometimes the custom in the Western style: 'Let's get together sometime' or 'Drop by anytime for a coffee.' It is better to say: 'Can you come for a coffee tomorrow morning about 11.00 a.m.?' Also, Indians prefer that the invitation should state specifically who is invited: the individual, the couple, the children, or the whole family!

2. *Punctuality* Indians are usually punctual for invitations and appointments so Western guests should also strive to be neither too early nor too late. In the Western tradition, it is polite to come about 15–20 minutes late in order to give the host/hostess time to make the last-minute preparations. In Singapore however, it is better to arrive on time. Some Singaporeans like to tease their very close personal Indian friends about 'Indian Rubber Time', meaning that time can be stretched.

3. *Shoes*
   - Remove shoes in the house – Most Indians do not wear shoes in the house. Indian Muslims, of course, never wear shoes in the house because of religious restrictions. Hindus do not have religious restrictions about shoes, but they do not like dirt being tracked in. Leave your shoes outside the door, to the right or left. Some modern Indians may not follow this custom. Always look to see what the family does, and do what they do.
   - Remove shoes if there is a prayer room – In many traditional Indian homes there is an area set aside for prayer, a *pooja* (prayer) room. Statues or pictures of Hindu deities are found there. Shoes must never be worn in a house that has a *pooja*. Indians believe that shoes must be removed for prayers.

4. *Some general rules*
   - Always dress modestly while a guest in an Indian home.
   - Guests can bring some fruit or sweets for the children if they know the family well.
   - Unless offered a tour of the house, guests should not wander about. Guests are entertained in the living room. Unlike Westerners who love to take guests on a general tour of the entire house, Indians usually do not do this.
5. *Sitting*
   - Wait to be seated – In the Western home, guests are often informal. They come in and find a seat for themselves. When you are a guest in an Indian home however, it is polite to wait to be seated. The host will find a place for you.
   - Sitting on the floor – Seating is usually on chairs, but if chairs are not provided, as in funerals, weddings, etc., guest sit cross-legged (men), or with knees together to the left or right (women) on the mats provided for such occasions.
   - When elders are present – In the presence of elders, do not cross one leg over the other, or drape yourself over the sofa. Always show respect for them: rise, or at least half-rise, from your chair when an elder enters the room for the first time. Even adults are highly respectful of elders. One important older man high in the government says: 'When my father comes in, my leg automatically goes down!'
4. *Conversation* Talking between men and women is generally kept to a minimum. Usually women talk to each other and men do the same. Conversation should not include sex or risque jokes.
5. *Segregation of the sexes* In many traditional Indian homes, the wife does not sit down when male guests are present. She may serve them but otherwise she will stay in the kitchen or some other part of the house. In more modern homes, the wife may sit with male guests, especially in the business circle.

When men and women guests are present at the same time, it

is common to see the women sitting together in one part of the room or house, and the men in another part of the room or house. If Western guests are present, then the family might entertain men and women guests in the same place, i.e., not segregated.

ON BEING A HOUSE GUEST

Some of the more traditional customs described below may no longer be practised by the more Westernized, younger generation of Indians. However, it is useful and interesting to know these traditional ways in order to understand the culture more fully.

1. *Observe family customs* Many allowances are made for a Western guest in an Indian home. The Indian host is mostly concerned that the guests make themselves one of the family. Guests should observe the family etiquette and customs and try to fit into their routine, for example, if the family does not wear shoes, then follow suit. The Indian host loves guests who are adaptable, flexible, and good-humoured. Eat heartily! The hostess is pleased if she knows that you enjoy good food and that you are a good eater.

2. *Offer to help* Women can offer to help with housework and chores.

3. *Inform host/hostess of your plans* It is not considered presumptuous to do things on your own, but polite guests should inform the family of plans to do things independently.

4. *'Go and come back'* When a member of an Indian family leaves the house, for any purpose, the others do not say good-bye. It is not a good omen. They say instead in their mother tongue: 'Go and come back.' The one leaving says: 'I'm going and I'll come back.' If you are a house guest in an Indian home, it is a good idea to follow this custom so they will not worry about you.

5. *'Calling a person back'* Indians do not call a person back into the house once they have gone out of the the door. If they must go back into the house for something they have forgotten, they sit down for

a spell, and have a drink of water, etc. They prepare to leave all over again, as if for the first time. They feel that it is not a good omen to disregard this custom.

6. ***Three people leaving the house*** Three people do not leave the house at the same time. Two go out, and the third follows a bit later. They feel that the venture will not be successful if three leave at the same time.

WASHING AND BATHROOMS

1. ***Traditional bathing*** In Singapore, standard-type showers are common. Some people may use a tap and a bucket. In traditional homes, it is the custom to stand and rub oil all over the body and the hair. A special plant scrubber (made from the fibrous skeleton of the loofah gourd) is used to rub the oil into the body. Then soap is applied. All this is then washed off with water from the shower or bucket. This treatment keeps the body soft and supple.

2. ***Women's beauty treatment*** Before bathing, Indian women apply a paste of a special flour and water to the hair and skin. It is said to keep the skin young-looking and soft to the touch. Today, women are likely to use commercially prepared ointments. These beauty treatments seem to work very well; observe the skin of both men and women.

3. ***Toilets*** Most homes have a Western-type toilet today, but some may still have the squat-type of toilet. Toilet paper might be provided for guests, but Indians usually think it is cleaner to use water. The left hand is used for cleansing.

BREAD-AND-BUTTER GIFTS

Among themselves, Indians do not give bread-and-butter gifts. They would wish for a return of the hospitality at some future date. Since Westerners may not have an opportunity to return the invitation, it is a polite gesture to give some lovely gift for the home: a pretty serving dish filled with sweets, a lovely bowl filled with fruits, or a basket of delicacies for the elders and the whole family. If there are children, gifts for the children are always appreciated. A thank you letter and flowers are always in good taste.

GIFTS IN GENERAL

1. *Opening the gift* Like their fellow Singaporeans, the Chinese and the Malays, Indians do not open gifts in front of the guest. It is good manners to set gifts aside until after the guest has departed. You should also set a gift aside if one is presented to you. Do not look greedy as if you can't wait to open it.
2. *At festivals* Gifts of sweets, fruits, or flowers may be brought for the family altar at festivals such as Deepavali.
3. *A gift may be reciprocated* If you give a gift to an Indian friend, it may be followed up by an invitation to a dinner, or it may be that you are given a return gift.
4. *Colours* White and black should be avoided. Red, yellow, green, and all bright colours are happy colours for Indians.
5. *Money* Odd numbers are usual when money is given as a gift. A dollar is usually added to the amount to make it uneven, and lucky: $11.00 or $21.00 as the count always begins with the number one. It is a symbol of progressive growth. It is also to add just a bit extra – to show that you go just a little bit further than you need.
6. *Frangipanni* Do not ever give frangipanni. These are very fragrant blossoms which look much like bridal bouquets. They grow on trees in clusters and they are very common in Singapore. (These flowers are called *plumeria* by Hawaiians who traditionally make festive flower leis from them). In Singapore however,

these flowers are made up into wreaths and sent to funerals. It would certainly be bad luck to give them to friends as gifts of joy!

7. *For Sikhs* Do not give gifts of cigarettes or ashtrays to Sikhs.
8. *Use the right hand* Remember: always offer a gift to an Indian with the right hand. The left hand can be used to support the right hand.

FOOD AND DRINK

The habits and customs mentioned here apply mostly to Indian Hindus and Sikhs. For the religious food customs of Indian Muslims, follow the advice under the section on Malay Muslims.

1. *Meat* Most Indians do not eat beef as the animal is venerated in their religion. The cow is considered to be a sacred animal because people consume its milk; analogous to a human mother who gives milk. In many Hindu homes, meat is not cooked or eaten on Fridays. This restriction may not be observed in restaurants because many non-Hindu patrons enjoy going to Indian restaurants.
2. *Vegetables* Indians tend to like everything, including vegetables, well cooked. This is probably why salads are not too common at their meals. Singaporeans are getting used to eating them, but Indians from India usually do not favour raw vegetables.
3. *Yogurt* Indians are very fond of yogurt. Yogurt is served and consumed in many different forms, but one of the favourite forms is *lassi*. It is a cooling drink made by blending some plain yogurt with a little water and crushed ice. Salt is added (by South Indians) or sugar is added (by North Indians). It is thought to aid digestion.
4. *Sweets and fats* Indians generally enjoy very sweet and rich desserts made from evaporated and sweetened condensed milk. They also like fried foods, and foods fried in ghee (clarified butter), which in the past, they had associated with nutrition.

Recently, the Indian community has been trying to get Indians to modify their diets in order to improve their cholesterol levels and to strengthen their hearts. Doctors are advising the community to cut down on oily foods, cholesterol-rich coconut oil, fried foods and fried snacks, fatty mutton, egg yolks, and sugar.

5. *Food preferences*
   - Vegetarian food – Many Indians (from the North, South East, West) are vegetarians. Brahmins are vegetarians. They belong to the highest caste. They are the priests and philosophers dedicated to the study of the sacred books. Among their various duties they must be vegetarians, they must bathe twice daily in flowing water, and they must wear the sacred thread that is a symbol of their status. Jains are vegetarians. The first of their Five Commandments of the Soul, given to them by Mahavira is: Do not kill any living thing; do not hurt any living thing by word, thought or deed, even in self-defence. To observe the first commandment in the spirit in which it was given to them, Jains became vegetarians. They never eat meat, even when it is a question of health or survival. Always ask when you are entertaining Indians what types of food they prefer.
   - Wheat and pulses – Northern Indians love lentils (*dahl*) and wholewheat breads (*chapatis*, etc.) Wholewheat products form a staple part of their diet.
   - Rice – Southern Indians, on the other hand, love rice. They do not feel that they have had a proper meal without it. They also make breads from ground pulses (*gram*) and rice flour.
   - Spicy foods – Indians love spicy foods, so a bottle of hot chilli sauce on the table is appreciated by Indian dinner guests. It is no use preparing subtle sauces and delicate flavours for your Indian friends: 'Very bland' they say while politely trying to pour hot chilli sauce on the 'tasteless' food to give it some character!
   - Colours – Indian food is rich in colour: red (chilli), brown (curries) and yellow (turmeric) enhance the appearance of their food. Pungent aromas are the most enticing part of the

meal. The rich colours and spicy fragrance of Indian dishes help to whet a great appetite!

6. *Food Indians do not enjoy* Indians tend not to enjoy European type cheeses, clams and other shellfish, and they particularly do not enjoy boring, colourless, and lifeless boiled, steamed or otherwise bland food.

7. *Beer and wine* Indian women tend not to drink alcohol, and wine is not ordinarily a part of an Indian meal. Some Indians seem to enjoy beer, but most Indians drink lassi, coffee, tea, and water.

TABLE ETIQUETTE

1. *The table setting* This varies of course, but in general the following applies to homes and restaurants: Serving bowls of food are generally placed in the centre of the table. Each bowl has its own serving spoon. Plates are commonly placed on the table as in the Western style; each person has her/his own plate.

   In traditional Indian homes there is no cutlery on the table, except for serving spoons. If Western guests are present, then forks and spoons are available upon request. The food is prepared in bite-sized pieces so no knives are necessary.

2. *Seating* Informality is the key note. There is generally no special place of honour, but the father of the family usually sits at the head of the table. The host generally invites the guests to sit where they please. The host may place a guest next to him or opposite him.

   Men and women generally do not sit and eat together. Women generally serve the men first, then eat when the men are finished. For Western guests, an exception may be made.

   At informal functions, if there is a buffet-style meal, the women generally serve themselves first, then the men do the same. At these buffet-type meals, seating may be mixed.

3. *Serving and eating*
   a. Hands should be washed before the meal. In an Indian restaurant, there is always a place to wash before and after eating.

b. The Thanksgiving offering: The devout Hindu quietly sets aside a small portion of food as a thanksgiving offering to his God before beginning to eat. You can also do this if you wish.

c. Guests should wait for the host to begin. The host generally picks up the serving dishes and hands them to the guests so they can begin to serve themselves. Sometimes the host may serve the guests himself. The host serves himself last.

d. The person serving is careful to put the food on the plate without touching the plate with the serving spoon.

e. Eating with the hand is not a haphazard affair! The food is eaten with the fingers of the right hand. Never use the left hand to handle food, although you may use it to hold a spoon or glass or to pass dishes.

At festivities and celebrations, it is good manners to use the right hand for eating, rather than to ask the hostesses for a fork and spoon, which may not be readily available during all the hustle and the bustle.

f. Some Indians press and roll the food which is on the plate or leaf into a tidy bundle. They neatly convey this bundle to the mouth by turning the hand upwards. The tongue sticks out slightly to receive the food which the thumb then gently pushes into the mouth. Some Indians are adept at flicking the food into the mouth without dropping a grain. This is more difficult than it looks.

g. Bad manners:
   - Do not drop any food or rice onto the plate or table.
   - The fingers are never soiled above the second knuckle.
   - Fingers should not be sucked or put into the mouth.
   - Fingers are never licked.

h. Elbows should not be placed on the table in an upright position, as if to hold up the head. The elbow of the left hand can be rested on the table, with the hand dropped out of sight, towards the lap.

i. The practice of trying a bit of food which is on the spouse's plate is not done in an Indian home. This is because not only is it considered unhygenic but it is also considered bad table manners.

j. Indians love to see a guest eat heartily, second and third helpings are not unusual. The hostess is not pleased with a picky eater. If you wish more helpings, you can serve yourself, smiling all the while, and commenting on how delicious the food is! You must eat all you dish out to yourself.

k. Sometimes meals are served on banana leaves instead of plates. This is common in some restaurants. The leaf is generally square cut, and larger than a normal place-mat. The glass, (and a fork and spoon – if asked for) are also placed on the leaf. The leaf is larger than necessary to give plenty of elbow room at the table. A variety of sauces and curries are placed around a mound of rice which is in the center.

At the end of the meal, the leaf is folded in half. Most Indians I have observed fold the leaf in half away from the body. But, other Indians have said that it is a sign of appreciation for the good food if one folds the leaf towards the body. Engage your Indian friends in their idea of the courtesy of this custom.

l. After the meal, forks and spoons, if used, can be placed on the dinner plate. There is no special way of arranging them as there is in the Western culture. Simply place them side by side.

Indians wash their hands and often rinse out their mouths with tap water after eating. You can even see this being done in restaurants at the tap which is usually available for patrons.

Guests do not leave the table until everyone has finished eating. After dinner at an Indian's home, guests do not leave the home immediately (as is common in the Chinese culture). As in the Western culture, they usually sit and talk for some time in the living room.

PUBERTY CELEBRATIONS

Many Indians in Singapore celebrate their daughters' coming of age. The ritual is called *Chamathi Chadanja*. It is usually carried out at the time of the girl's first menses and originates in Sri Lanka. It is carried out on an odd numbered date, e.g the seventh, ninth or eleventh of the month.

The girl wears a new sari with no black colour in it, black being the colour associated with evil. She is brought to sit among her relatives. Three women who are happily married with children attend her. Their presence promises a similar happy life for the girl. One of them if possible is the wife of the girl's mother's brother, whose son was often her ideal marriage partner.

Twigs, mud and leaves are place at the girl's feet to symbolize the impurities which will be washed away during the ritual. The girl's mother's brother holds a pail of milk (symbol of purity) containing coins (symbol of wealth) and grass (symbol of fertility). He splashes a little of it over her. The three attendants and some others, adding up to an odd number, do the same. The uncle then breaks open a coconut. If it breaks with no jagged edges, it foretells a happy marriage.

An odd number of married women, usually nine or eleven, carry trays to the three attendants. They contain many symbolic items including a bamboo container of padi (unhusked rice) filled to overflowing which assures her of a long and plentiful life; a sharp knife standing upright in the padi symbolizing protection against evil (a girl is thought to be in a special state of spiritual danger from evil spirits at this time); and a lighted lamp to symbolize gaiety, brightness, and cheerfulness in her personality.

The trays are passed from one woman to another around the girl starting at her right side and travelling over her right shoulder. Finally, the girl is given a container holding a whole coconut with some husk still covering the shell. It sits on some mango leaves and has a red dot painted in its centre to ward off the evil eye. She gives this to her mother's brother and his wife as a form of thanks.

215

Family and friends then give her gifts of gold or money (in an envelope, in uneven amounts). Afterwards the girl is taken to be bathed and her sari is given away so that she can never wear it again. The guests are invited to eat a vegetarian meal. The ceremony is usually only attended by close friends and relatives. If you are invited to this ceremony, bring the traditional gift of gold or money. Women dress modestly. Men dress casually in slacks and sports shirts.

COURTSHIP AND DATING

Young Indian men and women do not ordinarily mix socially or date as it is known in the West, unless they are engaged. They often meet each other socially in groups at school or university, or at work, but single and casual dating is not encouraged. Even to this day, women are strongly protected by their families and their virtue is highly prized.

Most Indian marriages are still arranged by parents with the young people's consent, and there may be no objections if the young people choose their own partners; however, it is hoped, that the children will choose as the parents would have chosen, i.e., the hope is that they will fall in love with someone of the same class, caste, education, ethnicity, age group, and community. When this does not happen, the parents may refuse to give their blessing, and the children usually abide by their rules.

In the case of one young university couple, close friends of mine, who fell in love across the ethnicity line (one was Tamil and the other was from Sri Lanka) the parents withheld their blessings and the young couple waited patiently to marry for over seven years before both sets of parents gave their blessings – but wait they did! And today they are blissfully happy and they have beautiful children.

Some modernized and Westernized Indians, university students for instance, may be more liberal in their attitudes towards love and marriage than their parents, but even so, they are careful to observe the traditions and values of their own cultures – which sanctions the separation of young people until marriage. Indeed, it is a problem in today's Singapore that the young people are caught between the old and the new. With rapid social change taking place, many of the traditional structures have broken down, and as a result Indian marriages are also down.

Today many eligible men and women are still single. Of the 25,000 marriages in 1988, Malay marriages increased by 7%, Chinese went up by 6%, and Indians went up only by 1%! Among Indian graduates from university who are between the ages of 20-39, 53.2% of the men and 50.8% of the women remain unmarried! Some Indians say that the only opportunities for a woman to meet an eligible man today are at weddings, cultural shows and religious festivals such as Thaipusam. Some parents only allow their daughters to date after they have turned 35, but by then, it may be a bit too late!

The Indian society has recently taken steps to try to reverse this trend. Some temples are setting up committees to help young people meet and mix with each other, with the object of marriage in mind. These temples set up programmess for young single people with 'O' and 'A' level education, and others set up programmes for unmarried university graduates. The temples provide a respectable setting which parents approve of, and therefore the young people are cautiously being allowed to join each other for monthly outings, dinners, and dances. In this case, the temple has taken on the role of the traditional Indian matchmaker! Do not even ask to date Indians unless you have marriage in mind.

ENGAGEMENTS

For many Indians in Singapore, the engagement takes place a few months before the wedding, and it is almost like a small wedding itself. A close family friend acts as a go-between (it is considered indelicate for the parents to handle negotiations themselves). A priest looks at the horoscopes of the couple in order to choose an auspicious date for the wedding celebration. The engagement is held at the girl's home and the boy's party (his parents, relatives and friends) are officially welcomed by the girl's parents.

The girl, dressed almost like a bride, sits on a mat with her parents on either side. A tray of coconuts, flowers, and oil lamps is placed before her. A priest may be present to bless the couple, and the go-between announces the engagement as the couple exchange rings. From this point on, the couple may date. Propriety must still be observed however, and the girl has to be home at a reasonable hour, and both should behave virtuously.

Family and relatives bring gifts, but friends usually do not. Women dress modestly, and men dress casually.

WEDDINGS

Traditionally, Indians marry within their own caste, clan, class, community, and educational group. This may be difficult in Singapore because of the small number of Indian people here who fit the ideal criteria.

In the past, dowries determined whether a girl married or not. Parents made sure their daughter was provided with a suitable dowry to match the wealth of her potential husband's family. Today, dowries are less important than the love between the young people. Dowries can now take the form of furniture for the new couple's house, or of gold jewellery which would belong to the girl.

Most marriages are negotiated by a go-between on the instructions of the parents and with the consent of the children. The average marriage age ideally is around 22 years for girls and around 27 years for boys. However, as we have seen, more than 50% of the young university people between 20 and 39 are still unmarried, and among non-graduates, 54.2% of men and 37.2% of women are still single.

Marriage in the Indian community is seen as sacred and eternal, lasting through life. The symbols of a South Indian woman's marriage are a red dot on the forehead and the *thali*, a gold chain that the husband ties around his wife's neck at the wedding. North Indian symbols of marriage are bangles on the arm and a red streak on the woman's hair parting.

While all ceremonies vary according to the religious beliefs of the families they all reflect Indian cultural rituals. Before the wedding, the bride is given a bath of 'gingelly' oil which is thought to have a cooling effect on her nervousness. Another traditional form of cooling the bride is to paint the palms of her hands and feet with henna.

Some Indians have very simple ceremonies; some modern couples going to the extent of requesting the priest to shorten the ceremony to the barest minimum time possible. Traditional South Indians however, have elaborate affairs, sometimes lasting several hours.

In some families, there is also a tree-planting ceremony. The young couple plant a small tree in a little pot to symbolize their new life. If they have a garden, it is replanted there and it is a good sign if the plant flourishes! After the tree-planting, the couple change their clothes. The bride wears a completely new outfit, given to her by the groom. It symbolizes that she is now his responsibility.

Women who are noted for their happily married lives are the ones chosen to dress the bride, for the belief is that some of their happiness rubs off on her. The main part of the ceremony is when the couple walk around the holy fire, which represents a purifying element.

When the *thali* is tied, drums are beaten wildly to drown out any noises, sneezes, howling of dogs, etc., which are considered to be bad omens. Guests then walk past the couple and throw yellow rice, a symbol of fertility, on them. As they pass, some may give presents of money or jewellery if they have not already done so.

A Roman Catholic wedding between Indians looks like a Western wedding but the tying of the *thali* by the groom is still observed.

The wedding night is spent in the groom's home. They are greeted by a burning oil lamp and they step into the home with the right foot in order to get off on the right start. A warm, loving and sensual married life is highly valued in the Indian community. When a newly-married couple visits friends and relatives, a sweet is popped into their mouths to symbolize the sweetness of their sensual life together.

WEDDING ETIQUETTE

1. Guests should arrive on time and leave about half an hour after dinner is over.
2. Guests should take care not to sneeze while the *thali* is being tied. It is a bad omen, in fact, to sneeze during any important occasion or business deal. It is a sign that the venture will fail.
3. Gifts may be brought to the bride at her home before the wedding, or a member of the family may accept them at the wedding itself or at the reception afterwards.
   - Gifts for the home are appropriate, but something ornamental as well as functional is preferred.
   - Money can be given in an envelope with a traditional wedding

Tying the thali. The thali is as symbolic of the Indian wedding as the ring is of the Western marriage. At this sacred moment, the guests are careful not to sneeze as it would be regarded as a bad omen. Photo: Munshi Ahmed

card. The amount is up to the discretion of the giver, but odd numbers are more auspicious than even numbers for Indians. A dollar is added to an even amount to make it uneven: $21.00, $31.00, $41.00, $51.00, etc.

4. Western women should dress up more formally for an Indian wedding, but still modestly. Indian women usually come in beautiful glittering saris and heavy gold jewellery.
5. Bright colours are correct for weddings. Red is very auspicious.
6. Shoes should be removed at the door if the ceremony is held at a temple. Heads of both men and women should be covered in case of a Sikh or Muslim ceremony, and uncovered for the other Indian groups.
7. The reception may be held at a local hotel, a restaurant, or in the temple itself. If it is held in the temple hall, vegetarian food will be served. The style of the meal may also be more traditional, i.e., eating with fingers of the right hand; sitting on the floor, or standing up if there are only a few chairs available. If long tables are provided for the wedding lunch or dinner, do not leave the table until the persons on either side of you have left.

BIRTHS

Most babies today are born in hospital in Singapore with the mother returning home after a few days. After the birth of a child, a priest is consulted and he prepares the child's horoscope; he may suggest some auspicious names for the baby based on this horoscope. Also, the horoscope is kept by the family to be examined at other significant times in their child's life, such as an engagement.

For twenty-eight days after the birth of a baby, both mother and child are considered to be in a state of spiritual danger. The mother has many restrictions placed on her: she is put on a strict diet; she is not allowed to leave the home, not even to visit the temple; her body is wrapped every day, and during the bath, hot water is thrown on her stomach to help shrink the womb. Today, some of these rituals may

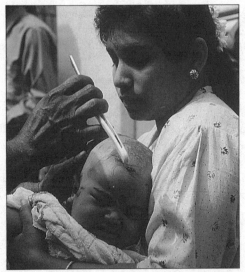

In thanksgiving for a safe delivery, babies are brought to the temple to have their heads shaved as a fulfillment of their mother's vow to the Divine Mother. Photo: MITA

be short-lived because of the call of the work force. (51.7% of Indian women are in the work force.)

Although the registry of births allows only fourteen days for parents to give a name to a child, the parents of an Indian child do not call him/her by name until the 28th day. At this time, the child is considered to be out of danger and there is usually a celebration to which friends and relatives are invited. The child is placed on the father's lap, or on the lap of a relative, and his/her name is whispered gently into the ears. From then on, the child is known and called by that name. At the first opportunity, usually during the naming ceremony or at one of the major festivals, the grateful mother takes her baby to the temple to have the head shaved of birth hair. This fulfills her vow of thanksgiving to the Divine Mother for the safe delivery.

For the first six months of their happy lives, babies are given a special bath every morning. First they are gently rubbed with 'gingelly' oil. After resting for a few minutes, the mothers cradle them on their legs while they lovingly caress and massage the head, face, arms, legs and body. This is followed by a soothing bath, then the babies are fed, and finally, laid down for a long morning nap.

The massage is worthy of note. The mother gently rubs the head to mould it into a perfect shape; the forehead is smoothed and flattened, the upper lip is shaped, and the bridge of the nose is massaged to thin and refine it. The child's eyes are rubbed with Eye-tex every day, in a circular motion around the rim of the upper and lower lids. The skin at the side of the eye is gently stretched. This is believed to make the eyes large and round. An older woman teaches the new mother how to do these things.

ETIQUETTE FOR BIRTHS

1. It is acceptable to visit a new mother and baby in the hospital, but do not visit on a Tuesday; it is not an auspicious day for a visit.
2. Gifts are usually not brought for the mother. Gold jewellery – a small chain, bracelet, or anklet, is often given to the baby. Today, baby gifts can include little toys, stuffed animals (no dogs for Muslims) little outfits, in bright and cheery colours – not black or white.
3. The new mother often gives a sweet to visitors to express the joy and sweetness in her life.

LIFE AFTER LIFE – THE KARMIC LAW

In the Karmic Law, all humans are part of the World Soul – Brahman – God. It is as if in the beginning, God broke off a piece of His own light and planted it in the soul of each being. The soul longs to return to the perfect light from whence it came, but it must be purified before it can exist in the pure vibrations of the World Soul.

In order to purify itself, the soul must go through numberless reincarnations until it is finally released from the Karmic debts it owes. The body is ruled by passions and desires and meaningless ambitions. It must struggle to rise above these things so that the soul can be set free from the endless cycle of births, deaths and rebirths.

Hinduism believes in the Law of the Deed, called Karma. This law teaches that 'From good must come good; and from evil, evil.' Every thought or act is either good or bad. Each is compensated or punished accordingly; if not immediately then in a subsequent incarnation. What we are now is the result of our thoughts and actions in past incarnations; and what we will be like in the next incarnations. This is Karma. The end of birth is death and the end of death is birth. When a body dies, the soul is reincarnated in the body of a newborn baby. Though reincarnation is a facet of many Eastern religions, the idea of immediate death and rebirth in a continuous process, combined with the Karmic Law is particularly Hindu.

FUNERALS

Indians believe that when a person dies, the soul leaves the vicinity of the house only on the sixteenth day. Some who are especially attached to their families may linger as long as 40 days. This is why an oil lamp is left burning in the home day and night (the light is the symbol of the soul); it is a gesture of respect to the soul. The funeral is usually held in the home of the deceased. Someone in the community who knows about funeral ceremonies is called in to help with the formalities.

The oldest son usually bathes the father and women bathe the body of a deceased woman. The body is dressed in new clothes and laid in a wooden coffin and silver coins are laid on the eyes to close them. Two oil lamps are placed at either end of the coffin. Grandchildren and children walk around the coffin carrying lighted candles.

The body does not remain in the home for longer than twelve hours. Most adults are cremated, children are not. When a man dies, a woman who has also lost her husband steps forward to remove the *thali* from around the widow's neck; it symbolizes the ending of the woman's married life. The red dot symbolizing her marriage is ceremoniously wiped off her forehead. The Northern Indian widow strikes her bangles against an object to break them. She will not put bangles on again. Although grief is expressed, there is usually no loud wailing or keening.

ETIQUETTE AT FUNERALS

1. The caller pays respects to the widow or widower first. He/she then stands by the body. It is appropriate to clasp the hands and to bow the head. A silent prayer can be said. The caller then moves away to make room for other visitors.

2. It used to be that only males went to the crematorium, but in Singapore today, there is now a trend for female relatives to attend the funeral as well. The custom of cleaning the house after the deceased has left the home, can be done by a maid if there is one.

3. Funeral floral wreaths can be sent to the home. It is not usual to give gifts of money.

4. Sombre colours are appropriate: white, black, greyish or pale colours. Avoid bright and cheerful colours.

5. Visitors leave after paying their respects.

FUNERAL TABOOS

1. *Do not visit the family on certain days* A visit to the family of the deceased should not be made on a Monday, Tuesday or Thursday. It is believed that the sorrow would come back to you.

2. *Bathing after the funeral* After a funeral an Indian does not enter the home before washing with some water left outside for this purpose. Sometimes water is sprinkled on the head and body. In fact, the Indian will not drink, eat, talk, or touch anyone until the bathing has been completed.

3. *A wedding and a funeral in the same period of time* Indians do not attend a wedding and a funeral during the same period of time. They have to choose one or the other. Indians believe that bad luck

would come to the couple if one of the guests had attended a funeral during the same period as the wedding.

4. *Mourning* A widow cannot visit the temple nor attend any social functions for a year after the death of her husband. A child may not go to the temple for a month after the death of a parent.

5. *Abstaining from meat* The family observes a vegetarian diet for a certain period of time after the death of a family member. This would vary from one Hindu group to another, but a period of 16 days is generally accepted, because the soul of the deceased is believed to linger within the vicinity of the home for this period. After the 17th day, prayers are said and the diet is normalized.

HINDUISM AND SOME FESTIVALS

Hinduism has no founder and no fixed creeds, but it has a number of beliefs which are held by most Hindus. They believe that there is only one great Universal Spirit called Brahman (World Soul). Brahman is a Trimurti God (a Three-in-One God) with three major manifestations of the same divine reality: Brahma – the Creator; Vishnu – the Preserver; and Siva – the Destroyer. They are not separate; they are only different aspects of the same divine Unity.

Other divine attributes of the triune god are symbolized by different gods. For example, Lord Murugan represents youth, bravery, virtue and power.

It is interesting to look at and understand the rituals and festivals which give meaning and purpose to the lives of Hindus.

THAIPUSAM

One such festival is Thaipusam. Thai (month of January or February) and Pusam (festival) is dedicated to Lord Murugan. According to R. Raj Kumar, who researched this festival while studying at the University of Singapore, the festival reinforces the solidarity of the Hindu community. Hinduism believes in a caste system; but ideally on this one day, the caste system is removed; every Hindu enjoys (for a moment in time) equal status with every other, from the poorest to the richest, from male to female, and from highest to lowest. The pressure which the caste system puts on the society is thus released through the reversal of the caste system through the prescribed rituals! The festival is much more important in Singapore than it is in its original home of South India.

Female devotees do not carry spiked kavadis *because they are not allowed to expose their bodies. Photo: MITA*

The story of Thaipusam is a story which upholds the veneration of children for their parents. The legend says that the sons of Siva, Murugan and his brother Vinayagar, were tested by the god Narada. Narada said he would give a golden mango to the youth who could go around the world the fastest. Muragan, being young, brave and impetuous, jumped on his peacock and flew off immediately, but the less impetuous and cautious Vinayagar asked the god if there was any difference between the world and one's parents. The god of course, replied no. Vinayagar then walked around his parents and won the golden mango. A golden lesson!

Today, Indians who wish to thank Lord Murugan for a favour granted, or to ask for a petition, or even to make up for some deed, vow to carry a *kavadi* on their shoulders. This is done as a sacrifice, and the *kavadi* is seen as a sort of demi-chariot where the devotee carries the God upon his shoulders. The *kavadi* most common in Singapore is the *Alavvu Kavadi* which is a large semicircler object, rather like a bicycle wheel. It is really a simple structure, but the Indians decorate it lavishly; it sometimes weighs up to 18 kilograms.

Some Indians even have flashing lights intertwined among the peacock feathers and flowers that adorn it. Metal hooks or spikes attached to the kavadi are fastened onto the Indian's skin, or through it. Devotees may also pierce the tongue and cheeks with a small silver *vel*. The *vel* is shaped like a spear. The head of it is in the form of a heart and it denotes purity of heart. The shaft symbolizes closeness to God. It is a symbol of victory over evil and of purity and bravery.

The people who go through this ceremony are not mystics or holy men. They are normal, average, everyday Indians, and sometimes one can see people of other ethnic groups participating. The executive and the student may walk side by side. Women do not carry a spiked *kavadi* because they cannot expose their bodies to be pierced. There are strict rules that devotees must follow in order to purify themselves before carrying the *kavadi*. For at least three days, but more likely, one to two weeks, the devotees fast from meat, fish or chicken, and they abstain from worldly pleasures, like sex, smoking, and alcohol.

During this festival, they go into trance, ordinarily feel no pain, and, oddly enough, rarely bleed or scar. Some Indians carry the *kavadi* for one, three, five, or seven years in succession. Some vow to carry it for life. While the *kavadi* is being carried, the devotees walk the entire distance of about four kilometres barefoot. Along the way, people wash the feet of the bearers. Family and friends, and even total strangers, accompany the bearers; they heartily support them by singing, dancing, playing music, and chanting: 'Vel, Vel, Vel!'

DEEPAVALI

Deepavali is the Festival Of Light. It is one of the most beloved of all Indian festivals. It is celebrated by Hindus all over the world (and by the North Indian Hindi-speaking community, the Tamil and other South Indian communities, and by the Gujeratis, Sindhis, and other trading communities in Singapore).

Deepavali is known as the Festival of Light. An oil lamp is lit in celebration of this festival. Photo: MITA

229

It is celebrated on the darkest night of the year, according to the Hindu almanac (on October/November, on the new moon night of the month of *kartic*). The theme of Deepavali is that light conquers darkness and that good conquers evil! By lighting oil lamps (*deeps*) to turn the darkest night of the year into the brightest night of the year, every Hindu reaffirms faith in the triumph of good over the forces of evil and ignorance.

Deepavali is a time of celebration! As such, the social aspects of Deepavali are significant. Ritual offerings of sweetmeats, flowers, fruits, yogurt and ghee are placed on the family altar along with the oil lamps; the house is ritually cleaned, new clothing is put on, and children pay ritual homage to their parents. People pay visits to friends and family to reaffirm their ties of solidarity.

This day also marks the beginning of the new financial year for the 1000-strong Gujerati business community in Singapore and the large Sindhi business community. New cash books, ledgers, invoices and other books of account are placed on the altar at the feet of Lakshmi, the goddess of wealth, or Ganesh the Elephant-headed god, or Maha lakshmi. An odd number of books is considered auspicious. The books have red covers (to ward off evil) and are opened and placed in front of the altar, together with brand new red pens; they are placed at the same level as the goddess so she can 'walk through' them. There are other rituals performed which are intended to make their business successful during the coming year.

— *Chapter Seven* —

CULTURE SHOCK: THE MYSTERIOUS MALADY

When I first wrote this chapter fourteen years ago, very few expats could define Culture shock; even fewer knew that there were symptoms, side effects, stages, and various reactions connected with it, and hardly anyone at all knew that they were victims of it! Those who did know about it, didn't know what to do to prevent it, mitigate it, or to recover from it. Today, much of this has changed. Expats are generally sophisticated about the mysterious malady of culture shock, so what we shall briefly do here is to go over the main points for those who wish to update their information or for those who would like to learn more about this peculiar and universal occupational hazard.

231

WHAT CULTURE SHOCK IS NOT

Most people who misunderstand its nature think that it has to do with being angered, disgusted, outraged, fearful, dismayed, appalled, revolted, distressed, scandalized, offended, and/or shocked by the actions, behaviours, and beliefs of the people of the new environment. These answers are wrong! Culture shock is not any of these things. It is true however, that people in the throes of culture shock can feel some of these emotions, and it is also true that there are connections with the above feelings to culture shock (they may be reactions to it) but anger, disgust, and shock, etc., are not culture shock!

WHAT THEN IS CULTURE SHOCK?

Culture shock is a perplexing phenomenon which affects all strangers in a strange land. It can be experienced by those who move to a new neighbourhood, a new town, a new state or a new country. It causes mischief and misfortune to all who are exposed to it. Culture shock has two elements in it:

1. It is a near permanent psychological state of stress, anxiety and disorientation; a disturbance to the equilibrium, balance, or inner harmony of a person; and a disturbance to the mental and emotional faculties.
2. It occurs in those who have been uprooted from their own familiar culture and transplanted into a strange and alien culture.

Experts have defined it as: a disease; a malady; an illness; a deep-seated feeling of anxiety or euphoria which takes place when one's cultural milieu is changed; psychological stress; a feeling of inadequacy which results from not knowing how to act among strangers; and a pronounced reaction to psychological disorientation experienced when one moves into a culture markedly different from their own.

WHAT CAUSES CULTURE SHOCK?

Culture shock is caused by being exposed to a thousand and one differences in the alien society; in other words, it is caused by losing your cues to these differences. Losing your cues is worse than losing your cool! For instance, Kalervo Oberg, the anthropologist who first defined culture shock, probably defined the agony of losing cues better than anyone else. He said:

'...these signs or cues include the thousand and one ways in which we orient ourselves to the situations of daily life: when to shake hands and what to say when we meet people; when and how to give tips; how to give orders to servants; how to make purchases; when to accept and when to refuse invitations; when to take statements seriously and when not. Now these cues which may be words, gestures, facial expressions, customs or norms are acquired by all of us in the course of growing up and are as much a part of our culture as the language we speak or the beliefs we accept. All of us depend for our peace of mind and our efficiency on hundreds of these cues, most of which we are not consciously aware of.'

'Now when an individual enters a strange culture, all or most of these familiar cues are removed. No matter how broad-minded or full of goodwill we may be, a series of props has been knocked from under us. This is followed by a feeling of frustration, stress and anxiety.'

WHAT KINDS OF CUES DO WE LOSE?

Lost cues come in three major areas:

1. Lost cues in the personal, social, cultural, and business environment. We don't know how to behave appropriately any more! This is by far the most common and the most serious, and it causes the most problems.
2. Lost cues to our own value and belief system. We may lose faith in our own cultural values and beliefs by being exposed to the alien ones. This is more common in Westerners than it is in Asians because Westerners see things in black and white: 'If their system is right, then mine must be wrong!' Asians on the other hand, see things differently: 'We can both be right.'

233

3. Lost cues in the physical environment. We don't know how to take care of our common physical needs anymore. We don't know where to get a haircut; or where to buy our favourite foods; or how to adapt to the climate, housing, clothing, etc. This is by far the least harmful and the easiest to overcome!

WHAT ARE SOME OF THE PSYCHOLOGICAL SYMPTOMS OF CULTURE SHOCK?

Because culture shock is composed of anxiety and stress, it sometimes disguises itself as other illnesses. An expat may be experiencing a full-blown case and not even realize that he/she has it. Some psychological symptoms include: a belief that the new environment is dirty, particularly bedding, water, food, dishes and crowds; fear of physical contact with foreigners; overdependence on other nationals; irritation and unreasonable anger over delays and other minor frustrations, out of proportion to their real causes; refusal to learn about the new culture; fear of being cheated, robbed or injured; excessive concern over minor ailments; homesickness, boredom, withdrawal; compulsive drinking or eating; need for excessive amounts of sleep; difficulty in eating or drinking; exaggerated cleanliness; marital stress, family tension and conflict; loss of ability to work effectively, unexplainable fits of weeping and depression; feelings of being crazy or weak; headaches; absent-mindedness; and a vacant and faraway stare!

It is important to note here that these symptoms are common and even expected in those who have been uprooted and transplanted into a strange culture. It is very much like having the flu; if you don't have the headache, upset stomach, fever, and

muscle pain, you don't know that you are suffering from an illness. It is very much of a 'normal' reaction to experience symptoms and side effects of culture shock! It is also good to know that these things are temporary and transitory and that they clear up as soon as the causal factors are removed i.e., as soon as the lost cues have been found!

WHAT ARE SOME OF THE SIDE EFFECTS OF CULTURE SHOCK?

In addition to the symptoms of culture shock described above, the side effects of culture shock include: increased prejudice, hostility and intolerance (those most under the influence of culture shock have the most problems with prejudice and hostility towards the host people); cross-cultural misunderstandings and break-down in communications; culture conflict and clash (the potential for conflict, mayhem, strikes, and business breakdowns increase when one is in the throes of culture shock); feelings of, and actual episodes of incompetency, impotency, boorishness, foolishness and inadequacy. These side effects clear up as soon as expats learn how to find their lost cues and *accidental* cultural clashes and conflicts disappear.

WHAT ARE SOME INTERESTING FACTS ABOUT CULTURE SHOCK?

The results of a survey of expats in Singapore revealed the following interesting facts:

1. *Culture shock builds up slowly after an initial honeymoon stage.* Strangers often feel a sense of euphoria and excitement at first. This euphoria is called the honeymoon stage.

2. *Culture shock returns for a second attack after about one year.* There is an initial impact after the honeymoon stage, then it levels off after several months. It then returns for a second attack after about a year, with an even greater impact. Without training and orientation to help replace the lost cues, culture shock gets worse as time goes by.

3. *Women suffer more severe culture shock than men.* There are several reasons for this: they may not be able to work in the foreign culture if only the husband is employed. They may feel a loss of status because servants take over many of their duties and roles. They may have too much time on their hands and nothing of importance to do. They may have no cultural training or orientation.

4. *Men suffer more loneliness than women.* Oddly enough, men were seen to experience more loneliness than women. They missed family at home more than their wives did; perhaps they are more tenderhearted than most people realize.

5. *Culture shock is much worse in the physical areas at first,* but much easier to cope with in the long run. Physical areas such as different food, clothing, shelter, toilets, transportation, sounds, sights, smells, tastes, and so on cause a loss of balance as the family struggles to right itself in the new environment. However, once the physical setting has been mastered (in just a few months), it is not difficult to build up a tolerance for the physical differences.

6. *Culture shock is much more painful in the cultural areas (the lost cues) in the long run.* It is not easy to notice cultural differences – they are often invisible to expats. One must be culturally trained to discover them. Learning to read the cultural map of the mind is not anywhere near as easy as learning to read a road map of a physical area.

7. *The first experience in a strange land is always the hardest.* A person who has never lived in a foreign culture before has more trouble with culture shock than a person who has had experience living and working in foreign cultures.

8. *Cross-cultural changes are more difficult than cross-national change.* It is much more difficult to move from a Western culture to an Asian culture (Canada to Singapore) than it is to move from one Western country to another (Italy to Australia).

HOW DO MOST PEOPLE REACT TO CULTURE SHOCK?

Most people react in predictable ways; they go through two stages:

Stage one: The honeymoon The initial honeymoon is exciting. People spend their time getting settled; finding a new home; enrolling in school, meeting with other expats, and so on. After settling in, they begin to discover their surroundings; they explore the sights and sounds of the new culture. Then, when they are fairly comfortable and their physical needs have been met, they begin to notice a decidedly different way of thinking and doing, and they begin to discover that they are not nearly as effective as they were at home. They wonder why! Stage Two begins!

Stage two: When the honeymoon is over The following patterns are constructs; boundaries overlap; no one fits the patterns exactly; some fit one pattern at one time, and then switch patterns later. The type of response an expat makes is usually determined by the psychological nature of the individual; some expats are natural-born adapters and they do very well in foreign cultures with very little help, and some never learn to survive (let alone thrive) even after copious help. The type of response an expat makes during the early stages often determines the type of expat the individual turns out to be. Cultural orientation and training can alter a negative response. The following information was developed from a survey of 66 expats in Singapore in 1978, and updated and revised in a repeat of the same survey on another group of expats in 1992.

There are three basic cultural types which develop after the honeymoon: The Encapsulator, The Cosmopolitan, and the Absconder.

THE ENCAPSULATOR

(67% of Expats in the survey identified themselves as Encapsulators.) This is the most common. Expats who follow this path adapt to the expat community. They join the culture bubble where they meet and mix mostly with expats like themselves. They have minimum contact with the host people. They learn very little about the host people or culture. They attempt to recreate their home culture about them. They reject the host culture because it is too frightening and too confusing and because it causes them pain when they cannot understand it.

They join expat clubs; live in expat areas, shop for expat foods, send their children to expat schools, set up expat football games, and make expat friends. They really never leave home. Support groups (culture bubbles) can be beneficial by helping expats to settle in, but they can also be harmful in the extreme because they can make it too easy to survive within the culture bubble without learning how to thrive in the host culture. It is interesting to note that the reactivation of culture shock usually occurs with encapsulators only.

Reactions of the encapsulator to the host culture Expats react either with 'Flight' or 'Fight'.

1. **Flight** – Some expats run away from what is strange and unfamiliar to them. There are three stages: rejection, regression and retreatism.
   * They might *reject* the host people and sit around with like-minded friends complaining about them.
   * They might *regress* back to when they were happier at home, remembering only the good times until a trip back home brings them to their senses. (This is a critical stage; if they can find their lost cues during this stage, they can go on to a successful adjustment, if not, then they usually go on to the final stage).
   * Or they might *retreat* into the third and final stage of the flight pattern, where they may remain for the duration of their tour of duty. They retreat deeply into the expat community and isolate themselves from the frustration, failure, pain, and suffering of trying to cope with a culture which they cannot understand – not even in their dreams.
2. **Fight** – Some expats may also experience the 'fight' syndrome in reacting to culture shock. They respond to the differences in the

new culture with anger, hostility, dismay, disgust, disapproval and frustration. Host people have strange habits of their own which are different from theirs. They break the expat's habits, and this is not pleasant. The expats then begin to blame their troubles and unhappiness on the host people and the host culture instead of trying to account for conditions as they really are – a sad situation caused by lost cues.

THE COSMOPOLITAN

(27% of Expats were identified as Cosmopolitans – they were the most successful type). Cosmopolitans are culturally ambidextrous. They quickly learn how to become skillful and competent in both the host and the home culture. They meet and mix equally with people from both cultures.

They retain their own values and beliefs, but they stretch their behaviours to include those of the host people. They may never learn to love everything about the host culture, but they are considerate and respectful towards the people, and they develop an appreciation for their culture.

Cosmopolitans are identified by their optimism, enthusiasm, humour, and positive regard for individuals regardless of ethnicity, sex, religion, or political affiliation. Gordon Allport, the famous psychologist, called these people 'tolerant personalities'.

Reactions of cosmopolitans Cosmopolitans react to culture shock with cultural empathy, curiosity, interest and understanding. They learn about the culture; they learn about the behaviours and the values; and they find their lost cues! They learn to operate within the culture without stress and anxiety.

Although there may still be moments of strain, culture shock disappears with a complete grasp of the cues to social, personal, and business interactions. They experience much fewer problems than their Encapsulator compatriots, and they usually prove to be very successful in their dealings with Singaporeans.

THE ABSCONDER

(Only about 6% of expats fell into the pattern of Absconders.) This type of expat is the rarest of all. Absconders go native. They restrict their relationships to those with local people. They have minimum contact with people of their own culture and make their maximum adjustment to the local culture.

Reactions of the absconder They may marry into the local culture, take up citizenship, and put down roots. To them the local community becomes home and they abandon their allegiance to their country of origin. They cease to be expats according to the definition of expat in this book: A foreign national living and working in another foreign country for more than six months who considers his/her country of residence as alien and his/her country of origin as home.

WHAT CAN YOU DO TO GET OVER CULTURE SHOCK QUICKLY?

TRIGG.

1. *Find your lost cues in personal, social, and business interactions*

As in any illness, the cure depends upon eliminating the causal factors. Since culture shock is caused by losing the cues to everyday behaviours, then the way to cure culture shock, of course, depends upon finding the lost cues.

It is imperative that you learn as much as you can about the personal, social, cultural, and business patterns of behaviour, and that you learn them as quickly as you can.

Unfortunately, much of your study must be self-oriented. Most of the orientation programmes offered by multinational corporations stress physical orientation, which as you know by now, is not the most serious problem; and while some cultural specialists focus on raising the cultural consciousness of people, they may not stress finding the cues to behaviour in specific cultures. For instance, some programmes raise consciousness for all cultures so that you get the same information whether you go to Singapore or to France. To cure culture shock in Singapore however, you must find the cues which relate to Singapore specifically. Generalized information, while always helpful, does not cure culture shock – and this is your task. Some self-help methods are:

- Be aware. Cultural awareness is the key to cultural survival. Be aware that you have lost your cues. Try to find them. Seek out information on the dos and don'ts and especially the whys and hows. The whys are critical. They provide the logic, motivation, and reasoning behind behaviours.

  If you can see the sense to a behaviour, you tend not to judge it as bad simply because it is different from your own behaviour! Always aim for the 'Ah ha!' reaction: 'I see, so that is why they do that!'

- Ask foreign nationals for advice about how things are done here. Ask the three critical questions:
  1. What is it that foreigners do that is wrong here;
  2. Why is it wrong;
  3. What should they do instead?

  Most of this book was written with information gathered from these three basic questions.

- Remember that knowledge is a two-way street. At the same time that you learn about Singaporean ways, explain your ways to the Singaporean friend who teaches you. This way, you both become culturally ambidextrous.

- Share what you learn with your family and friends.
- Attend classes in the culture and the languages of Singapore. The department of Extra Mural Studies at the National University of Singapore offers such classes.
- Read books to give yourself an insight into the local culture. Cultural anthropology books about Singapore are excellent. Also, other books on the background of Singapore, its history, origins, culture, wildlife, and so on are helpful. (Some titles are suggested on pages 273–274.)

2. ***Make at least two or three Singaporean friends*** This may seem to be a strange way to cure culture shock, but it works. The friendships should be on an equal-status basis and they should be based on shared and common goals.

   We have found that if you can make at least three firm Singaporean friends of each main ethnic group on an equal-status basis, then you will have a positive regard for Singaporeans of those ethnic groups. There is no 'spill over' effect, i.e., friendships with Chinese do not guarantee a positive regard for Malays and Indians. You must have friends of each ethnic group in order to experience the positive effect. Your level of respect and acceptance of Singaporeans will be about equal to the positive tolerance levels associated with successful training and orientation.

MUST YOU GIVE UP YOUR OWN WAYS IN ORDER TO LIVE AND WORK SUCCESSFULLY IN SINGAPORE?

This is a very good question, and it has been asked to me by both Asians and Westerners many, many times. It deserves thoughtful and considerate attention. In the search for lost cues, the differences in appropriate and acceptable behaviour between Asians and Westerners become strikingly obvious. For example, what is polite here may be insulting in the West, and vice versa! What is simply a social greeting hug and kiss in the West – can be taken for a grossly rude and unwelcome amorous advance in Singapore. In answer to the question, first of all, the object of any type of cultural orientation is not to make anyone give up his/her own culture – it is to help people to function with skill and expertise in both cultures, the home and the host culture.

To cure culture shock, we focus on finding lost cues. When the cues are found, then it is advantageous to stretch one's behaviour to include the appropriate behaviour of the host people – in order to avoid potential pitfalls, conflict, misinterpretations, and misunder-standings. Finding lost cues permits symbols to be synonymous, thus setting the stage for proper cultural communication and meaningful cultural interactions.

To be more specific, there are basically three areas of interaction to think about in cross-cultural communication:

1. *Cultural laws, rules, legal practices and deep social conventions* In this instance, expats do not have a free choice. Expats must follow the rules and laws of the host culture. In this book we have listed a series of laws that expats must be aware of. There are even more, but these are the ones that Westerners usually come into contact with.

   Anthropologists know that one of the best ways to establish a basis for friendship and cooperation when in a culture which is different from one's own, is to learn the laws and rules which regulate behaviour, and to follow them. To do otherwise is to invite problems and disaster.

2. *Superficial behaviours, habits, customs and courtesies* Expats have a choice here. These behaviours, once learned, can either be kept or stretched, depending upon the situation.

   • When dealing with people from your own culture, use your own patterns of behaviour.

   • When you deal with the host people who do not know your behaviours, then of course, you must stretch your behaviours to conform to the host culture. The onus is always on the guest in the host culture; this is not only more polite, but it is more

CULTURE SHOCK

practical. The guest has to learn only one new cultural response (or three in the case of Singapore), instead of multiple cultures like French, German, Dutch, Chinese, Russian, and English, etc., as the host people would have to do. The old maxim: 'When in Rome, do as the Romans' is as true today, if not more so, than it was in those old days.

This is similar to learning a new language. One does not give up one's own language when learning a new language. One simply uses language to communicate, i.e., one speaks Chinese to those who speak Chinese, and English, to those who speak English! Nothing is lost; communication is gained. It is the same with culture. One 'speaks' the cultural behaviour of those who can understand it.

- When dealing with people from the host culture who know your customs, both parties have a choice. This is the ideal situation. Both sides know and understand the meaning of each other's behaviours. You both decide which cultural code to work with. No one gives up anything – both gain tremendous advantage.

3. *Fundamental values, beliefs, morals and ethics* These do not have to be given up. One should think deeply before giving up one's cultural beliefs and values. However, it is often the case that many cross-cultural people develop a cosmopolitan and cross-cultural mind. They often heavily weigh the two opposing cultural views with which they have come into contact. The cosmopolitan can then make use of freedom to expand or contract his/her mind.

Freedom, in the true sense of the word, means the ability to make intelligent choices based on a careful study of the existing alternatives. The cross-cultural experience affords one this luxury! Beneficial values may be kept and/or added; and negative or destructive values may be tempered and/or changed.

Industrializing and modernizing do not necessarily mean Westernizing. The West has developed many problems in its quest for science and technology. Human beings have become increasingly lonely and alienated as they become more materialistic and as they become gradually replaced by machines. The challenge of the West is to humanize science and technology. The cross-cultural experience affords both Westerners and Asians an opportunity to learn from each other and to contribute that which is their best to each other. Westerners in Singapore may well learn how to impose some basic humanistic group-centred Asian values onto a foundation of an oftentimes cold and impersonal scientific ego-centred value system. Both sides gain, nothing is lost.

Chapter Eight

SURVIVAL IN SINGAPORE: A GUIDE FOR EXPATS

When individuals decide to live the expat style of life they face the prospect of clashing with a double-edged sword. They are not only exposed to the shock of living and working in a foreign culture, but they are also exposed to the shock of living in an expat culture.

Expats do not live the normal, everyday style of life that is to be found in most countries of the world. They move from one place to another; they have no real place to call home; they are forever saying 'hello' and 'good-bye' to loved ones; they have to adjust to leaving old and new-found friends behind; and they have to cope with making new friends all over again. For them, nothing is permanent; they are like the wind, blowing through people's lives, with never a place to settle. They take their children with them, until the children reach an age when they must return home, and then they go on without them!

These modern-day nomads help to bridge the gaps between the cultures of the world; they bring science and technology to developing countries; they hold the potential key to international peace and understanding; they create business for their compatriots and companies at home, and thereby create jobs for them too. They also teach, train, organize, and guide foreign nationals to achieve economic independence. In the end, they leave a highly industrialized and modernized core of local technicians and industrialists in their wake – then they move on.

The presence of expats in a foreign culture however, does not automatically lead to the fulfillment of potentials. Indeed, it can have an opposite effect. Culture-shock problems can delay, block, or prevent the promise and the potential of the cross-cultural venture. The expat of the future will be the one who is culturally enlightened and trained to be culturally ambidextrous.

A LOOK AT THE PROS AND CONS OF EXPAT LIFE

Before deciding to live the life of an expat, the family should consider carefully the problems/pains (cons) and benefits/pleasures (pros) which are reported by expats living in Singapore. Each member of the family should be aware of the pleasure and the pain which accompany the life-style of the expat; it is easier to do this before leaving home!

An honest account (neither of the 'glad hand' type; nor of the 'Ain't it awful' type) of the pros and cons of the emotional, physical, and cultural aspects of life in Singapore does much to help expats make an intelligent choice. Without looking carefully at the pros and the cons, people are not free to make an accurate assessment of whether or not they are prepared to adjust to the changes which are to be encountered. If after having reviewed both sides carefully, the potential expats do not feel they can go on with the assignment, then they should be allowed to bow out gracefully without penalty.

Some expats report: 'The company was very unprepared in assisting us to understand the situation; there are so many differences' and 'The company could have done much to help our adjustment by having a vigorous programme to prepare us for the changes in culture and behaviour.' One expat perhaps even goes a bit too far: 'Anyone coming to Singapore should be required to take a six-month orientation course and read ten books on Singapore, also a personality profile is important...and they should get as much information as possible about the good points and the bad points of living in Singapore; and they should be saturated with proper cultural information on proper behaviour and differences in the culture, especially the differences in the business structure.' (This advice is actually very good!)

In a recent survey of over a dozen American corporations who send expats overseas, it was seen that only 25% of the corporations tried to give an accurate account of the pros and cons to potential expats. Contrary to this, it was seen that 95% of 22 expats living and working in Asia said that it was absolutely necessary.

To assist you in decision making, we asked expats living and working in Singapore about the pros and cons. In 1978 we asked 66 American expats (44 women and 22 men). Today, in 1992, we asked the same questions to a new group of expats. We asked 14 American businessmen; 13 expats from England, Ireland, Scotland, and Canada (10 were in international business and 3 were professors at NUS National University of Singapore); 25 expats from Asia:13 from the People's Republic of China (scholars at the NUS) and 15 from Malaysia, Thailand, Philippines, India, Burma, and Brunei.

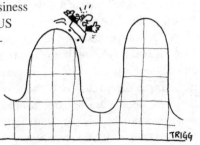

WHAT ARE SOME OF THE PROBLEMS THAT EXPATS ENCOUNTER WHILE LIVING OVERSEAS?

1. *The first problems are emotional* Frustration on a daily basis is high on the list of occupational culture shock emotional problems. The following quote from a suffering expat explains the pain of frustration: 'I have found that the feelings of frustration build up over a period of time (six months for me) until the need to leave is overwhelming. However, actually discussing leaving shows us that we are better off here, so we start again at the bottom of the frustration hill once more.'

   Loneliness, anxiety, anger, depression, disorientation, and even disgust and ethnocentrism are normal sufferings experienced by most expats. The disappointments in cross-cultural communication and the lack of cross-cultural understanding lead to many of the following problems. They are a part of the pain which is to be expected when one is uprooted and transplanted into a strange and alien society. We notice that there have been some changes since 1978. Frustration, anxiety and depression seem to be more prevalent in 1992 than they were in 1978. Loneliness seems to have decreased. Westerners suffer from more frustration, but Asians suffer from more anxiety!

	1978	1992	
	Westerners	Westerners	Asians
Frustration	76%	85%	80%
Loneliness/homesickness	81%	71%	76%
Anxiety	58%	71%	92%
Anger/hostility	71%	61%	
Depression	56%	66%	69%
Unease/disorientation	66%	65%	
Disgust/disapproval	66%	50%	
Ethnocentrism	52%	46%	

On the other hand, expats try to overcome these emotional problems by trying to be tolerant and understanding of the differences in the cultures; they try to learn more about the culture; and they try to accept the culture for what it is. Many come into the culture riding high on the wings of elation and euphoria.

	1992	
	Westerners	Asians
Tolerance and understanding	90%	73%
Try to learn the culture	76%	84%
Acceptance	76%	53%
Elation/ Euphoria	57%	39%

So many of the problems are directly related to culture shock, yet in the 1992 survey we found that only 23% of expats and spouses received some form of cultural orientation, and of these, several mentioned that the 'Culture Shock' book was the only training they were given. On the other hand, 42% received some type of physical orientation, which does not help with cultural adaptation, nor does it help to relieve the strain of culture shock. The international corporations have a responsibility to offer more help in the way of training and orientation to their expats in order to relieve the problems inherent in crossing cultures.

2. *Other common stress-related problems*
   • Drinking – Expats often consume large amounts of alcohol as part of their leisure-time activities. Excessive drinking can be a problem for men, women and teenagers because of stress, and because of the difficulty of adjusting to the role of the 'stranger' in a new society.

   Hard work, long hours away from home, the frustrations and disappointments inherent in cross-cultural operations, and the requirements for mutual entertaining make alcohol an occupational hazard for expats.

WHEN YOU CAN'T PUT THE CAN TO YOUR LIPS, YOU'VE HAD ENOUGH.

TRIGG.

- Marital problems – Such problems have a tendency to multiply because of the stress of an unfamiliar and non-supportive culture. The maladjusted family in the homeland has many more escape routes in which to accommodate its needs. Antagonistic elements, vaguely recognized at home, can become accentuated abroad. Extra-marital affairs can multiply when the lonely spouse is left alone for long periods of time while the partner spends considerable amount of time on the road. (32% of the 1992 expats said that the husband spends less time with the family since living the expat life.)

3. **Problems which have to do with the expat life** While all members of the family have their own specific problems, falling victim to culture shock and the separation from family and friends are problems which are common to all members.

a. Adjusting to the physical and cultural difference – 100% of expats suffer from some degree of culture shock: either mild, medium, or severe. Most of the problems are in the cultural areas, but the physical areas can be a 'shock' especially at first.

b. Some physical shocks some expats complain of:
    - The same weather 365 days a year – hot and humid.
    - Too many ants, bugs, cockroaches, mosquitos, and other insects. Ants in the sugar and weevils in the flour every day.

- Mildew in the closets and on all the leather bags, shoes, etc.
- Potato chips, nuts and snacks are wilted within 20 minutes of setting them out unless you live with the air-conditioner on.
- The squat-on-the-floor toilets are dirty. (This will soon end because there is a big fine for not flushing; see section on 'Laws' and they now have many 'automatic flushing devices' in public toilets!)

- The shock of seeing live animals killed for food; i.e., chickens, fish, etc., in local markets.

c. Cultural problems – The biggest problem is that although culture shock problems are preventable or cureable, they are often ignored by the corporations who send their expats into the field.

d. Separation from family and friends – This is the most frequent problem mentioned by expats. (93% of the 1992 expats said that they missed being away from family and friends.) This is an increase from 74% in 1978. One expat spoke for the others: 'The most serious disadvantage of the expat life is the separation from dear ones, especially family when they are in trouble or have any illness 12,000 miles away.'

4. ***Problems of the primary wage earner*** (Usually, but not always, men) As with their compatriots at home, the primary wage earner's problems revolve around business, spouse, and children. Primary-wage-earner expats report few problems in living the expat life. They say that they have challenging experiences; a built-in family of business and professional associates; and increased job satisfaction.

a. Problems with the business culture – Their problems are those of culture. The biggest problems reported are: poor cross-cultural communication and culturally inappropriate treatment of host nationals. In addition expats complain of not understanding the culture, its values, its work attitudes, its business etiquette, and its business structure. One expat explains: 'Our biggest difficulty is in believing that Asians think as Westerners do.' They also report distress in not being able to cross the cultural curtain. Some expats try very hard, and they experience pain and suffering because they know that they are always a stranger in a strange land, and they know that they are not always accepted.

b. Loneliness – One expat summed up the feeling of loneliness: 'There is not much chance to make close friends here. We are on a two-year contract, and, as everyone knows, we'll be leaving soon.'

c. Personal problems (9%).

d. Being away from the latest changes at home – Expats complain of losing touch with their own culture and of being 'out of the loop' of the corporate headquarters at home.

e. Mildew – One expat wag sums up the big problem many expats have in Singapore: 'Mildew!'

5. *Problems of spouses* (Usually, but not always, women)

a. Inability to adapt and adjust to the host culture – Most of the problems for the primary wage earner is the inability of the spouse to settle in. When an expat wishes to leave the assignment before the tour of duty is up, it is usually because of pressure from the spouse and children. The overseas spouse plays a much more crucial role in the success or failure of the expat mission than she/he does at home. A spouse who cannot adjust is disruptive to the company; harmful to the career; complains long, loud, and bitterly; and exerts a negative influence on other expats.

When the spouse cannot adjust, family problems spill over into business. Robert Kohls, one of the leading experts in the inter-cultural field, reports that in four out of five early returns, the decision to go back was made by the spouse, not the employee.

This was because of failure to adjust and adapt to the host culture. Research also shows that spouses experience more culture shock and related problems than employees do, and therefore they have a definite need for better selection, training and orientation, but they rarely get the help they need.

b. Expat life-style changes – The life-style of the expat changes dramatically in a foreign culture. The expat family often finds itself living in the upper or middle-upper classes of the society, rather than in the comfortable middle class of the homeland. This can cause discomfort to egalitarian Westerners who find themselves dealing with servants and household help. Thirty-four percent of the 1992 expats complained of problems with servants and the household.

c. No separation of home and work life – The spouse is involved in a whirl of entertaining, hostessing, and socializing. While some spouses enjoy this, others find it excruciatingly painful. Forty-eight percent of the 1992 expats complained of problems with the social life of the expat life-style.

d. The head spouse (Usually a wife) – In the corporation social circle, the spouse enjoys the same position and social standing as that of her husband. For instance, as the chief manager is head of the employees, so the chief manager's wife is the head of the spouses. If she has negative views of the foreign nationals, she can adversely affect the entire corporation, and all of the other spouses, through her leadership and position as the chief wife. If she has been well-oriented and well-trained however, and if she has a positive and tolerant view of the foreign nationals, she can do much to help the corporation succeed in the overseas assignment.

e. Life in the fish bowl – Unlike life in the home country where there is strict separation between the work-place and the home, life in the expat community is just the opposite; it is a life in a gold-fish bowl. The behaviour of the spouse and the children are no longer just a matter of family concern. The family's behaviour is now open to public and corporate scrutiny; it reflects on the employee, the company, and the country. This often causes problems for privacy-loving Westerners.

f. Expat employee travels too much – Fifty-three percent of the 1992 expats said that their husbands travel too much and that the family spends less time together. Some husbands spend up to 60% of their time out of town. Many of the husbands in the off-shore drilling business are home only one or two weeks out of the month. The spouse is left to cope alone.

g. Loss of spouse's identity – If the primary wage earner experiences a sense of mission or accomplishment, the spouse usually experiences a loss of identity. Many spouses are well-educated and highly-trained, but they may not be able to work in Singapore. One expat says: 'I can't work here, I miss my financial independence.' Another says: 'I only need a few more credits to finish my degree, but its not possible to finish my schooling here.' Another says: 'I have a servant and a childminder now – but no job, so what am I to do?' Women have more freedom and more household help, but maids, cooks, drivers, and gardeners may take over many of the traditional duties of the pre-expat life. A serious existential problem exists in trying to find a purposeful and meaningful life.

It is important to note that there have been changes in this problem since 1978. Today it is possible for many expat spouses to work in Singapore. If you have the qualifications needed here, a firm can get you an employment pass. Nurses and teachers and professionals are in demand. Also the British Council offers courses in teaching English as a Foreign Language.

6. **Problems of younger children** Children suffer most when the family is not emotionally healthy and stable. A loving and supportive family is the most important factor for a happy adjustment in a foreign culture. Children's problems often reflect the presence or absence of parental problems.

Parents have said that some of the most distressing problems for them are those concerning their children. They complain about education being too expensive; about not having opportunities for their children to attend higher education in Singapore; about rearing spoiled children who are given so much and who are so privileged, and who are indulged by servants; they also worry that their children are losing touch with their own country and culture; and some are very concerned about strangers who make such a fuss over their beautiful children, and who want to touch their hair and to pat their cheeks – they fear that this will make their children conceited and that they will come to expect adulation.

Parents worry about their children becoming too insular, i.e., mixing only with other expat children They don't have much opportunity to make friends with local children, so they lose the opportunity to expand their cultural world.

7. *Problems of teenagers* Teenagers have special problems which are both similar and dissimilar to their compatriots at home. Some of the problems they mention in order of frequency are:

a. Missing old friends and making new ones – As with adults, this is one of the most difficult problems with which to cope. Learning to love and then leaving the loved one causes grief. Some teenagers try to avoid this pain by refusing to make close attachments. One young man plaintively explained: 'I really like Mary, but it is no use asking her out and starting something. I know that I'll be going home to college this summer, and she will be going on to a new culture.'

b. Adjusting to a new culture – Culture shock affects teenagers too. There are new habits to learn, new customs, new people, and new ways of thinking and doing which they must face up to if they are to make the most of their cultural experience. This problem is compounded by the lack of cultural information available to them which prevents or cures culture shock (i.e. information on lost cues to behaviours and beliefs). Many solve this problem by avoiding friendships and contact with host nationals. Few teenagers report having more than two local friends. It is the same with their parents.

c. Ethnocentrism – As a result of such little contact with locals, ethnocentrism is a common problem among expat teenagers. From surveys conducted with teenagers in expat schools, it was seen that only about 29% of teenagers who have never been exposed to cross-cultural classes and/or cross-cultural friendships expressed tolerant attitudes to Chinese, Indian, and Malay people. By 'tolerant', we mean a positive regard for human beings, regardless of race, ethnicity, creed, colour, sex, or age. On the other hand, about 90% of teenagers who had been exposed to cross-cultural education and cross-cultural friendships exhibited tolerant attitudes. A dramatic example for all of us!

d. School problems – The fourth problem mentioned is the problem of coping with a new school. It is not easy being a new kid in a new school in a new country in a new culture, especially when this pattern repeats itself every two years. School work suffers as a young expat is taken out of one school system and transplanted into another. A teenager may find that he has to unlearn the math system he learned in the last country, while struggling to learn a new system in the new country.

Some teenagers report that the challenge of a new school helps them to do better because they try harder. One teen explained: 'When you come into a new school, you try harder because you don't want the others to think that you are dumb! No one knows you; you have a new and fresh start; you don't have to live down any poor reputation that you might have had before.'

e. Losing touch with home – Many teens felt that losing touch with their own culture, music, food, activities, etc., was a problem for them; however, one teenager stated that returning home was indeed a bigger shock than when she first came to Singapore. 'There's so much violence and degrading sex on T.V. back home!

– I was shocked at the number of people maimed and killed on only one night's viewing – and I had forgotten that it is not safe to walk about at night at home.'

f. Problems with parents – Only 2% felt that problems with parents were worse than they were before the expat experience. Four percent said that they were not close to begin with; and 94% said that their relationship was just as good, and even better, than it was at home. They are philosophical about expat family life. Fifty-four percent said that if they had more serious adjustment problems than their parents, it was only because they had typical 'teenager' problems to cope with on top of the expat life. They actually felt that it was more difficult for parents to live the expat life because: 'Kids are used to new things; they don't know anything different. Parents are older and more set in their ways; leaving home for them is a bigger thing because they are not used to change.' One teen thought that even though fathers were often away from home, it gave the teenagers a chance to help out more. 'My father travels a lot and it's hard on my mom, but I can change all the fuses in the house and I can stop the washing machine from leaking. I also took the "tarantula" out of my mom's closet.'

g. Not having part-time work – Teenagers and their parents cannot work in Singapore without work permits. (29% of teens said that they were definitely unhappy about not having a part-time or weekend job.) One teenager put it this way: 'At home, I had a week-end job and I was able to pay my own way on dates. It's sort of degrading to have to ask your parents for a hand-out every week. It's like going back in time a few steps.'

There have been some changes in the above since 1978. Today some secondary schools now try to organize vacation work for students in hotels or fast food restaurants. Also today, as in 1978, some of the expat shipping companies even put young aspiring able-bodied seamen to work on the tankers and ships which cruise the South China Sea during summer holidays. In addition, many young expats do modelling for magazines and T.V. or movie work for advertising agencies in Singapore.

h. Drugs – There are severe penalties for drug use and there is a death penalty for drug dealers. Teenagers who use drugs take their lives in their hands. They risk disgracing the whole family, the corporation, and the expat community. They are subject to a jail term and/or deportation. Parents are warned to be vigilant in preventing their children from coming into contact with any drugs at all. One teenager expressed the feeling about drugs: 'You'd have to be a fool to use drugs here!'

i. Alcohol – The legal age for drinking here is 18 years, but the problem is that Western teens often look like they are 18 when they are in fact much younger. Drinking can be a serious problem for young expats here, as it is for their elders. Caution is advised.

WHAT ARE SOME OF THE PLEASURES AND BENEFITS OF THE EXPAT LIFE?

There are many pleasures and benefits to living the expat life, especially in Singapore. Some of them follow:

1. *The joys of Singapore* There are many joys of living in Singapore! Let's look at how expats describe them. Some of the quotes come from expat teens:
   - 'The schools are excellent!'
   - 'There is an endless summer in Singapore.'
   - 'Water sports are available and inexpensive all year round.'

- 'In just a few hours one can travel to mysterious and exotic cultures.'
- 'You can take a girl out for a date to a food stall for satay and a cold beer, and it can be really cheap.'
- 'The city is beautiful; it's full of flowers and trees.'
- 'The service at the good restaurants is great: they give you the red-carpet treatment and it really impresses your girl.'
- 'The night life is good; you can get to anywhere in town and then walk home at night; you don't have to worry about getting mugged either!'
- 'There's a lot to do here; you can get a group together and hire a boat to take you out to an island for the day.'
- 'The food in Singapore is the best!'

2. ***The expat family is closer*** One of the most pleasant benefits for expat families is the close relationship which develops between parents and children. In a study by Ruth Hill Useem, she reports that an overwhelming majority of Third Culture Kids like, respect and feel emotionally attached to their parents. (She calls expat children TCKs because they belong to a 'new' culture – neither a home nor a host culture, but a cosmopolitan culture which belongs to the world.) Useem reports about 90% of kids feel close to their parents, our survey shows that 94% of the kids reported a similar closeness! Why should this be? The following are some reasons:

a. High mobility of the family – The high mobility of third-culture families, who often move every two or three years, seems to have the effect of bringing individual family members closer together. They share the experience of moving into unfamiliar territory and they offer each other mutual support in the face of change and strangeness. Parents are often the only people with whom the children have a continuing relationship as they move from one place to another.

b. Families spend more time together – While only 21% of the 1992 expats say that they spend more time together as a family than they do in their home-country, they say that their time together is not taken up with common and everyday activities. They take more holidays to exotic places together and they plan more activities as a family.

c. Mothers are home managers rather than housewives – Since servants help with the household chores, mothers can spend more creative time with the children. One mother says: 'It's amazing how pleasant children can be when one is not frantically trying to get supper on, answer the phone, and nag the children to pick up their clothes.'

d. Expat family members support each other – Another bonus is that expats are closer as a family. Social scientists say that members of a family in a new and strange situation are pulled closer together. The foreign experience heightens family cohesiveness. The family pulls together and relies on each other to get through the culture shock experience; they give each other mutual support and emotional sustenance. However, in our survey, only 50% said that they are closer now than at home. This is higher than the 39% figure we had in 1978, but it is still low.

Perhaps this low figure in Singapore is a reflection of the highly-developed and organized expat communities which exist here. The expat family is not really a stranger in a strange land, it comes into a highly structured 'culture bubble' i.e., the American Club, the Tanglin Club, the Swiss Club, etc. It may be that the family in Singapore relies more on the expat community than it does on family members.

3. *Children have benefits too!*

a. High motivation to continue the expat life – Children are highly motivated to continue in the international footsteps of their parents. (75% of teens reported that they hope to travel in their life's work as expats, rather than to stay put in their home country.)

b. Expansion of the cultural consciousness of the children – Many expats report that the expat experience gives their children a chance in a lifetime to expand their minds and to learn about other cultures. Many of the expat schools try to help teenagers to expand their cultural consciousness by providing field trips into the heart of the cultures of Southeast Asia. The young people live with host national families in traditional areas where they learn to harvest padi, to tap rubber and to be a polite person in the culture. These are incredible cultural experiences which instill cultural empathy and cultural compassion in the hearts and minds of the young expats.

c. Expat teens say they have a better social life – The social life of teenagers here depends upon their acceptance into the established system. Some teens report that it is difficult to penetrate the school cliques which have been formed before their arrival. On the other hand, teens say that their social life is better than in the home country because of the fierce support group which develops. 'We rely on each other more for mutual support.' Sixty-two percent felt closer to their friends here than to their friends at home.

d. Expat teens are flexible and positive – On the whole, teenagers are flexible and positive about the experience of expat life. They see the better parts! One teenager says: 'At home, everybody is going to football games, but we've learned to survive in the jungle, climb Mt. Kinabalu, and how to tap rubber. I can speak Malay, and I can bargain in shops better than many locals.' Another teen reports: 'I travelled all through India, Nepal, France, Germany and England with two other friends on our way back home for home leave last year. We had to take care of our own passports, arrange flights, and handle all the details. Not many kids back home can do all that.' One last word from a teenager which sums up the teen experience: 'Living the way we do doesn't have too many problems really; we learn to build up a tolerance for differences!'

4. ***Development of a cosmopolitan world view*** The teenagers' mind-broadening experiences of living as expats spill over into the adult

community. The majority of expats reported a development of tolerance and open-mindedness. Successful adjustment to living in a foreign culture, the learning of new languages; the exposure to other people's views, values and life-styles contribute to a cosmopolitan 'world-view' which gives both parents and children a deeper understanding of the more important things in life. In 1978 the percentage of expats reporting an increase in the cosmopolitan world view was 70%. In 1992, that number has increased to 83%. Some of their quotes follow:

- 'You get to know other people from different cultures, and learn from them.'
- 'You learn to grow in flexibility, creativity, and tolerance from your experiences with Singaporeans.'
- 'I have discovered in the last year that the comfortable and "superior" American can learn to be humble – and to be in last place – and this has helped me to be in tune with my inner self, rather than with the material possessions I have acquired.'

5. *The opportunity to travel* Expats have an opportunity to see new and exciting places, to experience new things and to live a life of travel and adventure. An expat wife says: 'There are the financial benefits, of course, but I think, more important, you get a chance to see and live as other people do. Seeing the world first-hand is a wonderful thing!' An expat husband says: 'Living the expat life offers a better perspective of all cultural values and behaviour. I only wish I had done this twenty years ago.' Seventy percent of women and 89% of the men said that travel, adventure, and excitement were some of the greatest pleasures of expat life.

6. *Professional benefits* There are many professional benefits for the expat employee. Expats report that there is greater job status, more prestige, more job satisfaction, more opportunity for creative work, more job autonomy, and more responsibility. Expats in 1978 and in 1992 said that they chose to live and work in Singapore because of:

	1978	1992		
	Americans	Americans	Europeans	Asians
Professional benefits/career	73%	57%	69%	60%
Greater financial rewards	72%	28%	23%	53%
Desire to escape uncongenial surroundings at home	0%	0%	38%	19%

Most Americans (57%) and Europeans (69%) come for greater professional benefits; most Asians (53%) come for greater financial rewards; and the most expats who desire to escape uncongenial surroundings at home are Europeans (38%)!

Other reasons for coming to Singapore in order of frequency:

- A love of travel;
- A sense of vocation;
- A sense of mission. Many expats mentioned a sense of mission and fulfillment in their work. 'I had a sincere desire to help others to develop, that is why I came here';
- A wife's identification with her husband's career;
- A love of constant variety. Many expats mentioned this: 'You get out of a rut and you avoid humdrum', 'You have the opportunity to make a new start', 'You can get rid of old habits and make new ones, eating habits for example' , 'You have a richer, fuller and more exciting life – there's something new every day!'
- Many expats also speak of the joy of 'Big Frogism' as being an important factor in being happy overseas. One expat explains the joy of being a big frog in a small pond: 'I have to know every detail of the operation. At home there would be four or five men in the same office doing the same thing that I am doing here. I would not have the control that I have here. There is so much satisfaction in being in charge of everything. You can do something and know that you did it.'

7. *Tangible benefits* Expats say that they have tangible rewards too:

| | 1978 | 1992 | | |
	Americans	Americans	Europeans	Asians
A better house	28%	14%	50%	53%
Make more money	72%	43%	66%	69%
More household help	79%	71%	66%	17%
More social life	49%	71%	15%	30%

Only 14% of American expats have a better house in Singapore than they do at home. Also, we see a big change in motivations from 1978 to 1992 in American expats. Fewer Americans are coming to Singapore to make more money (from 72% in 1978 to 43% in 1992); and as a result, the motivation of greater financial rewards is now very small; reduced from 72% to 28%! It appears that the Americans are the most social group of expats (71% have more social life in Singapore). Europeans are the least social, only 15% have more social life in Singapore than they do at home.

TIPS FOR EXPATS: HOW TO THRIVE, NOT JUST SURVIVE IN SINGAPORE

THE EXPAT LIFE – IS IT FOR ME AND MY FAMILY?

Some comments on choosing the expat life:
1. Carefully review the pros and cons with the entire family; have a family discussion about them.
2. Children should be consulted on their feelings about making the move to an alien society. Encourage them by letting them know that expat teenagers report an easier adjustment than parents!
3. Do not make the move unless the whole family agrees wholeheartedly. It is particularly important that the spouse be 100%

behind the move. Because of the crucial role of the spouse, the success or failure of the venture depends upon a willing participant.

4. If both partners have a 'travel bug' type of personality, then the chances of success are good! Travel bugs can be identified by their love of travel for the sake of fun and adventure. One travel bug spouse says: 'I just like this life; I like the travel, it's fun; I would choose to travel even if my husband could not.'

5. The worst reason for becoming an expat is because of a desire to escape unhappy conditions at home. They somehow always seem to follow!

6. A move to a foreign country will not ordinarily patch up a shaky marriage; in fact it ordinarily adds more strain to a weak marriage.

TIPS TO CONSIDER BEFORE DECIDING TO RELOCATE:

1. The job design of the overseas position and the length of stay; its political and safety factors.

2. Health care packages; effects of climate on health problems such as childhood asthma. Getting back into the health care/pension systems on your return.

3. Selling or renting your house. Many expats are shocked to find that they can no longer afford the same type of house that they sold prior to moving overseas. Being out of their home country for several years keeps them out of touch with the spiralling cost of housing.

4. Taxes: a knowledge of both your tax status at home and tax regulations in Singapore is essential. In Singapore, taxes are paid in a lump sum at the end of the year and many expats who are not used to this system run into difficulties.

5. Allowances: for removal expenses; settling in costs; rent allowance; getting a car.

6. Travel and home leave arrangements.

7. Penalties if the contract is broken; legal advice.
8. Provisions for cultural training/orientation/language. If there are no allowances for these necessities, then perhaps they could be requested as a condition of employment.
9. The possibility of work for the spouse.
10. Schooling for the children. Education allowance for children and allowances for special needs such as dyslexia or a mental or physical handicap. All of these can affect your tax status in Singapore.

Living in Singapore, distributed by the American Association of Singapore can answer many of these questions for potential expats. This book can be obtained from the American Association of Singapore, c/o The American Club, 21 Scotts Road, Singapore 0922.

TIPS ON HOW TO BE A GOOD COSMOPOLITAN

The most successful stranger in a strange land is, of course, the Cosmopolitan! The Cosmopolitan has many wonderful personality traits, such as: optimism, humour, cultural empathy, tolerance, positive outlook, curiosity, interest, kindliness, flexibility, patience, trust, integrity, self control, love of travel and adventure, taste for exotic foods, ability to adapt, sensitivity, wisdom, and compassion. We also know that Cosmopolitans meet and mix equally with the host people; that they like them and develop close equal-status friendships with them; that (while they may not always agree with their habits and customs) they respect and appreciate their culture.

We know quite a bit about Cosmopolitans; and we know that everyone reading this book is probably one, or striving to be one. For those striving, how does one consciously go about trying to become one? I would like to thank my old friend Bob Wakefield, a trained counsellor from the Singapore Baptist Mission, and DeVere Pentony, Professor of International Relations at San Francisco State University, for many of the following suggestions.

1. Be aware that there is a problem! This is the first step.

2. Develop a plan to overcome the problem, to cope with it, or else try to live with it. By developing a plan which includes steps 3, 4 and 5 below, you can take the matter into your own hands. There are three stages in this: The first is when you do something to help yourself. The next is when you then do something to help your family, and the third is when you do something to help others who are suffering from the same problems.

3. Experience the joy of Singapore. Strangers in a strange land can add to the positive experience by thinking of it as a wonderful opportunity to discover and learn new ways of living, thinking, feeling, and doing. New foods, new sights, new technologies, and new adventures help to expand your cultural awareness and help you to feel comfortable and secure in your new environment. Get out and meet the local people. Develop a spirit of adventure; discover new foods, see the attraction in living in a unique culture. Share any new experiences and discoveries in the 'cultural-discovery hour'.

4. Have a cultural-discovery hour once a week. Invite family and friends. Gather information about the new culture. Share the information, and have others share what they have learned. Involve the children too. This is the time to become a cultural detective. Begin to look for lost cultural cues. Look for dos and don'ts and whys and hows. Look for differences in beliefs and behaviours, and importantly, look for the logic and motivation behind the differences. For instance, to say that Chinese rarely say 'no' can lead people to wrongly think that Chinese are liars. But if you discover the logic behind this courtesy, and if you learn how to tell the difference between a 'yes' that means 'no' and a 'yes' that means 'yes', then you will have come a long way in understanding the Chinese way. The more you can interpret, the more you will understand and appreciate the people.

   - Start a cultural scrap book wherein all members of the group can paste photos, drawings, and original stories about the places they have seen and the adventures they have had. Do not limit these activities to 'tourist attractions'. It is a good idea, for instance, to compare and contrast the shops and main street of a city or town you have visited, with the shops and main streets of your own home town. The children are particularly good about doing this, and they can make a real contribution.

- Make arrangements to visit a factory, a court room, a police station, a market, a busy office, a primary school, a temple, or some other area of special interest. Keep a diary of how it is the same or different from those of your own home town. Add the information to the family scrap book.

- Ask Singaporean friends to explain and interpret plays, drama, poetry, wayangs, sports, music, art work, history, handicrafts, etc. Invite them to join you for some of your cultural-discovery hours. Become a cultural learner, and ask your Singaporean friends to become cultural teachers.

- During the hour, bring out all the feelings you have experienced about the host culture. Draw out and focus energy on the good feeling and the positive aspects.

5. Have a 'worry' hour once a week to balance out the 'cultural-discovery' hour. Talk about the problems and other things which cause you nervousness or distress. Talk about those things which you don't understand. The object is to find constructive ways to understand the problems, solve them, and to cope with them. Do not let the 'worry' hour degenerate into a gossip, gripe or grouse session. Negative talk is destructive. Make your talk constructive.

TIPS ON WHERE TO GET HELP

If your average bout of culture-shock depression seems to be unusually severe or long lasting, or if you find it difficult to cope with the problems and the differences in the culture, you can get help from:

- SACAC The Singapore American Community Action Council

has trained personnel and counselling services available. Any request for assistance will be responded to. They deal mostly with teenagers, parents and individuals. (Phone: 733- 9322)

- Samaritans of Singapore has trained volunteers to answer a 24-hour answering service. They can put you on to where help is available for problems of alcoholism, despair, suicide, etc. (Phone: 221-4444)

TIPS FOR EXPAT PARENTS

1. Give your children close, warm and loving support.
2. Involve them in the decision to move to Singapore. Assign them the responsibility of finding out about the new country. Have them write to embassies, travel agencies, and tourist boards to gather the information. Have the children share their information with the family and praise them for contributing to the family's understanding.
3. Take an active part in the children's new school. They regularly ask for reading mothers or library help. Scout or guide leaders are always needed. The Parent Teacher Associations are very active. Use the opportunity to encourage more cross-cultural classes.
4. Help your children to make friends inside and outside the expat community. Keep an open house where their friends are assured of hospitality and a warm welcome.
5. Encourage out-of-school activities such as swimming clubs, judo, water skiing where they will meet and mix with children from Singapore cultures.
6. Make sure that the behaviours of your children reflect the ethics and values of the family, the school, and the country. Teach them to respect the local culture, and to be considerate and respectful in their dealings with the local people.

TIPS FOR PRIMARY EXPAT EMPLOYEE

1. Give your spouse more emotional support than ever before.

2. Do not take for granted the efforts she/he has made to ease the family into the new environment. Appreciate, praise, and encourage all efforts made to help the family settle in. Be aware of the importance of the spouse in the overseas assignment, and realize the critical role she/he plays in the success of the mission.

3. Encourage family participation in learning about the new culture and its people. Assume the head role in the Cultural Discovery Hour and in the Cultural Worry Hour. Set the standards as the head of the household in showing respect and consideration for the people of the host society.

TIPS FOR EXPAT SPOUSES

1. Be creative in finding ways to maintain your sense of dignity. Keep busy and find ways to experience the best parts of Singapore. Do what you can to help others. Do not indulge in gossip, gripe and grouse sessions, and do not condone them; they are poison. Develop a positive and infectious attitude that will influence your family and friends in the most uplifting manner.

2. Think of your stay in Singapore as a college education without the exams. Be a cultural learner!

3. Remind yourself of Monday mornings at home in the depths of winter. Think about your friends at work watching the clock. Then see yourself viewing a red and orange sunset, eating chilli crabs at the West Coast Highway, and attending a Malay friend's wonderful wedding ceremony.

4. Take stock of your personal life. Read and improve yourself as a person. Intensify your faith and discover the faiths of other human beings. Discover new ways of praying and relating to God.

5. Learn to like and accept yourself. Be generous about your short-comings. When you come to like and accept yourself, you will find that you like and accept other peoples and their customs. Make a point of forgiving anyone who has hurt you, and ask forgiveness of anyone you have hurt. This exercise is very good

for the soul; it opens the doors and windows of your spirit and lets the light shine through.

6. Do try to find work. Many spouses who have arrived in Singapore on dependant's passes are now able to practise their professions. If a firm can use your services, it can get an employment pass for you. Teachers and nurses are in short supply here, and opticians, accountants, lab technicians, pharmacists and most other professional people can find work here.

7. The volunteer organizations need help (the school for the blind and the Samaritans, for instance) and the expat schools need help.

8. Do not restrict your relationships to expats. Make friends with locals. Go where they go. Take a cooking class, or a language class or join the Kennel club. Offer to tutor in English for lessons in a local language.

TIPS FROM EXPERT EXPATS

Some comments from experienced expats living in Singapore.

- 'Take things easy to begin with. Avoid making instant judgements.'
- 'Just remember that Singapore is not home – but it is more like home than than anywhere overseas that we have been before.'
- 'Realize that this is not your own home…accept it …adapt.'
- 'Get acquainted with local people as soon as possible.'
- 'Beware of other expats who sound prejudiced and sour.'
- 'Do not keep comparing Singapore with your home country.'
- 'Keep your eyes open and your mouth shut!'
- 'Stay cool – be flexible – be curious.'
- 'Don't judge, criticize, or be negative.'
- 'Don't stay too closely inside the expat culture or you won't be able to get out of it to make local friends.'
- 'Put aside learned patterns and judgments. Observe other cultures and study them through cross-cultural glasses. Associate yourself with upbeat expats who are positive thinkers.'

TIPS ON ADJUSTING TO THE PHYSICAL DIFFERENCES

Most expats learn how to build up a tolerance for physical differences very quickly. Here are a few tips for newcomers to Singapore:

1. Rest and take things easy in the first few weeks. Let your body acclimatize itself to the tropical conditions.
2. Pamper yourself in the beginning as you ease into your new environment, but don't make a habit of it. Just realize that you won't have all the energy that you would normally have in your old environment. It will take a little time to adjust to the physical changes.
3. Relax! Slow down! Walk slower. Look around you. Enjoy a lazier pace of life.
4. Some of the doctors at a missionary hospital in Singapore recommend an iron and yeast tablet as a daily supplement.
5. Try not to depend on air-conditioners too much. It is difficult to acclimatize the body to the tropical climate here if one is constantly moving in and out of artificially controlled environments. Fans are very helpful.
6. Make allowances for the climate by preparing meals early in the day when it is cooler and you are feeling fresher. Use one of the slow-cooking pots, or refrigerate or freeze the meal and reheat it in the evening.
7. Don't be alarmed by the number of *cicak* (little lizards) in your home. They eat the mosquitoes and other insects.

TIPS ON GOOD BOOKS

Etiquette and customs:
- *Malaysian Customs and Etiquette* byDatin Noor Aini Syed Amir, Times Editions, Singapore, 1990.

Religion:
- *The Great Religions by which Men Live* by Ross and Hills.
- *What The Great Religions Believe* by Joseph Gaer.

Festivals:
- *An Illustrated Cycle of Chinese Festivities in Malaysia and Singapore* by C. S. Wong, Jack Chia-MPH, Singapore, 1987.
- *Festivals of Malaya* edited by Joy Manson.

History:
- *Son of Singapore* by Tan Kok Seng
- *Sinister Twilight* by Noel Barber
- *King Rat* by James Clavell
- *Syonan – My Story* by M. Shinozaki
- *When Singapore Was Syonan-to* by N.I. Low.
- *The Fall of Singapore* by Timothy Hall: Mandarin Australia, Octopus, 1990.
- *Lee Kuan Yew's Singapore* by T.J.S. George, Andre Deutsch, London, 1977.
- *The Malay Dilemma* by Mahathir Bin Mohammed, Federal Publications, Kuala Lumpur, 1982.
- *History of Malaysia, Singapore and Brunei* by Mary Turnbull, Allen Unwin, 1989.

Wildlife and nature:
- *A Colour Guide to Dangerous Animals* by the Venom and Toxin Research Group, Singapore University Press, 1990.
- *The Birds of Singapore* by Christopher Hails, Times Editions,
- *A Colour Guide to Dangerous Plants* by Wee Yeow Chin and P. Gopalakrishna-kone, Singapore University Press, 1990.

Fiction: There are many books now available in Singapore written by Singaporeans.

Living conditions:
- *Living In Singapore*, American Association of Singapore
- *Insider's Guide to Malaysia and Singapore* by Sean Sheehan, Novo Editions, 1992.

TIPS ON SELECTING EXPAT AND SPOUSE

Most expats who fail in their overseas assignment do not fail because of lack of professional skill,but because of lack of ability to adjust and adapt to the alien culture; up to 80% of failures are due to poor personal adjustment of expat or spouse. What can be done to ensure that corporations choose the right person and what can be done to ensure a successful venture?

1. *Select the right employee for the job.* Things to look for include:
   - Excellent professional job skills.
   - Positive personality traits.
   - Stability of marriage and family.
   - Selection of a suitable spouse.

2. *Tips on selecting personality traits of employee and the spouse.* Careful screening for personality traits can reduce the failure rate from around 40% to 25%. Experts also agree that the selection factor should account for more than 50% of the decision to choose the employee.

PERSONALITY	CULTURAL ADAPTABILITY
Good sense of humour	Cultural empathy*
Tolerant personality**	Love of exotic foods
Patience	Learn foreign language
Positive/optimistic	Ability to adjust/adapt
Ability to build relationships	Sense of wanderlust
Trusting, friendly, kind	Political sensitivity
Non-judgmental	Previous expat experience
Sense of mission (not money)	Positive to change
Healthy physically/mentally	Love of incongruities
Courteous and diplomatic	Tolerance for ambiguity
High self-esteem (not egotist)	Flexible/not rigid
Self control	Competence as teacher
Good communication skills	Appreciation of customs
Lateral thinker	Learning from locals
Integrity, honourable, ethical	Joy and fun in the culture

*Cultural empathy: the skill to understand the inner logic and coherence of other ways of life, plus the restraint not to judge them as bad because they are different from your own ways.

**Tolerant personality: a positive regard for human beings, no matter their culture, religion, sex, ethnicity, age, etc.

3. *More tips on selecting the spouse*. The spouse plays a critical role in the success of the venture, we offer some more clues in determining a potential successful spouse:

a. Look at the motivation of the spouse. If it is altruistic, it is good. If it is grudgingly to follow the primary employee, or to make more money, or to escape unhappy conditions at home, then it is not good.

b. Look at the attitude. If it is positive and optimistic, it is good. Bad if it is negative, destructive, complaining, or demanding.

c. Look at the expectations. If they are realistic, i.e, not too far above what can be achieved, then it is good. For instance, if they wish to expand their horizons, both culturally and personally, then this is possible. If expectations are far removed from what is possible – for instance, to patch up a shaky marriage, to escape problems at home, etc., then it is not good. The more distance between their expectations and reality, the more potential for conflict there is.

d. Look at their relationship in the marriage and in the family. A family which is not stable at home is likely to become more unstable overseas. The marriage should be well grounded and healthy. There should be love and companionship between the two. In the overseas environment they must depend upon each other for mutual comfort and assistance.

e. Look at their sense of joy and fun in travel and cultural discovery. These are invaluable assets.

4. *Look for 'travel bugs'*. The most successful adapters (both primary employee and spouse) are those who derive the most pleasure from living in an alien culture.

• They love travel for itself.

- They love to eat the local food.
- They are curious and open-minded.
- They like themselves and all kinds of people.
- They rarely get sick; few headaches or minor pains.
- They read a great deal on a wide range of topics.
- They are cheerful and optimistic.
- They are fun-loving and funny.
- They jump at the chance for an international move.
- They are happy cosmopolitans.

AN ENLIGHTENED WORLD

International people carry the tools which make for economic development; they also carry the tools for international peace, friendship, and understanding. It is through international people that the world will be enlightened and come to see that all humans are one.

The author (left) working with one of her many Singaporean friends in close cooperation to help bridge the gap between East and West. Cross-cultural understanding is always possible if you put your heart and mind to it. Photo: Mats Ekstrand

CULTURAL QUIZ

Now that you have learned to understand many of the Singaporean ways, perhaps you would like to practise your new skills. What would you do in the following critical incidents?

1. *TO SHAKE OR NOT TO SHAKE – THAT IS THE QUESTION!*

You occasionally do some free-lance writing while you are in Singapore with your husband who is working for a large multi-national corporation. You are in a shop one day when you see a young Indian man come in; he is an old friend with whom you had worked together on a project some time before. He is smart, modern, and has been educated in the United States. You are delighted to see him; it has been a long time. You rush over to greet him. What do you do next?

A   You give him a Western style social greeting hug.
B   You offer your hand, and give him a good firm, solid handshake.
C   You nod and smile at him, but you do not touch him.
D   You let him make the first move, watching to see what he does.

ANSWERS

Response (A) You might see that your friend has stiffened and held out his arms to ward you off. You would feel embarrassed and offended, because not only has he rejected your friendly and innocent social greeting hug, but he has mistaken it for a romantic gesture as well. Even if your friend is westernized and modernized, (A) would not be a proper choice because respectable Singaporeans do not casually touch members of the opposite sex (however, a handshake is not impolite), and they especially do not hug and kiss across the sex line in public. If any of his friends saw a display of affection in public you could cause him deep embarrassment, and if his wife heard about it, you could cause her grief.

Response (B) You have made a good choice. Indians do not have any religious or cultural restrictions against shaking hands with members of the opposite sex. And it is proper for you to offer your hand first.

Response (C) Just nodding and smiling is not impolite. If your friend was a Malay, it would have been the the most proper and polite thing to do because they have restrictions against physical contact with people of the opposite sex.

Response (D) is not polite. It is not kind. You see your good friend. You wish to greet him. If you stand there staring at him, waiting for him to make the first move, you signal that you are being stand-offish and cold. Show your warm feelings; smile, and approach him, and shake his hand warmly.

2. *WHERE ARE YOU GOING? WHY DO YOU WANT TO KNOW?*

You and your two young children are walking down a road in a secluded part of Singapore. You see a kampung-type setting where

some Malays are taking some coconuts down from a tree with a long pole. You stop to watch. A Malay says: 'Where are you going?' What do you say?

A   'Why do you ask?'
B   'Nowhere of importance.'
C   'To the store for groceries, and then home.'
D   You say nothing; you just walk away.

ANSWERS

Response (A) while perhaps appropriate in a Western culture, is not good manners in a Malay culture; it assumes that they are being inordinately curious about your comings and goings.

Response (B) is the most polite answer. The greeting forms of a society are a reflection of what the culture feels is very important or what the culture is very concerned about. In the Malay culture, travel and adventure are admired. 'Where are you going?' is only a polite form, like the Western: 'How are you?' The only answer expected is 'For a stroll' or 'Nowhere of importance.'

Response (C) would not be appropriate. It would be like if you asked someone: 'How are you' and they then proceeded to tell you all about how they were, and about the operation on their knee, and the pain in their shoulder, and the trouble with their stomach.

Response (D) would be impolite and inappropriate. After all, you are the one who stopped to watch them take the coconuts down. To walk away without responding would be unkind and discourteous.

3. *DO YOU WANT SECOND HELPINGS – OR NOT!*

You invite the Chinese business colleagues from your husband's office for a meal at your home. It is Thanksgiving, and you have worked all day preparing a turkey dinner with all the trimmings. You know that most Chinese do not tolerate milk very well, so you do not serve cheese, milk, or ice cream. Everything is delicious. You've served the first round of food and it is time for seconds. What do you say/do to offer more food to the guests?

A You ask if the guest would like second helpings. And if the guest says 'No-no-no', you stop offering the food because in your culture it is impolite to press food on people once they say no.

B You keep pressing food on the guests. You keep asking if they will have some more.

C   You start filling up the dish again, even if the guest says, 'No-no-no'.

D   You feel hurt because you have worked so hard and they have refused second helpings. You think that perhaps they do not like the food, or that they are very rude. You never invite them again.

ANSWERS

Response (A) might disappoint your Chinese guest. Polite Chinese guests are supposed to refuse first to show that they are not greedy. Do not stop offering your guest food after only one refusal.

Response (B) is the appropriate thing to do. You keep your eye on their plate. As soon as it starts to look empty, you ask if they want more. When they really do *not* want more, their eyes look at you, their voice drops down, and their hands cover their plates.

Response (C) is also a polite response. As soon as you determine that they really do want more food, you serve them again. Remember that Chinese do not ordinarily like large hunks of white meat, they feel it is dry and tasteless. Offer small slices of the dark meat, with lots of gravy, they should find it delicious.

Response (D) Chinese love good food. If you stop offering them food after only asking them once if they would like a second helping, those not familiar with Western ways might think that you are very rude and stingy for not giving them enough food! Both sides will be hurt when both sides were only trying to be polite!

4. *'YES'– I MEAN 'NO'*

You are working on a project with the colleagues in your office. The team is designing a new logo for a client firm. You come up with a brilliant logo. You show it to the team and ask what they think of it. You see them all smile and nod. One friend says: 'Hmm, not bad.' Another one sucks in his breath through his teeth, and says 'It is pretty!' Another colleague says: 'Yes, but there may be a slight problem.' You fully expect that the slight problem can be ironed out

whatever it is, and that the project will be accepted. And still another says nothing, but simply puts her hand over her mouth, and sort of giggles. Later you find out from the project leader that the design has been rejected by the team. No one however, came to you to point out the problems. Why didn't you know that the team didn't approve of your design – after all, they all said that they liked it? What should you do?

A   Conclude that Asians are deceptive. They tell you one thing and then go behind your back and do another thing. From now on, you don't trust them.

B   Decide to confront them head on and try to get to the bottom of the problem. You frankly and sincerely ask them why they didn't come to you with the problems, and you ask them why they lied to you about liking the design.

C   You ask trusted local friends or old-hand expats, or you take one of the team members (who is about your equal in status) out for a meal to see if you can talk about the problem informally. You learn about the Asian 'yes' and 'no' and about 'face' and you decide that you can work with the system because now you can understand it. You realize that this only scratches the surface, and you make more of an effort to learn even more.

D You give up trying to understand the inscrutable Asians. You hang out with the people of the expat community who talk your talk. You remove yourself emotionally, psychologically, and physically from any contact with Singaporeans except that which is absolutely necessary at work.

ANSWERS

Response (A) is inappropriate. It is an inaccurate assessment. You have culturally misjudged the situation; you need to learn to tell the difference between 'yes' and 'no', like Singaporeans do.

Response (B) is probably the worst thing you can do. Open confrontation and open criticism is taboo in Asia. You must be discrete and delicate in pointing out problems. Face is crucial to a harmonious working environment.

Response (C) is the best response. You should always seek answers to cultural problems which confuse and alienate you. In this case you found out that your design was very close to a symbol for cuckold. It would be a bad omen to have a symbol for cuckold as the logo for any firm. You both see the humour in the situation, and you become closer because of the teaching and the learning! But why did they all lie, even the girl who giggled behind her hand? *They did not lie*; they hinted that there was a problem with the logo. They did not point out your error boldly, as this would have caused you a loss of face, and it is important for the harmony of the office that no one loses face. They all thought you knew from their responses that they were rejecting your design.

Response (D) is the way many expats solve the cultural problems they encounter. It is unfortunately, the wrong way. A response like this puts the success of the venture in jeopardy and ensures that the mission of the expat will likely fail.

5. *HOW MUCH DID YOU PAY?*

There is a reception for the new lecturers at the university. You are one of the new unmarried male expat professors being honoured. Two women Singaporean staff members who have just been introduced to you, sit down to talk with you for a bit. You are delighted. One of the women is young, unmarried, and pretty. The older lady asks you how much the university is paying you and where you stay and how much you have to pay for accommodation. Then the younger one says: 'How much did you pay for that lovely car?' What do you do; what do you say:

A   You walk off in disgust thinking that these are the rudest people you have ever met, and that the young girl is a gold-digger.

B   You tell them that your rent is either $5,000 or $50,000 a month but you can't remember; and that you had the car shipped over and charged the expense to the university.

C   You choke back your anger, and tell them what they want to know.

D   You use the dialogue as an opportunity to start a conversation about cross-cultural miscommunication. You discretely try to find out why they asked such personal questions (about things – such as money and costs of possessions – which most Westerners never talk about).

285

ANSWERS
Response (A) is rude and inconsiderate. Whenever you are confronted with strange and peculiar behaviours which seem to be unfathomable, always suspect that there are cross-cultural implications in them somewhere.

Response (B) – the smart-alec answer, while salving your ego, is not a good response. Nothing is gained. The Singaporeans who might have been your friends have been put off by the bitterness of your answer.

Response (C) is not necessary. You do not have to tell things to strangers that you do not even discuss with your parents!

Response (D) is the best. Be a cultural learner and teacher. Ask: 'I am a newcomer here and I do not want to make mistakes; can you please explain something to me? I noticed that you asked about the cost of my housing and the price of my car. Is that a standard question in Singapore? Is it seen as impolite here?' When they, of course, say that these questions are normal you can say: 'Isn't that peculiar. In my culture, these are things we never discuss, not even with our parents.' Both sides learn and both sides teach.

6. *A GIFT IN THE HAND…*
Your child is in a Malay class at an expat school. You have been helping in the class from time to time, and you have developed a friendship with the Malay *cikgu* (teacher). She has invited you to her home for a meal. You are very pleased. You bring a small gift from your country. As you walk in you hand her the pretty parcel; she thanks you quietly and sets it aside. It remains unopened for the entire length of your stay. What is happening here?

A You have offended by bringing a gift to a Malay home.
B You did not wait until the friendship was more established before bringing a gift.
C You have caused 'lost face' by bringing a gift.
D You gift was accepted in the traditional and courteous Malay way.

ANSWERS

Responses A, B, C are all incorrect. You did not offend by bringing a gift. In fact, you were polite and caring in bringing a small gift 'for the children'. Your friendship was already established, so your gift was very appropriate. Your choice of something from your home country was well chosen. Your gift was deeply appreciated. You did not cause 'lost face' because you did not insinuate that the family could not provide you with refreshments since they did not even know what your gift contained.

Response (D) is correct. Your Malay friend has accepted the gift with courtesy according to her culture. Gifts are not opened in front of the giver. They are politely set aside and opened later. Unlike the Western way where the receiver tears open the package in front of the eyes of the giver with joyful abandon (to signal delight in the gift), most Singaporeans wait until the family is alone. It would be impolite to show 'greed' by tearing open the package; it would be as if they couldn't wait to get the gift, and it would signal that the gift was more important than the friendship.

7. 'DRIVING' ONE CRAZY

You are driving along the expressway in the middle lane at about 60 km/h, when a car comes up behind you; it then pulls into the inside lane to overtake you. As soon as it is just a bit in front of you, it pulls directly into your lane, cutting you off. It then goes merrily on its way. Do you:

A Shout and make a rude sign to the driver to show utter contempt for the poor driving skills.

B Report the incident to the police.

C Ignore it.

D Accelerate and retaliate.

ANSWERS

Response (A) is rude and uncouth.

Response (B) If you should try to report this incident to the police, you might be penalized yourself for 'hogging the road' (driving slower than the speed limit in the fast lane). Overtaking on the inside, is not officially acceptable but it is regularly done. Actually, the inside lane is for slower drivers and for vehicles which cannot go faster than about 50 km/h. The middle lane is for ordinary driving, at 70 km/h–80 km/h; 80 km/h being the speed limit. The outside lane is reserved for overtaking.

Response (C) is the best solution. Just ignore the situation and try to learn to function with skill in the Singaporean driving style. Be sure to learn the driving rules because you should not have been 'hogging' the middle lane in the first place. If you were only driving about 60 km/h, you should have been in the slow lane.

Response (D) is futile. Why allow someone the power to reduce your soul to bitterness!

8. *DOES THE SQUEAKY WHEEL GET THE GREASE?*

Your toilet is blocked. You phone the landlord to get someone out to fix it. Someone comes but they do not fix it. They leave saying that they will send someone else. No one comes. You ring again and are told that the plumber has already been there. You explain that he did not fix it. The landlord says that he will get someone there by 5:00 p.m. At 5:00 p.m. no one has come and the office is closed. The next day you ring back. What do you do?

A Keep your cool and explain the problem again. If this does not work; look for a 'middle person' – someone who can intervene for you.

B Get your own plumber and deduct the cost from the rent.

C Threaten to get a plumber and deduct the cost from the rent.

D Complain loudly and strongly.

ANSWERS

Response (A) To keep cool and look for an intermediary if necessary is the best response. Perhaps the company personnel director can put in a call and explain the problem delicately, saying that the company likes to maintain a mutually beneficial relationship with the landlord.

Response (B) is not a good idea. The shortage in your rent can be deducted from your deposit. A better thing to do would be to make careful enquiries about the landlord *before* you move in. Check to see if the landlord is a member of an organization which provides essential services, such as plumbing.

Response (C) is not a good idea either. Do not scold or threaten. You can *ask* if he would like you to call a plumber to repair the blockage because you fear that the damage to his home will be serious unless the problem is taken care of quickly.

Response (D) is the worst thing you can do. Remember the rule about face: 'The superior person never loses face, neither his own nor anyone else's.' A temper tantrum may irritate the landlord so much that he may purposely delay things. You can try an audible sucking in of air, to show that you are coolly controlling your emotions. Do not think that you are being singled out for this type of treatment; it happens to everyone, Singaporean and foreigner alike.

BIBLIOGRAPHY

ABC-Clio Kaleidescope, 'Singapore' in *Current World Data*, ABC-Clio Inc., Santa Barbara, 1991.

Advance Data Release, Singapore Census of Population, Department of Statistics, Singapore,1990.

Allport, Gordon, *The Nature of Prejudice*, Double Day, New York, 1958.

Cleveland, Mangone and Adams, *The Overseas American*, McGraw-Hill, New York, 1960.

DeMente Boye, *Chinese Etiquette & Ethics in Business,* NTC Business Books, Chicago, 1989.

Far Eastern Economic Review, 'Singapore', *Asia 1991 Yearbook*, Hong Kong, 1991.

Gaer, Joseph,*What the Great Religions Believe*, Signet Classics, The New American Library Inc., New York, 1963.

Hahn, Emily, *The Cooking Of China*, Time-Life International, 1970.

Hill, Hal and Pang, Eng Fong,'Technology from a Small, Very Open NIC: The Case of Singapore' in *World Development*, May 1991.

Holmes, W. F. and Piker, F. K., 'Expatriate Failure – Prevention Rather Than Cure' in *Personnel Management*, New York, December, 1980.

Lim Keak Cheng, *Social Change and the Chinese in Singapore*, Singapore University Press, Singapore, 1985.

Mirza, Hafiz, *Multinationals and the Growth of the Singapore Economy*, Croom and Helm, London, 1986.

Oberg, Kalervo,*Culture Shock and the Problem of Adjustment to New Cultural Environments*, International Publications, Foreign Service Institute, Department of State, Washington, D. C., 1958.

Ow, Chin Hock, 'The Role of the Government in Economic Development: The Singapore Experience' in *Singapore Resources and Growth*, Lim Chong Yah and Peter J. Lloyd (Eds) Oxford University Press, 1985.

Price Waterhouse, *Doing Business in Singapore: An Information Guide*, Price Waterhouse, Singapore, 1990.

Sharp, Ilsa, *Singapore*, The Guidebook Co., Hong Kong, 1988.

Singapore Business, 'The Rise of Woman Power' in *Singapore Business Magazine*, 14.11 November 1990.

Singh Sandhu, Kernial and Wheatley, Paul (Eds), *Management of Success: The Moulding of Modern Singapore*, Institute of Southeast Asian Studies, Singapore, 1989 – with specific reference to:

- Austin, W. Timothy, 'Crime and Control'
- Lim, Linda Y. C., 'Social Welfare'
- Ling, Trevor, 'Religion'
- Rieger, Hans Christoph, 'The Quality of Life in Singapore: A Foreigner's Reflections'
- Seah, Chee Meow, 'National Security'
- Shotam, Nirmala Puru, 'Language and Linguistic Policies'
- Siddique, Sharon, 'Singaporean Identity'
- Varaprasad, N., 'Providing Mobility and Accessibility'
- Willmott. W. E., 'The Emergence Of Nationalism'
- Yeh, Stephen H. K., 'The Idea of the Garden City'

Tham, Seong Chee, 'Tradition, Values and Society among the Malays' *Nanyang Quarterly*, Volume l, No. 4, December 1971.

United States Department of State, 'Singapore' in *Background Notes*, Bureau of Public Affairs, Washington D.C., 1990.

United States Department of State, *Singapore Post Report*, Office of Information Services, U. S. Department of State, Washington D.C., 1990.

Useem, Ruth H., 'The American Family in India', *The Annals of the American Academy of Political and Social Science*, Vol. 368.

AUTHOR

JoAnn Craig has travelled widely and has lived and attended university in many cultures, including the United States of America, Hawaii, the United Kingdom, Africa, Singapore, and the People's Republic of China. She was an honours student at the University of Singapore in 1978 when she wrote her first book: *Culture Shock! Singapore and Malaysia*. Part of the book was based on her academic exercise at the University of Singapore where she was reading Anthropology.

For over ten years until 1979, JoAnn was the wife of an expatriate executive. She lived the expat life with him and the six children they raised, while learning to thrive in their overseas assignments in England, Africa, and Singapore. Her love for the expatriate experience stems from that time.

Since 1981, JoAnn Craig has written numerous teaching manuals and textbooks for the Overseas Training and Orientation Program (OTOP) at the University of San Francisco, where she has been the developer, designer, and director of OTOP for the last ten years. As director of OTOP, she has trained countless Asian managers, executives, scholars, and students in the fine art of working and studying sucessfully in Western cultures, while at the same time, she has trained countless Americans in the fine art of working and studying successfully in Asian cultures.

Some of her manuals include: 'Success in International Relations', 'Better Business Behaviours in America – The Key to International Understanding' (A guidebook for Asians), 'Skillful Business in China: Successful Ventures', 'Welcome to Asia: The Golden Dao/ Dow – Everyday Business Courtesy in Asia', 'The Chinese in America – A Small History', 'Culture and Guidelines to Behaviour in the United States: How to Live in the USA'.

JoAnn is dedicated to promoting cross-cultural understanding, and to relieving the pain of those who cross cultures. She is happiest when she is helping people respect and appreciate other cultures.

INDEX